RADICAL DESCENT

Radical Descent

THE CULTIVATION OF AN AMERICAN REVOLUTIONARY

A Memoir

Linda Coleman

For Linda
from Linda

PUSHCART

Winner of the 2014 Editor's Book Award

Distributed by W.W. Norton Co., 500 Fifth Ave., New York, N.Y. 10110

ISBN: 978-1888889 – 74-1

In memory of my parents

"Those who make peaceful revolution impossible will make violent revolution inevitable."

JOHN F. KENNEDY

AUTHOR'S NOTE

Many people risked or lost lives, were injured, incarcerated, or spent years in hiding for anti-war protests and/or actions that helped to expose our government's rabid, illegal, and sometimes lethal efforts to quell political dissent through it's notorious COINTELPRO program in the 1960's and 70's. The cascade of events that propel this personal narrative are now one thread in that tapestry of voice and story, one part of our collective history.

I have had no contact with the people involved in these events for decades. As a result, to protect their privacy, I have changed names and some locations of events. Their politics and ideas may certainly have changed over time, as have my own, but the issues that drove our protest and distress—ever-widening socio-economic disparity, ill-begotten wars, rising rates of incarceration and civil rights abuses of poor people and people of color, along with heedless destruction of the planet—these failures of our system have continued to escalate. More hopefully, a multitude of movements and organizations of resistance and/or change have also emerged since then, and these give voice to those working towards a sustainable and peaceful world community.

In a deep sense this story blends a quest for home and authenticity, and, as well a quest to determine when, if ever, violence is a useful offensive response to oppression and exploitation. Given our current global circumstances, it seems a question that may unfortunately be asked again. And then, who will become the next revolutionaries to take up arms? What tactics will they use and who will be their leaders? And what will be their deepest motivations for taking on their chosen mission?

Che Guevara, a world-wide icon of resistance at that time, once famously said that "all true revolutionaries are guided by great feelings of love". A beautiful sentiment . . . one tremendously ambitious to actualize when wielding a gun.

I hope this story will find younger readers in a larger audience—those exploring the many ways to form a "more perfect union", as well as those who may feel alienated in their home or social circumstances and go looking for replacements. Perhaps it will remind them to take stock of their motivations while choosing their tactics for resistance and change, as well as the motivations of their comrades, and to be rigorous in investigating those most insistent in "knowing the way"—often, the seeds of violence are being sewn there as well.

Linda Coleman, June, 2014

United States Courthouse, Springfield, Massachusetts
January, 1989

Roland is in this courtroom, somewhere in this sea of faces watching me walk upright, holding myself upright, to be strong for myself and for the child inside, this second child now who is eight months in my belly. This is the moment that has been coming towards me for so many years. And then the next and the next—moments that relentlessly proceed as I walk to the witness stand in the carpeted hush of the packed room—a room crowded with my choices, my ambivalence and fear, their voices and murmurings.

"Listen, you're just one of two hundred witnesses called by the government in a trial that has been going on for months and will continue for many more," Laura, my lawyer had said to me that morning, patting me on the shoulder with her smiling reassurances. "Nobody's going to sink or swim based on what you say."

But those are empty words, filled with compromised values —platitudes to wash down this poison I am swallowing. 'Government witness' is branded on my back for all to see. Traitor!

I'd promised never to talk. "I'm not a rat," I'd told them. I'd told the FBI too every time they came knocking at my door over the last twelve years. But here I am.

"The most prolific left-wing terrorist group in the U.S.," the F.B.I. had called them. "The most successful leftist propaganda campaign of the 1970's," some radical press called them.

I will try to tell the whole truth and nothing but the truth . . . .

I want to say to each of them: I will not keep you as my judge and jury forever.

And still I hesitate . . . .

Portland, Maine
October, 1974

This is how it started, how I met them. Your life takes this turn, that turn, and then you're outside the bookstore with the crimson red star over the door, just the sort of place you've been looking for. Just around the corner and down the street from where you live now. And inside are a few people, people who look like they might be the new friends you've been seeking in this city of strangers. The books in the window are the ones you've been thinking about reading, about working-class struggles and women and the war in Vietnam. In one corner there's a spread of small pocket-sized pamphlets with creamy linen -colored covers and delicate red lettering: On Serving the People, On Discipline, On Criticism and Self-Criticism, On Self-Reliance and Arduous Struggle.

The teachings of Chairman Mao.

These books beckon you. Their titles lift your lost feelings, feelings that all the suffering and injustice in the world lie heavily on your shoulders. The sketched profile of Chairman Mao reminds you that there might be leaders in the world after all who don't abuse their power, who can be trusted after all to represent the needs of the poor and the oppressed. And so you go in.

CHAPTER 1

I've found it! It's just what I've been looking for. This bookstore—
a radical bookstore collective—and there's a death squad in town,
a real death squad. These four cops got caught planning to "dispose of" eight "undesirables". They had the times picked out, the
places to bury their bodies. They planned to toss them under the
new belt parkway that's being laid around the city.

That is evil. Purely evil. What I like about it for me is that it's
so clear, the right and wrong of it. I won't get stuck in the gray
areas on something like this.

The people who run the bookstore are planning a demonstration to protest the death squad. It's exactly the kind of thing I've
been looking for to get involved in ever since I got here. And I
think the bookstore might be someplace I could go back to, work
my way in slowly, maybe even volunteer some time. Inside there
are hundreds of books I want to read—books on Marxism and
Socialism, on women's liberation, labor history, and international
resistance movements. There's a bay window set up as a reading
spot and I can imagine spending days there, looking through

every book and learning all I need to know to become a revolutionary.

Things have to change in this country. The way I see it, capitalism is the root of all evil. I know this is true from my understanding of the ways the system works, from my studies of Marxism and Socialism in college, and from my first-hand experience growing up a rich, white Wasp in a three story brick mansion only two miles away from one of the poorest black neighborhoods in the country. If there was Socialism here, all the wealth and resources would be shared equally. People wouldn't be clawing at each other's throats for their piece of the pie and never feeling satisfied. All the wealth wouldn't be in the hands of one percent of the people.

Of course, when I argue with my capitalist parents, I can never defend my position the way I want to. They're always telling me we live in the greatest country in the world because of all the freedom we have, and how everyone has an opportunity to do what they want with their life and blahblahblah. I say "Freedom for who? Opportunity for who?" but then I need facts and figures to back it up. I need more information. I need more experience out in the real world with real working people who weren't born with the proverbial silver spoon. The bookstore is perfect that way.

I met some people who work there, and they're also the ones planning the demonstration. They were pretty guarded, not altogether friendly, but I knew beyond a certainty of a doubt that they're the ones I've been looking for. They're the kind of people I knew in an instant had never been near a private school or a private club. No trust fund babies. No Social Register on the coffee table. The man there had tattoos on his arms and a long ponytail, and the woman he was with, a woman definitely younger than me, had a baby on her back. Nobody I know has a baby. Nobody's even gotten married or pregnant.

There was a third woman there, one who looked like she could have been my sister. I recognized her square jaw and the profile of her nose. She had hair thick and long like my own, and wire-rims almost the duplicates of the ones I wear. She was the only one who actually smiled at me and who told me more about the demonstration. The man and the other woman kept their distance, looked me up and down more than once like it was their job to protect the place from people like me. But that's okay. In a way, they're right and I really expect as much. After all, if they knew where I came from, they probably wouldn't even let me in the place.

I realized something about myself after I left, as I was walking back to my apartment. I realized that I'm shy, and I'm not shy. I have the kind of shyness that makes my heart squeeze into my throat when I meet certain new people. Not just anybody—that's the not-shy part. I'm always sorting, categorizing, putting them into one of two groups—solid people or liquid people. The liquid ones are the not-quite-smart-enough word-stumblers, the ones you dismiss in a group. Their faces disappear from memory when you turn your back. I'm in that group. Solid ones fill a room, have this kind of quick-tongued presence, never disappear. I'm in that group too—I'm in both. I change at the flip of a coin. No, sometimes even faster—at the blink of an eye. I can walk into a room feeling solid, like my mother at her most dazzling, the way she can work a crowd at a cocktail party, but then if I catch a sidelong glance or feel squeezed out by someone bigger than me in some kind of way, I'm dirt on their shoe soles, let them do what they will with me.

That's the way I felt after I left the bookstore. On the way in I felt solid, and on the way out, all liquid, dissolved, ready to seep under the door back out to the street. But somewhere there must be a hard core of me, because I fully intend to go back, soon, and I'm definitely going to the demonstration.

The other good thing about the Death Squad, what makes it so perfect for me as a kind of cause to get involved in, is that it looks like the four cops are going to be acquitted. That says enough about the failures of the system right there, let alone that they were acquitted by a judge who I know. I don't know him exactly, but my grandmother does. I think my father even clerked for him one summer when he was in law school.

From all our summer vacations visiting here, I figure I've probably passed hors d'oeuvres to him, to the judge, at a party more than once when I was younger. I'm sure I've seen him shaking the ice in his Tom Collins highball, standing on my grandmother's patio overlooking all the sailboats at sunset. He'd be talking yachting with my father, my uncle, my grandfather, my great-uncle, my first cousin-once-removed, my second cousin's uncle. I'm probably related to everyone rich in this town, probably even to the judge too.

I can see the rainbow of their colored pants milling on her patio, all ruddy- cheeked and smooth shaven. They all smell like my father, Old Spice and Brylcreem. Their cheeks are soft when they kiss me hello, smooth cheeks and firm handshakes. They look you straight in the eye exactly as I've been taught to do. I know about that look, the one that feigns interest. They ask you politely what you're up to this summer, but if you answer with more than a sentence or two, their eyes wander and you know they're thinking about stock options or golf scores. Not about you at all. Not about death squads either.

I've clipped some of the articles to send to my parents, but not right away. I don't want to talk to them about this. I don't want to talk to them period. Not right now, now that I'm finally on my own.

It's enough that my grandmother, 'Mammy' we call her, phones me every day, sometimes many times a day, checking up on me, worrying about me, sending me picnic baskets with crabmeat and blueberry muffins she has her driver deliver. With all her attention, it can feel like I'm not on my own at all; and then too, it all piles up, the attention, so that I'm always at a deficit returning it.

I do love her, but then, aside from feeling suffocated by her hovering, I've started to learn more about crabmeat pickers. I've learned that they're the lowest paid workers in the state, second only to blueberry harvesters. The women who work in the shellfish factory sit ten hours a day in the stench of all that smell, cracking shells as sharp as glass, picking out the tender tiny slivers so careful not to mush it. I imagine their raw fingertips, their hands cut by shells, their aching backs, and I can't eat another bite.

Still, the baskets pile in the corner reminding me of how long it's been since I've been to Mammy's to visit. Every week I swear I'll go out and have dinner with her, or lunch even and a walk down to the bay. Her home is just a few miles away, on the outskirts of town, in the "estate" section. But I haven't gone.

My family is wealthy all around, on my father's and my mother's side. Old money—robber baron millionaires who made their fortunes during the Industrial Revolution in the early 1900's, and even before that. My mother is related to Peter Stuyvesant, the first governor of New Amsterdam.

I remember school trips to the Museum of Natural History in New York City where I'd linger at the huge diorama of my great ancestor trading with the Indians. I'd brag to my classmates about how I was related, how this was my "greatgreatgreatgreat grandfather," though even then he didn't look like somebody I'd like very much, dressed in his starched pilgrim uniform, with his peg leg and his hawk-like profile, and the way he towered over the Indians who knelt before him with their offerings.

A few years ago I learned from one of my first radical teachers that the man had singularly wiped out the Native American population on Manhattan by intentionally giving them all blankets contaminated with the smallpox virus. But by then it was too late to disown him, to disown the years of taking pride in that heritage. Instead I felt like an act of such great evil could be carried on in a bloodline like any genetic disease, and that maybe I carried that evil somewhere inside me; that all of his sins, and the sins of all my exploitive ancestors, were my sins too.

When I hear about things like the smallpox massacre, or the Death Squad, that kind of pure evil, all the fathomless wrong drags me down like an undertow, down to where everything is dark and suffocating, where it feels like the weight of all the water in the world is on my chest and the only way to get back to the surface, to breathe again, is to do something about it. I have to do something.

I remember how I felt the first time I saw the footage from the Nazi concentration camps. Everything stopped when I saw those images for the first time—my breath, my heart—time froze, and when it was over, when the film went off and the world moved again, I was different. My very cell structure altered and I knew I'd been changed forever. Beauty was different. Before, I could look at a snowflake on my window and know that it was perfect— an exquisite crystal, one fragment of what I had believed to be a perfectly ordered universe. But now, though the snowflake's still beautiful, still perfect, now it belongs to a darker place, a place that couldn't possibly be perfectly ordered. Now it's part of a universe that demands all the attention and efforts of the forces of good to keep it in balance. Now there's always this background noise, the evil I can't forget. The very evil I might contain.

Everything here is new for me, this being the first time I've been on my own, in my own apartment. Every morning I wake with the feeling that my life's an empty white canvas—here, now, to paint on. The simplest things feel like brushstrokes. The sun that hits my pillow in the morning, the smell of new varnish on the floors of my apartment, the coffee I boil on the gas stove with eggshells in it like a cowboy.

My coffee. My bed. My sunlight.

I've never lived alone before and I have the feeling that this is home for me in a way I've never felt at home, not ever in my twenty-one years. Not growing up living with my parents. Definitely not at the boarding school where they sent me. And not at college either. Never, really until now. I like my bare walls, all the possibilities there. The poster of Che Guevara that I bought at the bookstore is the first thing I've hung up. When I lie on my bed and look up into his eyes, I see that anything is possible—revolution, change, love. His eyes are kind and fierce at the same time. His bandanna and army fatigues, the way he wears his cap off-center, give him the untamed look of a rebel, and beneath his image his quote:

"At the risk of sounding ridiculous, I must tell you that all true revolutionaries are guided by great feelings of love".

I bought a book at the store the other day too, along with the poster. Prison Writings by Regis Debray. I've never heard of him, but I liked the jacket-cover illustration and what it said on the back. "While in prison for his association with Che Guevara, and under extremely difficult circumstances, Debray continued to write . . . "

I want to be like that—to have a passion that will survive extremely difficult circumstances, and to be a loyal friend to a great revolutionary hero. Or maybe I will even be a revolutionary hero someday. I think about that too.

I have a job at the hospital, the big medical center that serves this state. I'm training to work in the operating room, to assist in surgeries. I hand out the instruments, just the right scalpel and blade, the right retractor, forceps, or suture, into the palm of the surgeon's hand. So quick, I have to have it there before he even knows that's what he wants. I prepare the patients too, positioning them correctly after they've been anesthetized, washing and draping the correct body part.

I love it there. To me, when I enter that suite off the huge elevator, passing the Private: Authorized Personnel Only sign, it's like entering the spell of a great never-ending ritual. I'm cloistered in those pale green windowless hallways, all of us shuffling around so urgently in our scrub suits like so many worker ants.

I love the other-worldliness of it, all the new frontiers of sight and sound. I have permission to touch through that thin layer of latex, to hold and press and stroke a body like an old friend, but even closer, and still at a safe distance. I get to touch forbidden places, sink my hands into interiors that are deep and warm and full of life, and all the while I stay hidden behind my mask and gown. Just my hands convey how gentle I can be.

I'm called a technician, but I feel more like a sculptor's apprentice, smoothing and stroking the surfaces I prepare and carefully arranging the instruments they'll use in the creation.

I like open-heart surgery the best. Sometimes we work there for long hours in silence. When I'm the one to hold the retractors I can stare as long as I like into the deep heart-lung cavity. I feel that if I stare long enough into those heaving or flaccid dusky red organs, that they'll reveal some great mystery. And the only sound that links us all to the life suspended under the green sheets is the steady hiss and clunk, hiss and clunk of the respirator.

CHAPTER 2

Four months ago, on the morning of my twenty-first birthday, my father walked down the long hallway to my bedroom at the far end of the three-story Georgian brick mansion we lived in. By choice, mine was smallest room in the house, the "maid's room", the farthest away from where my parent's slept. That's the way I liked it.

My birthday is June 5th, the first early days of summer. I was home from college having decided I wasn't going back for my last year, and that instead I wanted to get into the "real" world where I thought maybe I'd belong. So far, belonging was a feeling that had evaded me entirely.

I was still in bed, reading, letting the slow day unfold with all its birthday grief—those days always falling short of what I imagined they might be. That morning I'd awakened to heavy humid heat already closing over me by nine o'clock, and had lain awake for a long time listening to lawn mowers in the distance, and mourning doves in the yew tree so close I could have touched them. They coo cooed with that throaty whistle that made you feel like everyone's gone and left you out.

I heard his steps, the exact firm timing and weight of them, but when my father appeared in my door, dressed in his tennis whites, I was still surprised to see him there.

"Happy Birthday, honey." He tipped his head, the way he did, in his 'everything okay?' gesture.

There was no chair in the room, so I moved over and he came and sat on the edge of the bed. I had the feeling the room was really too small for both of us. The fact that he was there at all made this an event of some significance, and I imagined it had something to do with the manila envelope he placed on my covers on his far side.

I couldn't remember the last time he'd been in my room. As I said, our house was very large and it was a long way to travel. I didn't know if he'd ever seen my Michelangelo "Prisoners" replicas lined up on my bureau, or my Guernica poster, or my books on Zen and Marx and women's liberation. He didn't know I wrote poetry in the journal beneath my bed, or that I smoked pot and cigarettes on the roof next to the dove nests outside my window. He hadn't a clue that on a few different occasions I'd shared that single bed with lovers—male and female—awake all night while he slept at the other end of the house. I don't even know what he'd have done, what expression he'd have on his face if I told him. He didn't really have that many. But with him there was still a chance that someday he would notice all of that, and that he would come down the back hall for just that purpose, to find out who I was. Of course that hadn't happened yet, but I was willing to believe that he loved me, more than just about anyone ever had, only what that love was made of, I couldn't really tell you.

My father is a man of few words, and I am "my father's daughter". That's what everyone says, and I'm glad to be more like him than my mother. I don't want to be like her at all. If anyone makes the mistake of saying, "Oh you look so much like your mother!" or, "You have your mother's eyes exactly!" I take it as an insult.

14

I want to shake them and say, "You're wrong! Look again! Can't you see I'm really much more like my father?"

Physically, I am much more like him—tall and square-jawed and rugged. We don't complain about anything. My mother, on the other hand, feels like she'd snap in two if you hugged her, which is something I just avoid these days as much as possible. And with her you can be sure she's always got problems that are bigger than your own.

He pulled a red folder from the manila envelope that had The Bank of New York embossed in gold ink on the cover. "I have something to give you, now that you're twenty-one." What it was was a $150,000 stock portfolio. I knew it was coming. I'd been worrying about it for a full year since I'd heard about it from my older sister.

"This is yours now. You should look it over and I'll answer any questions you have about it."

My father's voice is always pretty flat and gravelly, like somebody who's been taught to take life very seriously, who hasn't laughed until he cried since he played drinking games in college. Maybe that's why he insists that we all sing those alma mater songs that sound like football cheers at every holiday meal. My sisters and I roll our eyes but we cut him some slack. It's one of the few times he seems to get really animated.

My eyes swam down the long list of purchase dates and deposits. Twenty-one years of slow additions. They were all there— Mobile, IBM, Johnson and Johnson, Nestles Corporation. A line-up of thugs. No, worse. A thug is a thug. A CEO dines at elegant benefits for the Junior League while he sends children to work in mines for pennies a day. His hands stay clean, manicured, un-calloused.

I had Marxist friends in college who used to sing the Nestles song like this:

N-E-S-T-L-E-S, Nestles makes the very best . . . .death by far.

That was because Nestles had killed millions of babies in

Africa with their infant formula, dressing up like doctors and nurses and telling women it was better than breast milk. They knew the women didn't have any clean water to mix it with. They knew the babies would get dysentery and die, but it was an "infinite market"; and the deaths, "collateral damages". For years they did that.

My father didn't understand. I could say he chose not to know, or I could say he'd just grown up in a different time, that his re-education would be slower as a result.

He'd built his entire life around believing in all the golden opportunities and goodness of capitalism, whereas for years I'd been witnessing the very black heart of it exposed all around me. To take the money was to sign a pact with the Devil. That's how it felt. But how could I spit on all his work and good intentions with him sitting right there looking around my room for the first time, the weight of him pressing down the edge of my bed, so close I could smell his Old Spice smell.

"God, that's a lot of money," I said after I'd scanned all the entries down to the Net Value figure at the bottom of the last page. I kept my eyes there, not knowing what more to say, feeling small and mean that I wasn't jumping up and down with thanks and throwing my arms around his neck like he'd probably thought I would.

"It's not really. It's really a drop in the bucket. You'd be surprised how fast it could disappear. But if you're smart about it, it will get you going."

What he meant was that with that money I could make more money. The rich get richer, and the poor get nothing.

"One hundred and fifty grand is more than a drop in the bucket, Dad, at least to most people in the world." I couldn't keep the edge of accusation out of my voice. He'd have to agree with me there. But he sighed with that heaviness that always ripped at my heart.

"Listen, I can keep it for you until you're older if you don't feel ready for it."

People were playing tennis at the club down the street. Our club. The private one that still only allowed Wasps as members. I could hear the pop-pop-pop of the balls hitting racquets carried on the dense humid air. I could hear all of my parents' friends calling out to one another.

"Good shot!"

"Oooo yes!" and laughing politely.

Those were other sounds, like the mourning doves, that made me feel like life was just so for everybody else, made of neat lines and simple rules to follow.

In or out. Point or fault. Game. Set. Match.

I knew they all cheated one way or another but they wouldn't want me telling them how to play a fair game. They'd never listen.

"No thanks Dad, I can handle it."

CHAPTER 3

To get to my grandmother's house from my apartment in town, you drive down Congress Street, past the park and through the roundabout, then on to Route One out of Portland, north to the suburb of Falmouth Foreside. It's a strip of beautiful road across the tidal flat bridges that I've traveled since childhood, a comfortable habit of a road I never tire of. On the left, you look into the end of a cove, a darkly wooded shore where you can spot the long gray necks of the herons who live there. On the other side you can look across the bay and islands out to the ocean off in the distance. When the sun is out, it's blinding on the ocean side, the water jumping with sunlight, infinite and unexplored. Or that's how it seemed when I was younger, a passenger in the loaded station wagon on the last leg of the trip from New York to my grandmother's for summer vacation; everything waiting to be explored, everything possible.

All of the uninhabited islands are places I've been to one time or another with my family and cousins on evening picnics or daysails. We'd make fires on the beach and cook lobsters we bought straight from the lobstermen lifting their pots. I was always happiest in Maine. Maybe it was no wonder I was here again.

But today, on my way to my grandmother's house for our long overdue lunch, I can feel how I've changed since then. As I pass by the new construction of the beltway, I can't help thinking of the Death Squad, how in another month or two I could have been driving unsuspectingly over the murdered bodies of people I had met. Today there's a patchy fog and every molecule of air is saturated with the acrid paper-mill smell that sometimes comes up from the south. I can't see the ocean, and even the islands are just moody unpredictable shapes that might not be there at all.

My parents called me this morning and even though I didn't want to, I did tell them about the Death Squad. I had to know if they knew the judge, Judge Albright, and I was right about that. They did know him, and he had been to my grandmother's before, and plus, my father had clerked for him as a law student about twenty years ago and they'd been friends ever since.

"I wonder if you've got your facts straight honey," my father had said, meaning that I must be over-reacting and exaggerating like, you know, women do. And my mother had to warn me not to go upsetting my grandmother by getting into a "thing" about it—meaning she thinks I'm likely to be unkind, which I resent. By the time I hung up I wished I hadn't said anything about it at all and that I didn't have a relative around here for a hundred miles.

So when I get to Mammy's, and walk in to the still wealth of her home with all the oil paintings of relatives that probably hopped off the Mayflower, and the silver this and the mahogany that, a home big enough for five families, a home that is so safe and protected by the ten short miles I've traveled from downtown Portland, so safe and exclusive, of course I do want to say something about what I've learned about the rest of her home town. And while I'm at it I want to invite her sister, my Aunt

Margaret, who lives with her maid and her cook in another house right next door, a house big enough for ten families, I want to invite her to hear about it too.

The problem is I love them both. I think I do. I always have before. I do, but I get confused. Even while I'm ranting to myself about the unequal distribution of wealth and justice, I know it's not fair to blame them really, but I've decided that ignorance is not innocence. Just because they may not know about the poverty and foul play that's virtually just around the corner from them doesn't mean they're not partly responsible for it, living like they do.

When I hug Mammy hello she smells of carnations. She feels cashmere-soft like she always does. She's happy to see me finally and doesn't even rub it in that I've been putting off the visit for so long the way my mother most certainly would and always does. She doesn't chastise me for being a little late.

"Are you hungry dear?" she asks, and I say I am because I'm sure that I've held up lunch, so we go right into the dining room and sit down.

I do love Mammy but my head is spinning with all sorts of conflicts, and sitting in the dining room for lunch just makes it all worse. For one thing, the dining room is the most formal part of the house. The rectangular table seats twelve, a mahogany antique, perfectly polished, with a large glass dolphin for a centerpiece and silver candlesticks, silver place settings, and linen place-mats and napkins which all have to be laundered and ironed so I feel bad using them, especially just for lunch.

On one wall is a huge gilt-framed mirror that runs the length of the table and almost to the ceiling. The two of us are dwarfed in its reflection—Mammy in her elegant beige wool suit with her sandy blonde hair brushed smoothly in its understated but expensive way, and me looking dark and unkempt next to her with my long hair and wire-rims, a black turtleneck and jeans. My face in the mirror is as unfamiliar as always; a face that changes every time I look at it, never restful.

But the thing about the dining room that I really dread is the turtle. It's always there, just to Mammy's right, on the table, always within easy reach—heavy, brass, elaborately engraved, and when you press its head down it rings loudly for Bridget, the maid, to come in to serve you. Bridget has probably been with my grandmother as long as the turtle has, which means longer than I have been alive. She must be no less than seventy herself, small with blue-white hair in a bun, a crisp white apron and white nurse shoes that move silently from the kitchen to the dining room and back again, and that is about the loudest sound she ever makes.

When we were kids we'd fight for a turn to ring the turtle, holding the head down so long each time that you'd have to wind it up again to ready it for the next course. We'd ring for seconds to be served, or for more butter, or to bring more water or take the rolls back to heat them up, or for whatever was the complaint of the moment, because nothing was ever quite right as far as Mammy was concerned. She hasn't changed much in that regard and that is one thing I don't love about her, the way she treats her "help", as if they hugely compromise her standards no matter how hard they work.

Lunch is hard, right from the start. I try to second-guess Mammy before she rings the bell, so I'm jumping up and down a lot to help Bridget serve and clear because I just can't tolerate being waited on anymore, until Mammy tells me quite firmly to sit. "Please dear, it's her job!" she says, and holds my forearm in a firm grip. But then I have to tell her that I can't eat crabmeat anymore because the crabmeat pickers are the lowest paid workers in the state and unfairly exploited. I don't mean to be rude. I don't want to hurt her feelings, but you have to draw the line someplace, and now I just can't cross that one anymore.

21

I do feel like a brat though when she says, looking very seriously, very kindly into my eyes, "Well dear, I didn't know that. That's very interesting. You'll have to tell me what else we can get for you." She's just about to ring the bell again for Bridget but I catch her just in time. I have to tell her at least four times that I'm fine, really, I'm fine, there's plenty of food right here. But I'm already eyeing the blueberry muffins and thinking that the blueberry pickers may be even worse off than the crabmeat pickers so maybe I shouldn't eat those either.

We take a nice walk down to the point after lunch. It takes about ten minutes to stroll down to the end of the peninsula of land that Mammy and my great-aunt share. Open and grassy, with big granite lichen-covered outcroppings and huge old trees, a still cove on one side and the bay open on the other, it holds all of the best memories of my childhood.

We walk arm in arm and even though Mammy does this walk every day by herself, she leans a little on my arm as if she needed my support. She tells me stories about what it was like when she was my age and still took horse and buggy rides to visit friends. I forget for a few minutes about all the contradictions in her lifestyle that I have to challenge, and enjoy the familiar highs and lows of her voice, the deep blue of her watery eyes when they smile at me.

But as I'm getting ready to leave I remember that I'm flat out of gas, and flat out of cash too, so I have to ask Mammy if I can borrow a few dollars. She insists that I take fifty because that's the only size bill she has in her purse. I protest but she insists.

"You go buy yourself a little something for the apartment with the change," she says, patting my hand where she's inserted the folded bill. "I just wish I could climb all those stairs so I could see for myself what you need." She is so generous. I know it's mean and cold that I'm suspect of her generosity, but I am. After all, she can afford to be generous, I'm thinking while she's hugging me.

Her generosity is a luxury she has because she has so much, and what else would she do with it? It's a terrible thought, I know, but there's some part of me that still feels compelled to impress upon her that her lifestyle is exploitive and immoral, as if I could save her if she would only listen. I wouldn't expect her to turn around and give all her money to the revolution, but you never know. But I didn't say anymore. After all, I now had her fifty-dollar bill in my pocket, and I still had all those stocks in the bank too, so who was I to preach?

At least I could honestly tell my mother that I didn't talk to her about the Death Squad.

CHAPTER 4

The demonstration wasn't what I'd expected—not the turnout I'd thought there'd be. Who wouldn't protest a Death Squad in their own home town, that's what I wanted to know.

I thought there would be throngs, but it was small, maybe thirty men and women altogether, looking like they were all from the Hell's Angels; walking around in a circle in front of the courthouse, dwarfed by its lofty pillared presence.

Where was everyone?

But then I had to ask myself how many demonstrations had I been to?

One. This was my first, my very first. Looking out at the crowd, it was hard to believe. Where had I been? It was 1974 after all, and I'd spent my whole life with a bunch of private school white kids, who weren't getting drafted, who weren't coming home in body bags, and so why not spend my time in college holed up in a darkroom making artsy photos and smoking pot while thousands were trying to end this war, were rioting and dying and protesting, putting their lives on the line for justice and peace. I had certainly been living in another universe altogether—at least until a year ago. Thank you Malcolm X, Karl Marx, Franz Fanon. Thank you Rick Best for riding up into that sleepy life of mine on your Harley, fresh from a two year bit in prison for draft resistance, your pale troubled sadness giving me the final push right out of that petty nest into the real world. Then the fog lifted, the ground shook and there was nothing solid or simple or safe anymore.

"There's no turning back from awareness." I saw that in the bookstore too. Thank you George Jackson. Good. I never fit into that world anyway. I've always wanted out.

But I wanted in to this world, the world of the people at the demonstration. In to their dark, weathered looks, their long outlaw leather coats, in to their purpose and action, the way they all seemed to know each other, the way they all seemed to have been doing this for a long time in many many circles, round and round and never giving up showing up for justice.

We say no! Portland Police have got to go!

The bookstore people were there, and they seemed to know everyone else, and although I definitely felt self-conscious and out of place, like everyone was looking at me and thinking I was an enemy of the people because of my background, that they could somehow tell, could somehow see through me right into my stock portfolio, I stayed in there anyway, to the end, just like they did. It helped knowing that as we marched those four cops were inside the courthouse colluding with the judge

I slipped into the line behind one of the smaller guys, a wiry, red-haired man who was one of the more animated in the crowd, throwing his black-leathered arm and fist into the air over and over like an exclamation point.

Justice! When do we want it? he'd shout.

And we'd all yell back, "Now!"

We did this over and over and at first it was even harder for me than I thought it would be. He was angry and loud and little flecks of spit sprayed out of his mouth when he shouted. He was ready to fight, and why not? Maybe he was one of the ones on that hit list. He was right to be mad! I thought I was mad about it too, but I had to wonder what was wrong with me that I didn't feel angry enough to jump in the air, to shout and yell for justice.

I don't like to fight, but how could I be a revolutionary if I didn't like to fight? Or maybe I would like it, but I'd never had the right opportunity. I'd never even been in an argument with anyone, at least not a real one with shouting or throwing things. Angry, yes. But I'd keep it to myself, or at myself. I was good at that.

"Peace at all costs"—that was the motto I grew up with. In my parents' home, anger belonged under the rug even if it rotted the floors and the whole house fell down. Don't ever raise your voice. Be good. Be very good. Out of my three siblings, I'd laid claim to that role early on. I was not someone who liked to make mistakes, any kind of mistake. I practically made a religion out of getting things right.

But now the longer I was in the circle, the louder my voice rose. It got easier when I held onto the image of the dead bodies stuffed under the asphalt, of the judge inside the courthouse conspiring with the police, likely pardoning their murderous intent. And I thought of all the other odious abuses of power that went undiscovered in this country, about the Civil Rights movement and the Vietnam War and the shouting got easier still. The low dome of the gray sky and the intermittent gusts of wind seemed to accent the seriousness of the event, the righteousness of our presence. Maybe I did belong.

The woman from the bookstore, the one I thought looked like me, stood off to the side, out of the circle handing out leaflets and next to the couple with the baby I'd met that same day. Her long black leather coat flapped in the wind and her glasses were tinted an exotic pinkish hue that hid her gaze, but she saw me at one point as I made the rounds past her and she nodded her head in acknowledgement and a gave me a hint of a smile, which I returned. Be cool.

Justice! When do we want it? Now!

But after a while, people began to drift away. It got colder, and the wind picked up, blowing everything askew—people, papers, leaflets. I thought about slipping out so I wouldn't have to talk to anyone, but I didn't especially want to go back to my apartment either where it would just be me and the four walls again. As it was, the wiry man stopped his shouting and ended the circle right in front of that same woman, with me right behind him. He grabbed a stack of leaflets from her and moved away to another part of the courtyard, and since I was pretty much face to face with her, I asked for some too.

"I remember you, right? From the other day? Hey, thanks for coming." She handed me some leaflets. "I'm RoAnne." Her hair was a wavy strawberry-blonde cascade blowing across her face, the same color as my little sister's. The hair I'd braided in the mornings for years; the color I'd always coveted.

I told her my name, Linda. It sounded plain.

The couple with the baby had their backs to us, the man carrying the baby girl in the backpack. She twisted around to stare me down, red-cheeked and saucer-eyed, a tiny warrior expression to be reckoned with.

"That's Emma," RoAnne said, and then introduced me to her parents, Sarah and Devon, both just as handsome now as they'd appeared the other day, Devon with his full reddish beard and blue piercing eyes, and Sarah with that smooth porcelain skin and red lips; but today they returned my smile..

"She's really cute," I offered, nodding at Emma. And she was, with that intent expression and a fistful of her mother's hair in her mouth even while she twisted around in the pack on her father's back, connecting the three of them like that.

"Thanks," Devon beamed then, took her little hand and raised it up. "She's a fighter."

For a minute, we were just standing there, side-by-side, thrusting leaflets at anyone passing by. But soon everyone had left the square except for the marching leader I'd followed in the circle who now wandered over. He introduced himself like a politician I'd met once, pumping my hand like he'd known me all my life. He said his name was Nick and thanked me twice in one sentence for coming. There was nothing tight and angry about him anymore. He was smaller than the others, and not altogether handsome like they were either, with eyes too wide apart and almost no lips at all. In spite of myself, I dismissed him for his lack of poise, even while I knew I was grateful for his open welcome.

"Well that wasn't the turnout we'd hoped for, was it?" Devon's voice was deep and quiet, but the kind of quiet that had some thunder behind it.

"Yeah, well people around here like to live with their heads up their asses. What's new?" RoAnne offered me a cigarette and I took it, glad to have that connection. She lit hers, cupped against the wind on the first match, deft as she tossed her hair out of her way and then exhaling the smoke with a cool indifference.

"Do you think there's any chance they'll put these guys away?" I asked her.

"No way," Nick jumped in. "It's the 'old boy' thing, and the judge is like their big daddy. Maybe he'll slap their hands but they won't see any time. They'll be swinging their sticks at us again in a few months. And we'll be ready for them, right you guys?" With a goofy kind of grin, he spun around on his boot heel, a full circle that ended in a karate kick just shy of RoAnne's chest.

"Cut it out." She gave a half-smile, but I could tell she didn't like his antics, or maybe she just didn't like him. By the way they shifted slightly away from Nick, I guessed that Devon and Sarah didn't either. Maybe he wasn't on that death list after all. But then neither was I.

We were all but alone in the courtyard then when Devon nudged Sarah. "There's one of them . . . that's Carver right there, the one in plainclothes . . . that fucking pig."

Carver was walking across the square in our direction. There were two others in uniform beside him. They were all stocky, strutting in black shoes as heavy as combat boots, and they were looking at us. We were looking back at them, only I couldn't hold my gaze, and when I looked away I felt all of their eyes on me at once. This was something else I'd never done, to look at a cop from the wrong side of the fence. To have a cop look at me like I was trouble. I was blushing. I could feel the heat in my face, like an idiot, like a bad child.

I wanted to turn my head, hide my face so they didn't add my name to any of their lists. What a coward.

"It's fucking disgusting that they're walking around town as if they haven't done anything wrong, as if we're the ones who are wrong," RoAnne spat out, "and I recognize one of the others . . . that one on the right. He's the one who cruises the bookstore fifty times a day. I recognize him." She threw her cigarette down, ground it with her toe in disgust. "He's a fucking creep."

"Yeah, well you should invite him in next time for some tea." Nick said, exaggerating a British drawl, holding up a flyer for them, smiling and pointing to the black, bold heading about the Death Squad.

"Give it a rest Nick," RoAnne said, and I was relieved when he put the flyer down. I could already tell he was the kind of guy who never really does give it a rest. And then he threw his fist in the air and shouted, "Power to the people!"

It seemed stupid to provoke them like that, but just as stupid to be afraid of provoking them. The three of them stared over at us at the sound of Nick's voice and I thought I saw them shift their direction ever so slightly towards us. Their expressions, the cops' expressions, were as cold and hard as those that Devon and Sarah and RoAnne returned. They hated each other. And I wanted to be a part of it—to be swept away in that kind of certainty, not blushing and afraid to be seen. I had to learn to hold my ground, to really take a stand.

The three cops walked by, only twenty feet away. I saw Sarah put her hand on Devon's arm, a restraining hand. I saw Nick pointing at the flyer, and the cops staring us up and down. Maybe because we had a baby with us they passed us by instead of coming after us like they would have liked. I wondered, as Emma hopped up and down in the backpack, cooing and gurgling, if it was such a good idea to bring a baby to a demonstration.

As they passed to the other side of the square and entered the court building, I thought about how there was something else lacking in me, something I had to change. To be a revolutionary, I couldn't just love, I had to let the hate in too. I had to remember when I looked at cops, when they would walk towards me, or when they'd be running towards me with their clubs and their hoses and their tear gas, that they deserved whatever they got. They'd asked for it. Even if they hadn't ever come after me, or anybody I'd known in the past, that was only because I came from the very class they'd been hired to protect. They were, first and foremost a tool of the capitalists, protectors of capitalist property.

I had to choose sides, remember whose side I was on. How else would I ever get the courage I'd need to fight them?

* * *

Nelson Rockefeller deserves to die. If I want to learn to hate, I can practice on him first.

I saw the movie "Attica" a few nights after the demonstration, about the prison uprising there in 1971. The bookstore group sponsored the film as a fundraiser for the prisoners' rights work they do. Though I didn't know any of the details about the uprising, within the first few minutes of the film I knew what was coming, out of the sky, off the 30-foot high walls, down from the fourteen gun towers the cameras kept flashing on.

Rockefeller could have stopped it. The inmates were only asking to be treated like human beings, to be given the opportunity to read books, drink clean water, not be packed into over-crowded cells like rats. And hundreds of inmates made do for days in that courtyard peacefully, taking care of one another, being brothers. They cheered the team of negotiators that came into the yard to talk to them—an explosion of cheering—frantic, ecstatic. Someone is listening! Someone will hear us!

In the end, even the hostages asked Rockefeller to grant amnesty to the inmates.

But then you heard his voice—his officious pig voice on the phone talking about "the larger societal implications" of listening to their demands. You could see him, leaning back in his swivel chair, the leather chair behind the polished desk, delivering the slaughter command with a phone call, right before his two martini lunch.

Lies! From the bullhorn in the helicopter overhead you could hear those lies . . .

Put your hands above your head. Surrender peacefully. You will not be harmed. Put your hands above your head. Surrender peacefully. You will not be harmed . . .

But then they were shooting from that helicopter and dropping tear gas . . . shooting and shooting and the inmates with their hands in the air dropped one after another and then they were rolling on the ground in the grass and in the dirt jerking when the bullets hit them . . . Put your hands over your head. Surrender peacefully. You will not be harmed. Put your hands above your head. Surrender peacefully. You will not be harmed . . .

They killed thirty-one inmates and nine guards. They tried to say that the inmates had done it, that the inmates had slit the throats of the guards they held captive. They got that story out in a hurry. But it wasn't true. The autopsies showed that bullets killed the guards, bullets from their own pig guns. That's Amerikkka. Now I know why revolutionaries spell it that way.

When the lights came on, I felt so much disgust for Nelson Rockefeller that if he'd been standing before me right then and there and I had a gun I might have shot him.

Every day that passes I learn more about the way power works in this country, what color you have to be, what sex, what class or religion to have a place at the table, the dining room table. Otherwise, you eat in the kitchen. You eat leftovers if you eat at all. Every day my commitment to become a revolutionary deepens. Rockefeller was no different than Nixon who sent men to kill and be killed in a war that was never even officially declared. Every day he broke the highest laws in the land. Every day he dropped tons of bombs and napalm on innocent people, all those children burning in the name of "defending democracy". And Nixon was no different than the others before him, than all the presidents who'd signed more than four hundred treaties with Native Americans and broken every one while they massacred hundreds of thousands and stole this country. And the others who grew fortunes with the blood and tears of the slaves they owned— in the name of "free enterprise". In the name of "defending democracy".

It was all corrupt. It was all filth and greed and a despicable, cowardly abuse of power.

Of which I am a part: Nestles Corporation, 150 shares; Exxon Corporation, 250 shares; Standard Oil, 130 shares; IBM, 400 shares . . .

Chapter 5

———

When I first moved to Portland, I wasn't looking for love. When I think about lovers I've had in the past few years, it's as if they all belonged to the past life of some other person entirely. Now that I see the world through the lens of a revolutionary-in-training, through the divisions of class and race and gender that separate us, I feel as if different blood pulses in my veins—blood that will open my heart to an entirely different sort of person—certainly one with eyes wide open to the injustices that surround us.

I haven't been lonely here. At least I wasn't at first. In my spare time when I'm not studying or reading, I take long walks down by the waterfront, walk along the piers and watch the great commercial fishing trawlers bring in their catch. I check out the fisherman as the boat docks—hefty seamen flinging ropes and bags and lines and calling out to one another in gruff exotic monosyllables. Or I wander down the narrow cobbled streets of the Old Port district where women came piling out of bars arm in arm, or sit head to head in earnest conversation at the window-side tables of restaurants. Do I want a woman lover? Maybe. But for the time being it's enough to come home to my new home alone, pack a stack of albums on the record player, light up a cigarette, and then another, while I work on emptying last night's bottle of Lancers wine to add to my collection—lining the ceramic bottles along the walls on the floor giving the room a decorative flare. Nights home alone steaming vegetables and eating from the pot of brown rice I cooked up once a week—there was a kind of comfort in that. Love was beside the point now that I'd been fully awakened to the desperate circumstances of the multitudes on the planet, and when there was so much about me to hide from inquiring comrades.

"Behind every great fortune lies a crime." Balzac said that, and as I read about how my ancestors swindled fortunes from slaves, Native Americans, immigrants of all kinds, how they by-passed laws or created their own in order to amass the fortunes that continued to define the power elite, the very fortunes that I'd inherited, I couldn't imagine ever being able to re-pay our combined moral debt—to be forgiven, to be equal.

But now that a couple of months have passed since I arrived, I've begun to look at everyone I meet, male or female, with some level of hunger, some instant assessment to determine if I'm encountering a possible lover, or someone at least who will be my friend. It's not happening at the hospital where almost all the men who work in the operating room are doctors—a breed I quickly discovered was too high and mighty to appeal—and the women, almost exclusively nurses and aides, are more interested in talking soap operas or fashion trends during coffee breaks than about death squads, or how to build a socialist revolution, or what kind of moral debt I owe to poor people because I have inherited wealth. I had hopes that someone might surface there, but so far my only regular invitation for dinner is from my grandmother.

So I have my eyes on the others I meet by showing up at the bookstore from time to time, and attending events they sponsor, my heart pounding in my throat with every encounter from shyness and other amorphous fears of judgment. But it's a community I can imagine belonging to. There are women with women there, I can tell, and women alone, and men alone and with women—all about my age, all who know each other—a community I want to be a part of. But I play it cool, too cool to want anyone, to need anyone. At least that's how I hope I've appeared— independent, strong, a righteous warrior for the cause. That's how they all look, each in their own way with the same air about them, as if each one could be a male or female version of the Che poster in the bookstore. But the other night at another movie they sponsored, I saw a man, a man who my heart decided in that particular way it does in an instant, before thought even arrives, a man who might be just the one I've been looking for.

He was making rounds through the crowd as people found their seats in the school auditorium before the film. Was it the way he put his arm around that old man's shoulders, whispered in his ear and made him laugh out loud? Was it his opening remarks to the film, a labor history film, where he spoke with love and reverence about his French Canadian mother, "Me-mere", and his "Grand-mere" who'd grown up working in shoe factories and paper mills, who'd given their souls and their blood to the mundane brutality of factory work,—two women he "loved with all his heart". Or was it the way people were constantly approaching him with their attentions so that I sensed that he was a leader among them? Roland. Roland Morand. That sounded like a leader's name. A king's name in fact—though from the looks of it, it seemed he might already have a queen. It didn't escape me that RoAnne hovered around him like a bee, her arm on his when she could, her long hair cast over her pink-tinted glasses as she looked up at him adoringly. I promised myself that I would never fawn over him or anyone like that.

Many months later, when a friend of mine told me that Roland was "the most frightening person he'd ever met", I had to wonder why I hadn't seen him that way at all. True, if you looked only at his exterior you might back away from his black leather Winchester coat, Ho Chi Minh goatee and mustache, the dark heavy eyebrows that met in a fierce V beneath his Che beret, and his expression a confident, warrior remove. True, he had a scar on his face (a crescent moon over the left eyebrow), and moved like a lion ready to pounce, but sometimes it's possible to see through everything exterior into the heart of another, and his was a deep heart, filled and bruised with love . . . love and kindness and a deep burn, a hot flame fueled with desire for justice, all packed behind the steely façade that was the soldier's armor. At least that's what I saw.

After the film, our eyes connected for a moment and passed some kind of recognition—a guarded promise of more to come.

*　*　*

I have a job working at the bookstore three afternoons a week. I asked RoAnne if they needed some help, and she said sure, as simple as that, and I was in. I work with RoAnne, and sometimes a woman named Jo, abbreviated from "Mother Mary Jones" after the famous United Mine Workers organizer and, I suppose, because she has two young children. Her real name is Mary Jones and she's Devon's sister, as short and stick-boned as he is tall and broad, but with the same piercing small blue eyes that don't miss a twitch, and a fierceness behind the smile that says loud and clear, "Don't fuck with me!"

Jo and RoAnne show me how to make sales, check inventory, and place orders. They are each friendly in their own cool ways, giving me tasks to complete and then going about their own work. I want to know things about them—where they live, who they live with, how they've come to be revolutionaries. But while they aren't exactly unfriendly, there hasn't been one personal bit of information passed between us in two weeks. They seem content knowing only that I work at the hospital and that I have some family connections in the area. It isn't the way I'd

36

normally make friends with women, diving in with hours of revelations, but then I've never met women like RoAnne and Jo before—radical feminists, "champions of the working class", and since I don't feel like a champion of anything, I'm just as glad to take my cues from them about how to navigate in this new world. It's a guardedness that has its advantages at times. I knew that any question I asked either of them could be fired right back at me.

Where do you live? Where do *you* live?

Where did you grow up? Where did *you* grow up?

I had my secrets and it seemed that I wasn't the only one.

I do love everything about being in the bookstore—the freshly painted sign over the door with the red star on it, the tinkling sound of the bell as you open the old glass-paneled door, the dense radiator heat and the sun from the bay window where I can sit and read between customers. I love the books most of all—the aroma of their new ink as we unload them from the packing boxes, their smooth glossy covers, their infinite offerings, every one waiting to inform and change me in ways I haven't even yet imagined.

It's a small space, one room in front for the books, and then a small room in back with a table and chairs where we can do paperwork and store things. The storefront is actually on the city's main street, a street that is really only about a mile long, and though we aren't in the center of the commercial district, we are the only bookstore on Main Street. I think the freshly hand-painted sign over the door makes ours the brightest, most inviting storefront on that end of town. It looks promising, hopeful. Even in the few weeks that I've been there, customers are coming in more regularly, ten or fifteen a day. We don't make much money, enough to keep it going, but that's not the point. Everyone volunteers—we aren't in it for the money at all.

One thing it hasn't taken me long to realize though is that not everyone in town is so happy about a bookstore with a red star on the front broadcasting revolution on Main Street. I've come to find out that Devon and Roland were among the eight on the Death Squad hit list, and there's no question about the fact that the cops keep a hovering watch on us at the bookstore. So we work in pairs whenever we can; RoAnne says it's safer that way. I can tell that I've changed since the day of the demonstration just a few weeks ago when Carver and his cronies rattled me. Now that I have women like Jo and RoAnne and others as fierce as they are to toe the line with me, my fears have taken a back seat. We have a right to be here and I'm proud of the books we sell that offer truth and hope to the world, so I don't pay much mind to the police squad cars that sometimes cruise by slowly, their circular strobes lazily flashing, the cops staring in at us in menacing ways. It just proves to me that the status quo does not want change and will go to great lengths to protect their interests. A kind of war has been going on for years and I'm finally waking up to it and standing my ground. I think Jo senses this change in me and is warming to me because of it, though she's tougher and more ready to fight than I will ever be.

"Eat shit and die pigs!" she said the other day, while she smiled and waved at one of them through our window. She was smiling, but she spit the words out like curare darts, with cold and clear intent. I do admire her, at the same time that she scares me. She's half my height—ninety pounds of fire. When her jaw gets set in an under-bite, and her lips get pursed white in anger, I would definitely not want to be on her bad side.

"What if they read your lips?" I asked her, awed by her taunting. It's been permanently etched in my soul to be polite in every circumstance, whether it's called for or not. Another chain I have to break.

"Shit, if that pig comes in here I'll spit in his face," she said, never taking her slit-eyed expression off of him. And she would, I'm entirely sure of it. But I couldn't do that. I just don't think

I'll ever have that kind of courage. I can't even call a cop a 'pig'. When I try to say it—pig—it catches thick in my throat and stays there.

Over the next few weeks, I didn't see Roland that often in the bookstore and that was fine with me. I've been reading *The Dialectic of Sex* by Shulamith Firestone and wonder if I will *ever* have another relationship with a man! I agree with her that most leftist analysis alone is not radical enough. It ignores the sexual class system, that being the model for all exploitive systems from the beginning of "king"dom come. She calls it the "tapeworm" that must be eliminated first by true revolution.

I didn't know that eight million women had been burned at the stake in Europe by the Church as "witches". Or that, even after this country's Civil War, women were still essentially slaves, deprived of all rights, even to their own children! Or, that women were beaten, imprisoned, and some starved themselves to death to win our right to vote. Why didn't I know any of this? All my years of expensive education didn't include a word of it. What was it worth to be brainwashed by the male canon of history and philosophy and literature? No, I had to look at every relationship through the lens of the feminist now too, and that put Roland in an altogether different light. What did I want? A man to "save" me? No! A man who was a leader? I would look to a woman first.

But in my "un-liberated" heart, I looked to Roland as well.

I kept my focus on the bookstore work with RoAnne and Jo and occasionally some others in the group, and while I was aware of Roland's presence in the background, a presence like an epicenter, like an axis around which everything spun, I didn't have much opportunity to be around him. He was busy, always moving, and only occasionally would sweep into the store, cadre in tow, to advise us or to complete an order, arriving with the kind of energy that just might change the world. I couldn't deny that I felt some sparks jabbing my gut when he was around, that I avoided conversations with him out of shyness, but he seemed to be unavailable for anything so lowly as love anyway, what with the full weight of building a revolution on his shoulders.

He and Devon were equally intimidating in fact, as much because of their histories as their presence—both Vietnam Vets, and both ex-convicts who'd done time after coming home from Vietnam in the darkest of prisons for the most minor offenses (Roland caught with a five dollar bag of weed and sentenced to five years!) They were living examples for me of more injustice foisted upon the working class in this country—men of service who got screwed as soon as they came home, just as they had been screwed by the system before they left, and men the likes of whom I'd never met, who dwarfed all those I'd known before in stature and presence and purpose.

The more I learned about Roland, about how he started the bookstore, and a bail fund for prisoners, a radical statewide newspaper on prison reform, weekly study groups open to everyone, and free martial arts classes for women and children which he taught himself—the more I learned about him, the more my certainties grew that he'd never want to be with me anyway. I was, after all, "the enemy", a fact that was, I hoped, unknown to him and the rest of the people I met, but a fact I feared would be discovered any day and then I'd be out—if not literally out, at least shunned in subtle but definite ways.

But some days the not-so-shy part of me would kick in, the part that was independent, not afraid, a feminist who believed that there shouldn't be hierarchies of power at all, a "radical truth seeker" as my sister called me, who didn't listen or even recognize the belittling voice of her self-effacing other. She was the one who stared him directly in the eye from time to time, who turned away when others swooned over him, who was just as interested in finding a different lover as in scoring with Roland. But it was this part of me, ironically, that recognized something similar in us, who felt a connection slowly growing in spite of my resistance . . . slowly . . . from one brief interaction to the next.

As for lovers, any one of the new people I've met might be my next—male or female. It seems that partners come and go in this crowd. I would take any one of them to bed just to find out more about this new world of difference, just to show how ready I am to divorce myself from everything familiar and stifling in the world I'd grown up in. I loved them all without the slightest negative judgment for offering me just that.

And then there's the work. Every day that I come into the bookstore I'm reminded as I unload the tens upon tens of new books and flip through their contents, that I've come upon a great source, a deep well of teaching and knowledge of the causes that have created such inequality and suffering in the world, and I feel as if I can't drink fast enough or deeply enough to keep pace with the understanding I must acquire to become an effective part of the struggle for radical change. To rid the world of this country's gluttonous hold, that was what was required to bring an end to all the suffering our greedy ways inflicted on the planet. And all over the world people were waking up to the promise and necessity of an armed struggle—in South Africa, Angola, Mozambique, Vietnam, Chile, Nicaragua, El Salvador. The posters that decorate the walls of the bookstore celebrate their courage. Women with babies on their backs and rifles in their arms. Whole villages waving fists and calling out their determined resistance. No, capitalists would not let go of "their capital" without a war—capital which was the life blood of the people they stole it from.

And so I dive in—to the bookstore work, and soon after, I joined the study group too, and then the martial arts classes. But not because of Roland. Only partly because of Roland. He is a leader after all, and I still needed training.

*   *   *

I don't know what to write.

RoAnne's been scribbling away, letter after letter. She licks and stamps the envelopes in the same exact way she lights a cigarette, graceful and cool. I can see from where I sit at the other end of the long table in the back room where we're working that she has a neat flowing script and never crosses a word out. But I can't see what she's writing and I can't bring myself to ask.

It's quiet in the bookstore, dark outside. There are stacks of letters to respond to, letters that pile in from all over the country, from prisons with names that already strike ominous chords in me—Attica, Angola, Marion, San Quentin, Leavenworth. I study the handwriting, the small tight script, the backward slanted letters, and try to look into the eyes of the faces they belong to. Gilberto, Jerome, Tyrone, Vincent. I see the men in the Attica movie, the bodies dead in the courtyard. Their voices breathe on me. 'Miss Coleman' they call me, and sign off 'Your Brother in Struggle'. All the formality of the content, which is mostly political, makes the desperation I read jammed between the lines loudest of all. And, what really can I tell them about myself?

I don't know what to say.

Dear Roberto,

I've been told that if I write anything "too political" it will just be crossed out by the authorities. If I write anything too personal, my intentions could be misleading. I can't ask you questions about the prison conditions because you can't answer them. I can't ask you what you're doing time for, because I'm told you never ask an inmate about that . . .

42

Dear Roberto,

I've heard they have "behavior modification" units where you are in Marion. One brother told us after he got out of there that they strapped him naked to a stainless steel table twenty-four hours a day and every day that he was "good" they gave him one item of clothing back, and every day he was "bad" they took all the clothes away and made him start all over again. I wonder if this has happened to you.

I myself am going home to a nice basket of crabmeat and homemade blueberry muffins that my grandmother sent over to me. I have a trust fund, a new car, and I've never even had a detention at any one of the three private schools I went to for the last twenty years. How can I explain, and I'm afraid to even admit, that even with all of that I still feel "chained" too . . .

In the end, I can't help hiding behind versions of the same political rhetoric they send, about the necessity of raising consciousness among the oppressed masses and fighting the lies of the power elite and then signing off, Your Sister in the Struggle, and feeling like a hypocrite.

I write five or six with hardly a word of difference between them and just thank god that RoAnne doesn't ask to read one of mine. Or worse, that Roland doesn't appear to look over my shoulder. We don't say a word to each other while we work, but I guess that's okay.

"I'm getting ready to lock up," she says.

I'm getting ready to ask you if you'll go out and have a drink with me, to visit.

"I'm all done too." I can tell she'd say no by how she's rushing to get her stuff together.

"You coming to the study group tomorrow?"

"Ya, I think I can make it. "

"Great. See you then."

We part and walk our separate ways. I resist the urge to follow her, to find out where she lives up on "The Hill", that part of town where they all live.

*   *   *

Every week we gather for study groups in an old warehouse down near the waterfront—a group of twelve or so that fluctuates, new faces coming and going that I am slowly starting to recognize. RoAnne is always there of course because Roland is, and Jo too, her brother Devon or Sarah depending on whose turn it is to watch the baby, and sometimes Nick from the demonstration. There are others I'm getting to know. Bobby and Joel work at the newspaper and always come together, red-eyed and high on something even though there's a rule that you're not supposed to come to meetings that way. Joel has a gold front tooth and a big everlasting smile and Bobby is always doing a deadpan Irish comedy routine that lightens what can be a pretty stiff atmosphere.

And there are two lesbian women who come as a couple. They sit close together, thigh to thigh, and write notes back and forth. One of them, Lori, is an ex-con too, the first and only female ex-con I've met. She's sharp-eyed like a ferret but otherwise so young looking and small that I am awed at the idea of her incarceration. That is the word she uses—incarceration—when she talks about her prison time. It has a dignified sound to it, a certain power that I covet. Plus, she's a feminist too, "a radical dyke ex-con feminist" and so I think she must have a lot to teach me. There are moments when Lori looks at me, when she chooses me with her look, even while she's stroking her lover's thigh, and that's exciting too.

The study group is the only place I really get to study Roland because there, when he's talking, I have an excuse to watch him more closely. Roland the leader. Roland the most advanced student of Marxism in the group. We're not supposed to have "a leader" per se, and he doesn't presume that position, but it's there as an undercurrent, and most everyone seems to look to him for clarity whether he asks for it or not.

It seems effortless for him to have focus and direction. While each of us take a turn deciding on reading assignments, Roland's are the most difficult, the hardest to understand—on dialectical materialism, the economics of monopoly capitalism, the theory and practice of socialism. He says they're pieces that he's found helpful in understanding what we're working towards. He says that any of the great revolutionary leaders would counsel us that without a sound theoretical base, our own practice and efforts will fail. I think it frustrates him that everyone is so quiet during our "discussions", reluctant to jump in and talk about the parts we don't understand. He jiggles his foot and taps his pencil on the table during the silences, and we stumble through as best we can.

"The key conception of dialectics is the conception of contradiction inherent in the very nature of things—that the motive force of qualitative change lies in the contradictions contained within all the processes of nature and society, and that in order to understand, control, and master things in practice we must proceed from the concrete analysis of their contradictions . . . "

I would rather read the life histories of freedom fighters I found in the bookstore, real stories of oppression and liberation that make transformation seem possible. But I want to understand—I want to find the pulse of meaning in these readings. I think sometimes that Roland is the only one who understands how these abstract concepts apply to our lives, to our situation here, and that he, at least, has a plan for how we'll proceed to achieve our revolutionary intentions.

Read it again.

"The key conception of dialectics is the conception of contradiction inherent in the very nature of things . . . "

I wonder if those sorts of contradictions include things like me being a revolutionary with a trust fund, or me advocating violence against the ruling class but wanting to keep my family off the firing lines.

With these thoughts the fog just gets thicker. I'm farther and farther from anyone, anything familiar. In the fog I've abandoned my parents and family, and Roland and the rest are way ahead on the road to victory.

But which road? What kind of victory? The truth was I didn't have a clue what revolution would look like. Would we be marching on Broadway in a ticker-tape parade? Would there be leagues of bloodied soldiers and tanks? Would we be opening the mansions in my parents' neighborhood to hoards of hungry and poor?

"Come the revolution!" they all say.

Come the revolution there won't be any more rich people owning all the means of production, rich people living in big houses, rich people driving fancy cars, with stock portfolios, with nannies, with second homes, while millions have nothing. These were all the things that I believed should happen, could happen with leaders like Roland. Good riddance to all the mansions in my life—my parents', my grandmothers', my great aunt's. Turn them over to the people! My parents' bedroom alone could sleep thirty homeless. They could even sleep on the rug, my mother's precious white rug that was as thick as a mattress. And there were enough pillows on my mother's bed alone for everyone to have something. I'd be happy to give my bed away, to sleep in a tent in the backyard, to never go to my parents' ski chalet in Vermont again. And if it took force to make it happen . . .

By whatever means necessary, like Malcolm X said, and I could feel at times a kind of reckless excited readiness in me to take the quickest route possible to change everything around. But in my mind, in the picture of the revolution that was always half-formed in the fog, I knew that all of these events somehow occurred without bloodshed. I couldn't conjure a real war with firing lines and battles, with torture and maiming in the name of peace and equality. And yet it was the torture and maiming done in the name of capitalism and imperialism that turned my stomach, that made me want to reach for a gun to help defend the weak and abused victims of our system's ruling class. In everything I read, the same message was repeated:

Without mass struggle there can be no revolution.

Without armed struggle there can be no victory.

You have to take an elevator fifty-six floors to the top of the Chase Manhattan building on Wall Street to visit Dad at work. You exit into a large reception area, thickly carpeted and furnished with leather chairs and polished wood tables. No, you tell the receptionist, you don't have an appointment. He isn't expecting you. You just thought you'd stop by to say hi . . . but only if it's convenient . . . only if he's available. Already you begin to feel this was a bad idea, this little surprise you'd planned on a whim. You haven't been here since you were a child, accompanied by an adult. You're still a child. Already you feel that you don't belong, that all your entitlement to this visit was left behind in the elevator, that you should be dressed differently, that you should be different entirely to come here.

You walk on air, in the clouds, above the world surrounded by windows of sky. Your steps make whispering noises as you follow a perfectly tailored woman to the door with the brass plaque that has your father's name engraved on it. He greets you with a hug, calls you "honeybunch", your face pressed against his gray lapels, his scent of newsprint and faint aftershave. He is perfectly tall and strong. But as soon as you've entered his office you wish you could leave.

You don't belong here.

The man you know as a father is hardly the one before you and you wonder who he is. He is the managing partner of this law firm of two hundred. He has the biggest office. He is so glad you came by, he says, and you did see a certain light in his face when you appeared at the door. With his arm around you he in-

troduces you to some other men in gray suits who shake your hand, pat your shoulder, and hurry away down the hall.

He looks at his watch.

He takes you over to the solid wall of windows that face downtown Manhattan and New York Harbor. He says, "Isn't that view something to look at?" the same way you're certain he says to everyone who comes in the office. He says it just the same way because you know he's no good at small talk, just like you.

Together you spend a silent minute watching all the miniature comings and goings of the little lives down below and the great pale expanse of New York Harbor beyond. He jingles change in his pocket.

You're thinking that from way up here it would be easy to feel like the manager of everything. You're thinking that from the big leather chair behind the big mahogany desk that it would be easy to make phone calls, to sign papers that would change the lives of millions, to make the Nestles' kinds of decisions that make millionaires off of babies' lives.

Your new friends would call him a killer if they knew. They'd say he'd never give away his power without a fight. He's not a fighter, not the man you know, but you wonder what in a million years "peaceful alternatives" would ever mean to his corporate clients. You wonder again if the violence you talk about in your study groups is the only way to get their attention.

You remember what the professor who got you thinking in college said, about how violence needs to be re-defined. He said that the real violence is the mansion in the exclusive neighborhood, the private school, the all-white male corporate board. He said that violence is whatever creates profit and comfort for one at the expense of another, whatever places profit over human, animal, or environmental welfare.

Your father, his partners and clients, all the people you know who live off of corporate profit, along with your own self, all of you are the real killers. We are the violent ones.

He picks up the phone. "Let's order some lunch."

He tells you you can order anything you want, that the two of you can eat together in the executive dining room down the hall. It's a long way down to where you'd like to go with him for lunch—fifty-six floors down to the bench in the park where you can just barely imagine what it might be like to share a sandwich with him, throwing crumbs to the pigeons, watching the boats go by for a few minutes. Just the two of you. It's just more than you can bear to eat in the executive dining room, and you can't believe he doesn't know that about you by now. You don't want to hurt his feelings but eating there is just out of the question and you know you have to leave before it gets any more complicated. You tell him you're already late for lunch with a friend . . . you just stopped by. You wanted to see him, to see the view. It's been so long since you've been up here.

"Are you sure?" He looks at his watch. The phone rings and he tells his secretary to hold the call.

He walks you back to the elevator with his arm around your shoulder.

Love you honey.

Love you Dad.

You'll be home tonight?

I'll be home tonight.

*   *   *

Lately, I've grown aware that not everyone sees Roland as a leader. Nick, the red-haired man from the demonstration, comes often to the study groups, and when he does the tension can be razor sharp between them, a tension that apparently has been years in the making and now it's not hard to see the rift that's pulling the group into two camps.

It's hard for me to imagine that anyone would choose Nick over Roland as a leader. Nick was always standing up in meetings to make his arguments, and he uses his middle finger to point or tap the table for emphasis and I've always hated that. He tries to rattle Roland, and sometimes he comes close. I can see Roland's dark eyebrows gather together like a thunderhead and his jaw popping with tension, but he doesn't raise his voice. He's a lion waiting in readiness, only his tail twitching in anticipation of the moment he'll pounce and swallow his prey whole.

Whatever their personal differences, the two of them particularly lock horns around the issue of violence—whether we should promote it and support it as a necessary means to our ends. Nick holds firm that violence will turn people against the Left and ruin everything we've been trying to do. He says there are "peaceful alternatives" that will show people how the system is set up to oppress them.

"We need to raise awareness on a grassroots level, the very grass that may start the prairie fire someday, but not yet." He was referring to the motto, "One spark lights the prairie fire" used by the Weather Underground, a guerilla group that had been conducting bombings and other violent political actions in the U.S. for years.

Roland doesn't come right out and advocate forming a guerilla group, but you can tell that's where he's headed in his thinking. I'd heard him say more than once that peaceful alternatives are fine and necessary . . . that he'd spent the last ten years organizing and serving and educating the people with non-violent means of changing the system, but he always defended other groups around the world who'd chosen armed resistance in response to colonial tyranny and imperial control. In our last group meeting he'd become more vocal and vehement than usual. "Every group I've been involved in since I came back from Vietnam, wherever I've worked . . . no matter how small or how large an organization I became a part of, every one of those groups was under police surveillance. Every one of those groups experienced harassment of some kind. And it's just getting worse! People . . . organizers and activists are being locked up all the time . . . and some murdered! The Death Squad in this town is just one more declaration of war against the people. Some part of this movement has to be ready to defend itself against attack . . . *all* revolutionary movements need cadre trained in defensive tactics."

There was a nervous silence as he paused and looked around the table. A few heads nodded in agreement but it seemed that few could meet his look head on. My own eyes glanced off his urgent, demanding gaze. "Hey . . . wake up people! It's happening all over the world. I think the prairie fire *has* begun! You've just got to ask yourself, which side are you on?"

He didn't usually speak out so forcefully, but with his ancient warrior face and earnest command, I thought, even sitting in my own discomfort and uncertainty of which side I would choose, that he could lead an army of thousands to victory and he'd never leave their side—like Ho Chi Minh, like Che—he could be that kind of leader. But Nick, you just knew that Nick would be waving the white flag before the first shot was fired.

At least that's what Jo said about him. The next day, when we were at the bookstore together working, she said that Nick and the others who go along with him are just "armchair revolutionaries"—people who talk a hot line about social change but aren't ready to go the distance to make it happen.

"They make me sick!" she said with a fake spit on the floor. "You can never trust someone like Nick when things get heavy. When the pigs come after you they're the first to hightail it the other way. Or worse—they rat on you."

Still, I wasn't sure I could pick up a gun.

But listening to Jo, I was even more certain I didn't want to be like Nick, the way she talked about him, to be in any way associated with cowardice or insincerity . . . to be any kind of a hypocrite or an armchair revolutionary.

* * *

51

I had to give Roland a ride to the study group. He asked if I was going and what could I say? "Can I catch a ride?" he said, just like that, before I had a chance to get out of it. I couldn't pretend I didn't have a car. He knew I did by now—he'd just never seen it. No one had, even though I'd been working in the bookstore for three months, and going to the study groups almost as long. But Roland especially, I didn't want him to see my brand new car, to know that much about me.

Three months and I have never been alone with Roland. I'm never alone in the bookstore and he always has someone tagging along—a Roland Morand groupie is the way I've come to see them. Everyone wants a little of what Roland's got—his power, his vision, his hard to get laugh. It makes me pretend all the more that I don't want any of it. I'm not going to fawn over Roland. Besides, I don't forget for a second that my background represents everything that he's at war with. Still, the quick looks between us go back and forth whenever we're in the same room together no matter who's around. Shy and not shy. Proud and not proud.

So I barely look up when he comes in and I turn away a little so I can compose my face, take the startle and blush out of it.

"Hi."

"Hey Roland."

"You going to the study group?"

"Yeah, I was just closing up."

"Can I catch a ride with you?"

"Sure."

That's all we say until we're out on the street walking towards my car, until we're at my car, the red little Fiat that I got when I turned twenty-one, and Roland says, since now it's just after Christmas, "Oh wow . . . did your Daddy put that in your stocking?" He's teasing, not in a mean way, and I have to laugh, laugh out loud, because of course the ruse is up, and I've been "outed" after all this time, all the months I was sure none of them knew. Now that it's out I can tell he doesn't hate me, that he's flirting with me in fact, and that makes me laugh even more. I've been hiding my car up the street and around the corner for months . . . what an idiot!

Now, under the streetlamp, my little red car looks particularly red, particularly shiny and European, particularly new. And yes, I would have to say if I could speak at all, which I suddenly can't, that yes, my father did put it in my stocking more or less, my twenty-first birthday stocking. And what's worse, although I don't have to tell you Roland, I don't have to confess, that I chose it. I chose it on my very own and drove out of there like I was some kind of royalty, as high as a kite just on how cool it was to slide up and down the manual gears, my little coach so light and tight it floated on air.

But what I also want to say in my defense is that I've changed since then. What I'd really like now is one of those cars that your friends have, the old Chevy's with the split-leather interior and the rust inhibitor patches on the sides. I'm not kidding. If I could turn mine in for one of those without being such an obvious phony, I would in a minute.

You're laughing at me. You would be laughing if I could actually tell you all of this the way I sometimes talk to you in my mind. But you've swallowed the laugh for now. Now you're just sitting there, inches away from me in the passenger seat, with your leather jacket smell and your crescent moon scar waiting to be touched and your long thighs with the worn jeans stretched over them, your left knee brushing my hand every time I shift into third. You would be laughing if we could find our way out of these pretend places where we wear all these labels in layers— rich, poor, ex-con, ex-preppy, feminist, revolutionary. We resume our serious surface, neither of us knowing for certain if there is any room or any time left in the world of the revolutionary for fooling around.

CHAPTER 6

——•——

It's Sunday, visiting day at the state prison in Thomaston. I'm sharing a seat with RoAnne on the bus, a small yellow school bus our bookstore collective rents every week for the two-hour ride north. It's another Roland Morand initiative organized on the behalf of prisoners and their families, along with the bail fund he began, legal aide affiliates, and the statewide alliance to advocate for the rights of the incarcerated. There are about twenty other women with us, chatting away like schoolgirls on a class trip, and though I don't have anything to chat about, I'm letting the music of their voices lull me into a sense of belonging, like we're an extended family of women making the best of a bad situation, with me included.

This is my first time going with them. I'm going to visit Vinny, a man I've been writing to through the prison correspondence program. This is my first meeting with him. He is my first inmate 'in the flesh' and this is my first trip "inside".

I'm trying to pretend that everything's not a screaming first for me, that I've been on lots of rides with women to visit men in prison, that I've been inside before, been searched and locked in, that I've sat and chatted with this man, Vinny, and I have lots to say.

RoAnne is talking mostly to the two women in the seat across from us about news from Thomaston, about the recent crackdown on the inmates, the new and more restrictive visiting rules—no sitting on laps, no making out, no physical contact except handholding. She's telling them that Roland is helping to organize a prisoner's union inside to fight these new rules. Her tone has that familiar territorial brag to it, the one that stakes her claim on Roland with every woman she meets, even if they haven't even met him yet.

But today, I don't really care that I'm being reminded that they're together. I'm thinking about Vinny, the man I'm going to see. I'm a little relieved, a little disappointed, overhearing the new visiting restrictions, that there's no chance I'll be sitting on his lap and making out with him.

We've been writing for a couple of months, our letters formal at first, the same attempts to exchange political theory that I've been doing with others I correspond with, only at Thomaston the screws open everything. They'd turned our letters into fragmented pieces of sentences between long lines they'd blacken out with laundry marker, pages that looked more like a lengthy Morse code by the time they got through with it.

The prison system is an antiquated device that exposes capitalism's essential fallibility. What we need to do is . . . and then thick black marker lines would follow, running together so that you could feel the force of the hand that put them there.

The screws will have fun with this one, I'd write back, and send him long passages from Frantz Fanon or Karl Marx that they'd have to cross out. It was like a game we played—anything to taunt them with their abuse of power. Only my moves felt reckless to me, not knowing the stakes. It was like walking through a minefield you didn't know was there—like not knowing what a mine was.

To be honest, I knew these letters gave me a kind of license to puff up this image of myself as a "freedom fighter", a comrade of the oppressed. Even though I tell myself I don't know anything about their world, another part of me, a part I can't really share with him or with anyone, believes that I know what it feels like to be in prison, to feel trapped. I have chains to break too—long generations of chains to the bloodied events of my ancestors, to entitlement that I don't want any part of any more, and to a dark shadow of shame that's always with me.

Vinny's been inside for ten years, since he was seventeen, but it's only lately, since he's gotten political and started organizing the other inmates, that they've been really coming down on him. In the four months we've been writing he's been in solitary more than half of it, but every time he comes out he's more resolved than ever to fight back. That's what it seemed like, what I gleaned from his letters, especially the few I'd gotten hand-delivered, un-censored.

"They think they can silence me with their goon tactics," he wrote. "They think I'll leave here kissing their fascist asses—but every time they throw me in the hole, it makes me stronger, more determined to expose the system. It's like the brother George Jackson said before they shot him down, 'There's no turning back from awareness.'"

Then, about a month ago, little intimacies began to appear. He switched from signing his letters "In solidarity" to "Your loving brother in struggle." I took his lead and did the same, but cautiously. Given his circumstances I didn't want to be seductive. I didn't want to compromise or belittle our political intentions. I was diligent, tried to see my letters as assignments, part of my education in training as a revolutionary. We were studying to be warriors, not lovers. But I had to admit I began to have some fantasies about love, imagining what it would be like to be the shining light in his dark imprisoned life, and how he might take Roland's place and become my teacher about the struggle.

He asked for my picture. I dismissed any romantic ideas when I chose it. It wasn't a close-up. I was sitting on the bench outside the bookstore and about the only thing sexy about it was that my hair was long and shiny in the sun. Other than that, I looked plain enough. When I sealed the envelope I convinced myself that my thoughts were of friendship, kindness, and doing the right thing.

But once it had been sent, it was as if the envelope contained some physical part of me that bonded me to him. I imagined the ways he might daydream of touching me when he pulled the picture from the pages of his book, or pinned it to his bedside cell wall. I began to wait for his letters with impatience, and contained myself from replying too quickly. And somehow, without knowing what he looked like, I managed to hold his completely imagined body close to me as I fell asleep at night.

Thomaston looked as I'd imagined it, a mountain of a stone fortress shadowing a small surrounding village. There was a crowd of other visitors waiting when we arrived, and together we were herded into a screening area to be searched before we'd be cleared for entry.

I have a confession to make. I think I should have been filled with despair and outrage traveling through the multiple gates, the search, the lewd once-overs of all the fat bellied screws along the way, but that wasn't it at all. The further in I got, the more steel gates that echo-slammed behind me, the greater the swell of calm I felt inside. Like finally, after all my wondering who I was I'd finally landed in a place that defined me. Never mind that I was only the substance of opposition. That was clarity enough.

Now I watched Vinny shuffle in, a guard at each elbow. Big guards . . . and Vinny so slight, bird-like, air-boned, with a grayish-white complexion to match the prison walls. He had long, black Rapunzel hair and his expression was soft and sad in a feminine way, broken hearted.

That's what I saw to begin with. A small man—a boy really,

escorted by two huge men. It wasn't how I'd imagined him to be. I blushed to think of the ways he'd appeared in my mind—muscle-armed, broad and rugged looking. That's how all the ex-cons I knew on the outside were. Well what difference did it make anyway? When I looked in his eyes, when I saw in that first moment all the pride and resignation there, I had a terrible feeling, a wave of aching and wanting to take all of him in, to be someone that could love all the darker sides of another, mirror my own absolution without a stone cast. That would be freedom enough.

As the guards backed away from his chair on the other side of the table and the newly-installed Plexiglas partial wall that separated us, we exchanged a fist salute, a rote bonding among revolutionaries.

"Hey Sister. So we finally meet." His voice was quiet and whispery dry. And his lips were dry, cracked at the corners, the lower one split in the middle. I bet it hurt when he smiled. Don't smile then. It's okay.

"Did the screws give you a hard time coming in?" His eyebrows furrowed with concern and he leaned forward peering at me closely. He was ready to fight for me, I could see, beyond his gentle demeanor. He'd take them on if I said one word that they'd given me any trouble. I thought of him cornered by the guards I'd seen bringing him in.

Devon, who'd done time at Walpole, told me they'd come into your cell while you slept. One goon would grab your feet, another your arms, and they'd swing you into the bars over and over. Inmates died that way, but those in power were always able to cover it up.

"No, no trouble."

I didn't know how to begin. There was so much you could hide in letters that he wouldn't know until now. What did he see that he had to re-arrange from how he'd imagined me? Everything seemed dumb to talk about, or fake. Everything seemed to come back to the truth of the space between us that I couldn't move beyond. Where was our common ground—inmate from poor rural Maine and free-walking rich girl from New York? All the delicacy in his small hands toying nervously with a rubber band he held, and the way his eyes looked to me as if I might know the way—it changed everything.

We talked in short choppy exchanges, trying to find a rhythm. Sometimes his low voice was muffled by the background noise in the room, crowded with the voices of other inmates and visitors. Or we'd start speaking at the same moment and then stumble over who would pick up the thread of conversation that seemed so tenuous between us.

"Thanks for all your letters," he said at one point. "It made a big difference, being able to write to you. And thanks for the picture . . . You're . . . " He stopped, swallowed his words, and looked down at the rubber band, maybe even shyer than me, and I could see the hint of a smile he was trying to hold back. "You're a really solid sister."

It was what he didn't say that made me blush a bit, shy and giddy there with the table and the Plexiglas between us, almost as if we were alone for a minute.

You weren't supposed to ask why someone was inside, what they'd done. I knew a little of his story—armed robbery at a gas station with an empty gun and a car theft.

A small part of me wanted to know more, all of it, every detail of what he'd done then, the kid he'd been, what he felt with the gun in his pocket as he swung open the glass door, what he'd been telling himself—all the sadness in his eyes somehow like my own. I couldn't imagine him threatening anyone.

"Hey, what happened in the parole hearing you wrote about? You said you might be getting out soon."

"Yeah, it went well. I should be out in a few weeks."

I couldn't figure his expression—the same low sad tones of his voice hadn't budged at all.

"Jesus, really? You're getting out? That's so far out!" I sounded like a silly cheerleader. That was all wrong. Dumb of me. I could see he looked scared, unsure, the way my canary trembled when I drew her from her cage for her first flight around my bedroom, her fear light on my finger. She'd spun away, smashing into ceiling corners, getting tangled in the window drapes, her wings whirring a desperate insistence to stay airborne. And the small sound of her body when she finally dropped to the ground—there was nothing I could do to save her.

"Yeah well we'll see what happens." He chewed the corner skin on his thumbnail and looked right through me for a second.

I asked him where he was going to go when he got out. I knew there was no "home" to speak of—no family he'd mentioned.

"I don't know. Somebody will put me up I guess." He sounded matter of fact about it, like he didn't need much.

"Well, if you get stuck, you can stay at my place."

That's what I said, not as a come on. I wasn't thinking about sleeping with him then. I was thinking it would be good to take care of him, to feed him, let him take a hot bath and sleep for days long into the afternoon. He could have my bed and I'd sleep on the couch. Share the wealth. All that I'd been given and didn't deserve.

When our time was up, the screws whacked the metal doorframe with their nightsticks. One of the larger ones walked by our table, glared at me while he brushed by Vinny's chair. He tugged his hair—not hard, but he did it. "Come on princess, time to go." And then he winked at me.

Pig.

On the way home, the mood in the bus was more subdued. There were long stretches of silence when all you could hear were the seat springs marking every dip in the road, and when someone did speak their voice was barely louder than a whisper. But I felt that in the silence, our group of women was bonded in a deeper way now, each of us holding the images and sounds of the prison, its rank institutional air, its bullies and fear and the chill of its tyranny. Before today I'd felt certain that prison could never be the way towards the "rehabilitation" that it claimed to accomplish, but now I felt that my understanding had been entirely superficial. Going inside and meeting Vinny had exploded this feeling of wrongness into every cell of my body. Who had designed such a concept? What kind of mind could be so deluded as to think that such a dehumanizing system could ever accomplish any kind of healing?

Vinny and all of the men these women had visited had gone back to their cells, to their lives behind bars while we were surrounded by the huge expanse of forest and sky outside the bus, whipping through space at sixty miles an hour, infinite space, on our way home to prepare our choice of foods, to read our choice of books, to sleep in the quiet privacy of our warm beds. I could barely sit still with these contrasts. I cracked my window to breathe fresh air, the clean cold air of the un-boundaried expanse around me.

They'd had Vinny for ten years for his crime.

I had Soledad Brother with me, George Jackson's prison letters. I turned to a passage that I'd read over and over, the lines that I'd underlined and starred in the margins.

"Settle your quarrels, come together, understand the reality of our situation, understand that fascism is already here, that people are dying who could be saved, that generations more will die or live poor butchered half-lives if you fail to act. Do what must be done, discover your humanity and your love in revolution. Pass on the torch. Join us, give up your life for the people."

Chapter 7

— · —

Of all the people in the group, Jo and I spend the most time together, sharing the same shift in the bookstore. We're getting to be friends, I think, though I'm careful to stay in her shadow when I can, to let her take the lead, and to always be on the alert for any sign of her imminent explosion. Not that I've ever seen her blow, but you can feel the potential in the down turn of her mouth, the slight hunch in her narrow shoulders, and the way her eyes darken from pale blue to some deeper shade when she talks about injustice, or revolution, or of the pigs that cruise outside the bookstore door.

She has lots of secrets about her too, like they all do.

Sometimes we drink tea in the back room of the bookstore before we open up for business. Jo drinks Lipton's light and sweet and I'm getting to like the same. It's the time we talk the most.

"These are my kids," she said one day, picking up the picture frame that's always on the desk in the back room. She kisses each snapshot before she hands the frame to me for admiration. Blonde haired and blue eyed, she tells me they are both named after Black revolutionaries who've given their lives for the struggle.

She tells me they named Mark, who's four, after the Black Panther, Mark Clark, who was murdered by the FBI the same year he was born.

"And Lou, my baby, she's almost two, we named her after Fannie Lou Hamer."

I'm embarrassed that I can't remember exactly who Fannie Lou is, if I've got her mixed up with Rosa Parks, and that I'm not sure about the story behind Mark Clark's death. These are *my* secrets. It's another reason I let Jo do most of the talking.

When she says "we" I know she's referring to her husband, Sam, and Sam is one of the secrets about Jo that hovers around her. She's only mentioned his name on one or two other occasions, and then misses a beat—like she's said something wrong, like she's surprised to have said his name at all.

"Don't your kids live with you?" I asked.

"Oh they do . . . they're at home with Sam most of the time . . . or Devon and Sarah."

There it was again, the pause, the half-beat of hesitation. But she said his name with the same pride in her voice that she used with the pictures of her kids.

I know I have to measure my questions. I don't know why exactly, but I'm learning that you don't ask for information about anyone's private life, present or past, but I risked just one more question. I wanted to know if Roland was part of the shared living arrangement . . . Roland and RoAnne.

But when I ask, it's clear I've gone too far. She can tell I'm fishing for something and she answers with a flat "no" and a sharp look that makes me blush, and ends whatever inquiry I had in mind. I want to tell her she doesn't have to worry, that all her secrets are safe with me. I want to tell her that all I'm thinking about is how great it must be to be living together—one big extended family, sharing kids and meals and work, devoting their lives to building a better world, working together that way. They have everything that I long to be a part of.

One secret she has shared with me is about her having epilepsy. She told me about that a few days later. She didn't want to, but she had to because we work together so often.

"I figure because you're kind of a nurse you won't get all freaked out, but I'd appreciate it if you kept your mouth shut about it. I don't like the whole world knowing my business." She leaned back in her chair and tucked her shirt in a little more. Her shirt is always tucked in, clean and pressed, and her belt buckle pulled tight to the last notch. She was so very thin, matchstick thin, they probably didn't make belts small enough for her.

I told her of course that I wouldn't say anything.

"So have you ever seen a seizure?"

I had to tell her no, I hadn't, but that I knew a little about them.

"Well, I have seizures, just so you know. If I fall down sometime and start jerking like a motherfucker, just turn me on my side, and if you can keep me from splitting my head open on something that would be great."

She darted me one of her fierce looks, scanning my face for something—disgust or judgment of some kind. It seemed I had only a split second to re-assure her. I knew I'd be fine with the seizures. It was, in a way, one more thing to draw me closer—that made Jo different from anybody I'd ever met before and took me further from the world I'd grown up in. The way I felt at that moment was that I'd do anything at all to help her out.

I didn't have the words to say this so I just met her gaze head on. She laughed suddenly, and it was infectious the way she did this, always holding the back of one hand to her mouth to cover her teeth, which were grayish, she told me, because the medicine they gave her was slowly killing them one by one. Her high, tinkling laugh made me feel like we were actually part of the same secret.

"God, I'm not going to bite you! Besides, my fucking teeth would fall out if I tried."

I loved her courage. I looked forward to the time when I could help her through a seizure, when I could be as brave as her and share some of the authority she had about life that I felt so shy on.

We're together in the bookstore, having our tea in the back, when we hear a sharp rap on the door, like something's hit the glass. The store's open but no one's at the door when we come out front to investigate, only an envelope that's been passed through the mail slot—a sealed envelope without postage or address. Later, I'd think that it wasn't so smart to pick it up, to open it so naively without considering the possibilities, but for a few more moments, I'm as dumb and unsuspecting about real life as you can get.

The note says: *Get out of town you fucking freaks—or else!*

The letters are an uneven print, scribbled carelessly, and the paper lined and torn from a ringed notebook. There was a poorly drawn scull and crossbones at the bottom of the page.

"Jesus, not another one of these." Jo said without the alarm I felt rising in my chest. She handed me the note.

"Another one? They've been others?"

"Well, just one, maybe two that I can think of . . . the same kind of thing. It's probably the pigs trying to scare us out of here. Since we organized the publicity about the Death Squad, they're really on our case. I'll call Sam about it though. He'd want to know."

I was glad that whoever Sam was that he'd want to know, that Jo wasn't just going to toss the note in the garbage without so much as a second glance, the way she sounded like she'd like to. I didn't want to be scared by the note either, but just holding it made me feel like I was being watched, like someone was there behind the bookshelves, or in the back room crouched behind the book boxes—somewhere, someone watching us. So while Jo called Sam about it, I made myself go into the back room to get our coats, feeling like a kid that needs to look under her bed before she goes to sleep because after all, we'd just been sitting back there.

My heart was pounding as I as I stood there in a space that felt a million miles away from Jo's voice in the next room talking in hushed tones on the phone. It could have been a premonition, the fear I felt, of the next time I'd be in that room—of all the evil that would seep into every box and book back there, that would fill the room to bursting and then blow everything apart.

"Okay, I'm going home for a little bit. Sam wants to see the note. Do you want to come?" I jumped at the sound of her voice behind me, but it wasn't lost on me for a second that this invitation was another opening, another sign of trust that I'd be allowed into their circle of family, and that meeting Sam was part of the offering. Of course I wanted to go.

It wasn't a long way to their apartment, just up Main Street to the other end of town, up a long hill into the poorer neighborhood. Everybody from the bookstore and the prison group lived up there, on 'The Hill' they called it, except for me. A few times I'd driven up through the winding streets of that neighborhood and imagined that I lived in one of the old houses closely set with different paint colors peeling off of clapboard siding, the sagging front stoops buoyed by cinder blocks. We passed a cluster of houses where laundry hung on lines strung between the upstairs windows, frozen stiff in the wintry afternoon sun, and I thought how comfortable it would be to have neighbors who weren't afraid to let the whole world see what shape and color underwear they wore, if their socks were thin at the heels. I imagined that the people in these houses would be tolerant of imperfection in a way that I'd rarely experienced in my own home. I imagined "stopping by" and being invited to sit at the table for supper without having to swallow or cover or tuck in whatever it was about me that didn't quite measure up. That's the way it felt in my parents' home—that I never quite measured up.

Jo's apartment was on the second floor of a two-story house like any of the others. The staircase was narrow and dark with bare bulb hallway lights and steam heat banging in the hall radiator. Looking into the dark corners, I thought for a second about the note in the bookstore, of the breathless feeling I'd had standing in the back room. I was grateful to be with Jo. There didn't seem to be an ounce of fear in her, just fight, and now that we'd left the bookstore, the whole event had taken on some excitement, some impending drama that I was proud to be a part of.

"Now you see we're at war," she'd said to me in the car on the way. "Didn't I tell you? That's what 'cadre' means—warrior. I guess you've signed on now, sister." She poked me in the ribs and gave a little laugh. I liked that, the poke, the laugh, and thinking of us as warriors together.

More intrigue as Jo knocked a special coded rhythm that was greeted by a loud threatening voice on the other side of the door asking us to identify ourselves. "It's me, Sam."

At the sound of Jo's voice, the door was unbolted, two deadbolts, and even then, Sam checked us through the hook-and-eye latch before he opened the door fully.

I don't know which impression hit me first when I entered—the comfortable bright kitchen, full of coffee aroma and sunshine, the red geraniums on the windowsill, the bay sparkling in the distance, the entirely welcoming feeling of the small room, or Sam, his dark face, his skin permanently tanned and lined as if he'd spent his life in a desert, his eyes deep and small in their sockets inches away from me, scrutinizing me instantly as if I might have been the very one to leave the note. He wasn't tall, like Devon or Roland, but he was solid and powerful, all tension and readiness, his black beard, hair, and mustache complementing the severity of his gaze. In an instant I felt as if he could read every weak and counter-revolutionary thought I'd ever had, and some I hadn't formed yet. Like Roland, everything about him demanded respect. But in the next moment he smiled, an open smile, and shook my hand firmly, grasping my arm with his other hand in almost a hug.

"We haven't met yet, but Jo's told me about you. You're welcome here."

We moved into the room, and as there wasn't room for all of us to stand, I took a seat at the table by the window.

"Where're the kids?" Jo asked. She and Sam stood side by side, affectionately leaning into each other for a moment and I watched Sam reach up to gently brush her hair off her shoulder.

"In the back taking a bath. They're waiting for you."

Jo kissed him quickly on the cheek. "I'll just go say hi then."

I was too shy to be alone with Sam, and the room became instantly smaller as soon as Jo left, but there was no way I could follow her from where I was sitting. It was no relief when her brother, Devon, appeared in the doorway, moved over to the table with a nod of greeting in my direction and sat down opposite me.

I think I'm just not used to men—not real men, grown men, like Devon and Roland and now Sam too. Compared to them, all the male friends and the lovers I'd had before were boys, with none of the solid bulk, the weight of life to fill them out, to harden and weather them. These were men who stood their ground, who could take heat, who you just knew could deal with anything dangerous, anything at all.

Sam held out a mug of coffee to me and asked if I had the note. I fished it from my pocket and handed it to him.

"I know it's the same guy, that rat who's Carver's friend," he said. "Look at this one Dev, it's just like the other one." He handed it over and Devon nodded.

"You mean the cops?" I asked. "How can you tell?"

I saw Devon shoot a look to Sam, a look that asked permission, and Sam's nod okay.

"The last note, the one before this, I saw the guy who put it in the mail slot at the bookstore. He didn't see me—I was just crossing the street—but I know the guy. Like Sam said, he's a rat—a kiss-ass friend of the cops, probably cozy with the guys who planned the Death Squad. I saw him slip it in the slot and smack the door, just like Jo said he did this time. It was right after the whole Death Squad conspiracy came out and we'd organized the demonstration a few months ago."

"I remember that. I saw you there," I offered.

He had a voice, I thought, they all did, these men, calm and commanding at the same time. He reached a large heavy hand across the table and plucked some sugar cubes from the bowl.

Sam was stroking his beard, shaking his head, apparently considering grim possibilities. "I don't like it. I wouldn't put it past them to hit us hard somehow. They want us out of here and the bookstore's our most visible front."

He'd said "our" most visible front. I heard him include himself, but I wondered why I never saw him there, why I'd never seen him anywhere before now—not at the demonstration, or the study groups, or at the public forums. Still, I had the distinct impression that Devon was taking his direction from Sam, that Sam had some undisputed authority.

"Well, they never did get Roland and me buried where they wanted us," Devon said, "and now those guys are probably going to end up back on the beat again."

We all stared silently into our coffee for a moment, considering the heavy injustice of that possibility. Then Devon looked up at me again. He laughed a little to break the tension. "Better stay on your toes, sister, if you're going to keep working around the likes of us!" He winked. It was half a joke, half a challenge to see how far in I was willing to go. He'd called me 'sister'.

"Oh I'm not going anywhere," I said, and I liked the conviction, the confidence I heard in my voice, and I knew I meant it. I wasn't going to take off because of one little threat. With the prospect of those cops being acquitted, I felt even more aligned with the politics on display in the bookstore and with these people who had the courage to parade it all on Main Street.

Still, I had to admit that sitting there with the two of them sipping the coffee that Sam had poured us, I felt a sexual tension in the air along with whatever danger we might be in. Was it just me? It wasn't only because I found them both attractive, but also because I couldn't imagine what else of substance I might have to offer.

I wonder if other women feel that way. Sometimes I think I don't know how to be with men at all unless I offer up that sexual part of me like a leading card, an ace of hearts that takes the first round and fixes my place in the game. But then I'm sure they'll call my bluff on the next hand, which isn't so hot, where I fumble around without a strategy. Some feminist I am!

My mother, and some of her friends—they certainly have strategy. How many times have I witnessed their skillful flirtations? Like brightly colored butterflies they swoop and flutter, making men blush and croon to be next to them, how they throw their heads back to laugh in their low cut cocktail dresses baring their white necks, their sparkling jewels, resting their smooth and polished hands ever so lightly and briefly on a man's shoulder. But I have way too much baggage for that.

I'm not bad looking. I'm tall, not fat or thin, and I have an odd kind of angular face that looks good sometimes in the right kind of light. I have vanities, but every time one appears there's a ready troupe of gremlins that jump me from behind to offer their counterclaims, reminding me of my heritage as a Mayflower murderer, a Robber Baron blue blood, or of my commitment to the feminist struggle where make-up is a tool of the oppressor designed to encourage women to feel like display objects or something to be consumed by men. It's not a good revolutionary practice. So I buy my clothes in thrift shops. I wear little bits of make-up and keep it hidden in my bathroom closet behind the toilet paper rolls.

Jo wears make-up. Not a lot. But her cheekbones have that fake peachy-rose blush to them sometimes, and her lips a frosted glaze. I don't think she's self-conscious about it, but maybe she doesn't know that make-up is an un-liberated practice for a revolutionary. It seems unlikely that she wouldn't know, so I can't quite figure it out.

It was all too much anyway, more than I could take in all at once. Sitting there in their sunny, safe kitchen, alone with these two men for the first time, the police wanting to murder us all, wondering if Roland would be the next one to appear, and when Jo would come back so I could breathe a little easier. One thing didn't seem any less important than the next.

But then two naked dripping kids ran into the kitchen,—a round toddling baby girl being chased by a skinny boy. The girl ran laughing to Sam with her arms outstretched and he scooped her up, and the boy, making lion roars, clung to Sam's pant legs. His father reached down and swung him into his other arm, beaming at both of them. When he smiled I saw all the well-worn laugh lines at the corners of his eyes. He kissed each cheek and the little girl began to stroke his hair.

"That bad monster almost got you, huh Lou?" he crooned and kissed her again. The boy placed his hands on either side of Sam's face and turned his head to look away from Lou, and eye to eye with him.

"I'm not a monster . . . I'm a big lion!" He made his voice deep for emphasis and his eyes stretched wide. At that moment, I wanted to trade places with Sam, to be holding them both, to be rich like that.

Jo appeared then and grabbed Mark with a towel. "Come here big lion," and then threw another one to Sam for his daughter.

I haven't been around kids at all, not since I was a kid myself. To me they seemed as foreign as they were cute, but their entrance had changed everything. It was easy to watch them together— Sam and Jo rubbing down their kids in the sun-filled room, their pure-skinned naked bodies rosy from the bath. With the kids there wiggling and chattering, all the heaviness in the air lifted and I stopped feeling like I was such a big awkward presence there. I wanted to hang around then instead of disappear, maybe help out with their lunch or play games with them in the next room. I didn't want to go back to my apartment, or to the bookstore, or to think about any of that for a while. With the kids there, the note and the bad cops and the fear I'd felt in the empty back room—that all seemed like it belonged in another world, well at a safe distance, at least for the time being.

CHAPTER 8

———

Sometimes your memory just glances by trouble. Huge life shaping events speed by in a blur . . . you hear the sounds of it over and over again muddled at a distance, or you hear nothing at all . . . a great silence. Fragments hang suspended in time, small animated frames, a piece of sound, one bright color, and you wonder or you wait for all the other pieces of it to come together to reveal you to yourself, how you've been changed, rearranged.

Finding Jo in the bookstore was like that. There's the 'me' of before, and then there's the rest of my life after that.

It's the door sign I'll remember, the door sign swinging before me like a metronome as I stepped up to the entrance of the bookstore. Closed, closed . . . jogging a flash of unease, a slow thought: Why does the sign say closed in the middle of the day when I know Jo's inside? And why is it still swinging? But the question doesn't slow my entrance—I just go in.

First, there's the piece of calm, bright silence that belongs here; that's always here on a sunny afternoon. I know that piece—the one mixed with the new book smell and the old radiator warmth.

But the rest has all been all taken apart—the entire room, hundreds of pieces scrambled in a box.

Why are all the books on the floor and the tables turned over?

Why are the posters ripped off the walls?

Who spilled the soda on the counter and left a broken bottle there?

I stand as still as the books and tables, maybe for a second, maybe for as long as it had taken for all of this to happen. The soda drip, drip, drips on the floor. It moves like the door sign moves and the motion of it connects all the disarray in the room with echoes of great crashing, ripping, shattering sounds. It's all just happened, is still happening and Jo is here . . . I know she's here.

"Jo?"

There are small sounds in the back room—little crying sounds, moaning, alone sounds. She's there alone. I have to be with her and then I am, stroking her long wispy hair. My hands travel over her small, crumpled fetal shape. My fingers brush the porcelain white skin of her waist and hip, smoothe the creases in her un-buckled, un-zipped, jeans.

My hands will make her whole. My hands will brush it all away. Let them speak for me. Let them bring a strong mother into the room, one who knows . . . one who knows without asking why there is blood pooled on the floor by her hair, on her shirt collar, on her neck. One who knows what kinds of wounds a rapist leaves inside of unbuckled jeans, inside of porcelain white skin. A wise old mother who knows without asking about everything that can happen to a woman.

I am not old, not wise, but I have to take care. I can be the nurse who soothed my mother's pained body all my childhood, who memorized her scars and every tender spot. My hands are practiced, steady, unflinching. I blot the wound on her neck with my flannel shirt. I see its small crimson opening no bigger that a whisper. No deeper than a quick breath. Its edges are as smooth as the green glass edges of the broken bottleneck that glitters on the floor beside us, the sharp point that has pushed its way through her soft skin surface.

Open your legs! Open your legs!

I lay my coat over her. I want to cover her, put her in a warm womb, a safe close nest.

I make sounds with her, low moaning sounds in the rhythm of her deep shuddering and for a few moments we rock back and forth together, our knuckles white and locked together.

But then she moves away. Suddenly I'm not certain what to do, what she might want from me. Whatever spirit has guided me this far vanishes and I'm stranded back in my own self-doubt. I look away, worried that my own gaze will feel like another violation. But if I don't read her face closely, if I don't study her movements, her eyes, her tremulous mouth, then how will I know what she needs from me?

She sits up. Already her tears are slowing, her voice almost steady.

"Did you lock the door?"

She begins to fumble with her jeans trying to zipper and button her pants but her hands are shaking and the effort shatters whatever remnant of composure she had almost claimed and she falls back to the floor, covers her face. "Call Sam. Just call Sam, okay?"

When she says his name she begins to sob, a sound that comes from a place I recognize, that place of wanting to go back to before and having lost all trace of the path there. When she asks for Sam and the locked door I know that all my caring for her will not stop the man from coming into the room again. But Sam could, Sam would know just what to do.

The phone is on the counter in the other room. I move quickly across the floor, stepping between books to the door, turn the lock with a quick snap, and run back to the phone. It's while I'm dialing that I notice the stocking balled up on the counter next to me like some dead animal. No, not dead. Sweaty, spitty, teeming with his lower than animal life. It's then I feel his huge presence, his breath on my neck, his eyes staring at me through the plate glass window, his hand reaching for me from every hidden direction.

"Jo?"

"Yes?"

"I locked the door. I'm right here. I'm calling Sam now."

I get him on the second ring. I tell him what's happened, quickly, urgently, because all I want is to get back to Jo. That's where I belong. That's the only place I want to be.

When Sam arrived, I left the two of them alone for a while and started to pick up the books and put things back together for something to do to keep moving. It was getting dark outside, and in the bright overhead lights in the room I felt onstage to the outside world, his world, whoever he was, whoever they were. Jo said there'd been two of them—one to stand guard while the other one went to work.

She'd said they were big, both of them, and thinking of how they would fill this space with their stockinged faces and broken bottlenecks, I felt small in the room alone—smaller even than Jo in the back room with Sam. I scurried around, a mouse in a maze of debris, a small gray mouse that couldn't find a safe place to hide from the bright lights. I didn't know what to do.

I'd missed the note. I found it pinned to the poster of Che. It was written in the same uneven boyish script as the threat from the other day.

It said they'd get us all, every woman in the group, unless we left town. It said they already knew where we all lived. It was signed, "The KKK" with awkward looking curly-ques at the top and base of the K's, like whoever wrote it was still in grade school.

When Sam brought Jo out from the back, she wasn't crying. She was white, gray-white, and Sam was all but carrying her. She looked old and her eyes had an eerie glaze that didn't focus on anything, not on me at all.

"She just had a seizure. I'm going to take her home. Will you be okay?" Sam didn't wait for an answer; he was busy re-arranging her so she wouldn't fall down.

"Just lock the place and leave it. We'll deal with it later." He tossed a key on the counter.

I handed him the note. He read it quickly and said, "Yeah, well we'll just see about that," like he was talking to himself, and stuffed it in his back pocket.

Jo looked as sick as some of the people I see at the hospital. I'm learning what really sick people look like, and she looked like that—hanging so limp in Sam's arms. I thought of suggesting that he take her to the emergency room but I didn't. He had that voice that you don't argue with, the very quiet kind like Devon's that was more commanding than a shout. I didn't mind that he seemed to know what to do and I wished he'd ask me to come with him. I'd have to go to my apartment now. I'd have to because I didn't know what else to do.

"Lock your doors when you get home," he'd said. "We'll call you later."

After they left, when I was alone, when the door had clicked shut behind them, when I'd turned the deadbolt and the silence was huge, the lights like spotlights, and I was alone in the huge silence, I couldn't move. They'd left me! I wouldn't expect them to stay of course, how could they? But the windows, the bay windows were almost entirely black now, the last light was waning fast, too black to discern the outside shapes, and all I could see was my own form reflected back to me, that startling shape that had just moved, and the sound, the sound of my boot brushing a book on the floor, my sound, became the sound that would alert all the evil presence in the back room to come for me. I grabbed the key, flicked the lights off as I opened the door. I could see the lights in the back room were still on, knew that my coat was there on the floor near the pool of blood from Jo's neck wound, but I couldn't bring myself to go back there alone. The most important thing for the moment, and the moment was all I had, was to be out on the street with people walking by. Where could I go? I'd find someone small and feminine and safe to walk with. I'd follow her—go home with her.

Home. As I felt the first rush of the cold air outside hit my face, its grounding bite, I thought, I'll go home! Why not?

For a moment it was a possibility, but in the next, home—my parents' home—was too far away, involved too many decisions, too many miles of dark highway and a distance doubled by all that I would have to explain and defend when I arrived. I looked up and down the street for a woman, any woman to follow, but there was no one around, and at this end of town there were few street lamps and lots of shadows. I turned up towards the center of town where there were more lights and likely more people, but then hesitated, not wanting to be seen, and began walking instead towards the darker side-street near my apartment. I wondered if they'd be there waiting for me, the men who left the note who said they knew where I lived—if they'd be waiting in the foyer, behind the stairwell. I was cold, shivering without my coat, but I slowed my pace again, still uncertain which way to go.

If I went home, May, the woman who'd cared for me growing up, would be there—warm, kind, soft, her bed always big enough for both of us—but for all of my closeness to her, it wasn't May who I wanted. May didn't know men as lovers or as rapists, had not had babies . . . not labored that way. It was another kind of mother I wanted . . . it was my own mother, though I was surprised to think of her. I thought of holding her gloved hand as a child trying to keep up with the click of her high heels when we'd go to the city, and I was suddenly filled with a rage at her that made me sob out loud. She wasn't here, would never come if I called, was too precious, too *busy*. I was suddenly filled with her, couldn't push images of her away—her tone of voice, the way she swallowed, the shape of her toes, her perfectly lacquered nest of blond hair, her perfume smell, her breath smell like coffee, like gin, and her greased up Estee Lauder cheek at night that no one could kiss, nestled among all the little white lacy pillows that got closer to her than anyone was allowed.

Why was she always the one who was sick, in pain, who needed help? I could never lean on her—she was not wise, not old and strong, would not appear beside me and put her arm around me, wrap me in a warm coat, and lead me down this street, tell me where to go, what to do. And worse, she would never understand that it was because of her that I was here, working in the hospital, in the bookstore. Didn't she see how good I was being? Her "saint" she'd sometimes call me. But never the other way round—that was the covenant, wasn't it? I took care of her. It would never work the other way round, would it? So was it love at all? If it was love why did I hate her so? Why did I want nothing more in that moment than to feel her gloved hand in mine showing me where to go.

CHAPTER 9

———•———

That night they came to my apartment, Roland and Sam and Devon, into my home that had not had a man in it since I'd moved there six months before. Three men packing guns, their leather jackets squeaking as they moved awkwardly around my living room trying to all fit into that small space.

"We wanted to check on you . . . see how you were doing," Roland had said as he entered, his eyes catching mine for a second, that hot energy between us right away, even in the midst of all of this.

I wouldn't tell them about the fear, not after what Jo had been through. The fear squeezing me on my walk home alone on the dark streets, opening the entrance door to the building, waiting for the rapists to rush up behind me, cornering me on the stairs to my apartment, the interminable moments of fumbling to get the key in the lock and then once inside, pacing, then sitting, and then pacing again.

I'd made hot tea, then switched to wine, then more tea, trying to thaw the deep chill that gnawed at me. I ran a bath, but to take off my clothes, to lie naked and alone behind the closed door of the bathroom, I couldn't do it. Music would help, I'd thought, and had put on my new Tom Paxton album, but even the sound of his gentle voice made me jump, and then certain that the music would obscure the sounds of footsteps on the stairs, of breathing outside my front door, I'd turned it off.

I didn't hear their steps on the stairs, only the knock at the door and Roland's voice calling my name. "Linda, we're here to see if you're okay."

I was stunned, entirely and completely surprised that they'd come, still so convinced of my outsider status that I never would have expected them to have considered my safety or cared enough to make the effort. For a few moments, as I unlocked the door, as they brushed past me and into the room, I was afraid I'd cry. My throat ached with the sudden floodgate of relief, of fear, of whatever it begged to release. I swallowed hard.

Roland was by me in a blur, but Sam stopped to hug me as he came through the door, his black beard bristled against my cheek. And Devon rested his hand on my shoulder, gave it a little squeeze as he passed by. Until they found seats the ceiling hovered lower than before, the room became a small den—a girl's den, each one of these men a decade, a lifetime, older than me. Sam took the couch, Devon the wicker chair I'd borrowed from my grandmother. He raised his eyebrows as the chair complained about his weight and bulk as he lowered himself with a boyish grin. My canary, Flute, was next to him in her cage and he squeezed the tip of his large forefinger between the bars, making gentle clucking bird sounds at her.

Only Roland remained standing, taking in my home—my desk, my plants, my bird, the record albums on the table. I imagined it all through his eyes—all of my borrowed comfort on display. At first his warrior face held its hard unreadable edge, didn't budge, but then I watched it soften. His expression said he was glad to be here, that he'd wanted to come.

The energy in the room was confused, confusing. I wasn't sure how it should be given the circumstances, but in contrast to the weight of my fear until their entrance, it now felt as if their own combined adrenalin mixed with my surprise was making us all a little high, a little giddy. There was a smile hiding on Roland's face, the kind I was always looking for. He was ready to poke fun, to make jokes, to tease me at my expense the way I liked.

"So this is how the other half lives," he grinned. I was grateful. I blushed. I laughed inside. I knew right away that they all knew that I wanted to be with him, always had wanted him most of all, and I didn't care. I wanted to play, to forget everything and play with him. But not tonight, not after Jo had been raped and I could be next. Of course, not now.

"How is she?" I asked, and looked at Sam.

I wondered why Sam was here, and not at home with his wife, but as if he'd heard my thoughts he said, "She's okay. She says she's okay. She's home with RoAnne and Sarah and the kids." He didn't say any more than that. I could see it pained him to say that much, to remember. What makes a woman "okay" after being raped? The brevity of it hung there, as if none of us could handle the images that surfaced when her name was spoken. It was hard to know what to say or what to do, hard to make it real again except that they were here, the three of them sitting in my home. I didn't want to think too much about Jo; I don't know why I pushed images of her away, but already my memory had a strange story quality to it as if the attack was something I'd only just read about.

I did ask if she'd gone to the hospital. Sam said no, they'd decided it was better not to. He used the same voice I'd heard before, the one I'd never want to push against, but I was surprised, fleetingly wondering why they wouldn't choose to get that kind of attention. But then he asked me, looking up at me, his eyes suddenly seeking my authority, "Do you think she needed stitches?"

I told him her neck was okay, I didn't think she needed stitches there but I couldn't bring myself to say she might need stitches somewhere else. I couldn't even ask if she was bleeding there, or think about what it looked like. I didn't know that much about medicine yet, or about bodies or sex or what could be endured. What flashed through my mind was a surgeon in the operating room who I despised, and with the memory the feeling of having to contain my hate and disgust for him silently behind my mask and gown. He'd cut into women and rip things out from between their legs like so much dead meat, with not a moment's reverence, with no care at all, rattling on in his arrogant fool voice about last night's football scores, or his golfing vacation in Florida. He'd snap his needle-sharp clamps into pink membranes, squeeze the ratchets extra tight with his huge paw of a hand .The instruments hung from the vaginal opening—three, four, five, like a cluster of sharks, their pointed teeth clamped to tender flesh, pulling the tissue down, the organs out.

A few weeks ago, I'd handed him the wrong clamp. With one back sweep of his arm he'd knocked the whole tray over, had ripped off his gloves and slammed out of the room.

I didn't want to think about Jo.

"We think the cops could be behind these guys, maybe they even set them up to it, you know? So we're not going that route, to the cops, with this." Devon explained.

"Jesus. Of course . . . I hadn't thought of that." No cops to find the rapist for us. No hospital to take care of us. No one to turn to. But in an odd way I didn't mind—it brought each of them closer to me and into their circle.

"Listen, if you're scared, one of us will stay with you," Devon offered—a sincere offer, leaning towards me, his blue eyes looking intently, earnestly at me,—a Brother, Brothers, this is what they meant. I'd felt it as soon as they walked through the door, as if they'd linked arms around me to fortress me from all the dangers outside. It meant I was a Sister, and you just did that for Sisters, for Brothers. You showed up for them. You protected them. You'd even die for them.

As high as I was on their attentions, I'd never ask one of them to stay with me. It was best not to ask for help—to ask or to expect or to lean on anyone. That was my mother's territory, her insatiable need followed me everywhere, and I didn't want to be like her.

"No, thanks, I'll be fine . . . I've got good door locks."

I looked over at Roland. Had he wanted me to ask him to stay? He was flipping through the jacket covers of the record albums on the table, one knee jumping, his eyebrows touching in a dark furrow across his brow. Not tonight. We couldn't be lovers tonight, not with Jo's battered body right there between us.

He looked up as if he'd been waiting for my answer. His eyes were not a lover's eyes, not then, but full of duty—a soldier's eyes.

"Well, if you're going to be alone, we thought you should have some protection. I brought you a gun." He pulled out a small black revolver that he'd tucked in the back of his jeans and held it out to me. "You can keep this one for now. It's loaded."

I'd never seen a handgun up close, not out of a police holster like something wild out of its cage. It looked small in his large hands, small enough to pretend that it wasn't all that it was. I was surprised that it had appeared there so suddenly, but not entirely surprised. Somehow the gun fit into the course of events of the day, into the next frame of the scene after finding Jo in the bookstore, after the walk home and waiting alone for whatever would come next. The gun was next. The gun that would now be mine if I took it from him. But there wasn't any question that I would take it. It seemed a part of an already written script I'd readily follow, a simple direction. I reached out and grasped its handle.

I liked the way it felt in my hands, the heft of it, the solid black iron warmed by his body heat. I held it as if he'd given me his own warm hand to grasp. But in the next moment I was awkward with it, its foreign unwieldy power.

"I've never used one. I wouldn't know how."

"I'll show you."

I handed it back to him and he opened the bullet chamber, twirled it's cylinder to demonstrate its smooth action. I could see the flat brass plate of each bullet in the six chambers. He shook them out and then showed me how to check the chamber. With all the facility he had, I could tell he'd done this a thousand times before. He showed me how to push the safety on and then snap it back off.

"Leave it like this. Leave it off. If someone's coming at you, you don't want to be messing with a safety. Besides, this gun's not going to go off unless you pull the trigger." He was serious now, deadly earnest for the moment, and I was grateful for that as it made me even more certain that he knew what he was doing, and wouldn't have trusted me with it carelessly. "If someone's coming at you, you just point and shoot." He held his arm, elbow bent and tucked at his side. "You're going to aim for the center of his chest and you're going to keep pulling that trigger until you stop him dead in his tracks. Do you think you can handle that?"

We were standing next to each other, his intent expression of serious inquiry searching my face. Devon and Sam watched us from their chairs. What could I say? Of course I could handle it.

"Okay, now you try it." He handed it back to me. Our hands brushed again, our hands and shoulders and his chest just inches from my back now as he stood behind me.

"Aim at my reflection in the window and pull the trigger so you know how it feels, just once or twice—it's not good for the gun to dry fire it."

I aimed at the window, at his dark shape mirrored back at me. I wasn't afraid. I didn't close my eyes when I pulled the trigger. And then he watched me put the bullets back like he'd showed me, and check to assure the safety was in the off position. My hands were steady and I felt solid inside, solid like the three of them.

"Good," he said. "You'll be fine with that." And for the moment I felt certain that I would. Devon and Sam murmured their agreement. "You can keep this for a few days, but maybe you should think about getting one of your own. You should have one. We all need one now." I could see he was right—there didn't seem to be any other way, and if I had any doubts, they were quelled by the solidarity of these men, their combined strength, and what appeared to be their unshakable certainty about what to do next.

We spoke for a little while longer, the four of us in a tight circle in the small room, my canary our silent incongruous witness in her cage on the table next to the couch, her small head cocking from side to side as we spoke. Sam said they would all be "laying low" for a while, taking matters into their own hands. "We're going to find them," he said, his hand pausing from the nervous way he had of twirling his mustache, his voice quietly fierce. "We'll find them."

His eyes left little doubt what they would consider doing when and if they did find them. I should have said "Good!" at least for Jo's sake, but instead I looked away, queasy with the images that flashed through my mind. Would they kill them? Torture, beat, or castrate them? I didn't know what I hoped for—the rapists free to hunt down more of us, or to discover that these men, my new brothers, were capable of that kind of violence. And I wondered what Jo would want, if she would ask for this retaliation.

After the Death Squad, it seemed altogether likely that they were right about the police being involved, and if that was the case then I had to enlist, there and then, or else withdraw, take a back seat with the other "armchair revolutionaries" who would continue to be ignored, be silenced by evil powers such as these.

But I was so dumb and naïve about everything, everything, that I needed to transfuse some of their courage and resolve to quell the voices of dis-ease in my heart, small voices that wondered if more violence was the answer.

As they left, Devon backed out of the doorway giving me a power salute and a quick wink. Sam grasped my hand like a Brother, and his 'You take care now!' felt entirely sincere. And though Roland didn't touch me at all, the look he gave me filled the empty space between us with acceptance, maybe even respect, and possibility.

When they'd gone and I was alone again, I let the gun remain on the table where I'd put it down, lying amidst the other objects there like something that belonged to me. The gun next to the blue plate with the browning apple slices. The gun next to the little brass table lamp, the Tom Paxton album cover, the ashtray and the tea mug with the bluebird on it.

I paced around my apartment some more, picking up, changing for bed, fixing toast I didn't want . . . but always skirting the table, not touching anything there, and appraising the gun from different angles. Sometimes I'd look at it directly, sometimes out of the corner of my eye. Every movement I made seemed in relation to the gun as if in a dance that circled closer and closer until I'd readied myself to hold it again.

When I picked it up, I felt some of the same steely confidence I'd felt practicing with it before. And I felt something else, something that hummed inside me. It hummed with defiance, with a loud voice, an answer back, a curse right in the face of the cops or the rapists and in the face of whatever forces had come together to decide who I was and how I should behave. The gun charged me with that same thrill of finding out something entirely new about myself, something fierce and unafraid. It sliced me away from all I was supposed to be—good, quiet, a "perfect" child. I felt ready to lay a patch on all of that, scream out of the driveway and hit the road.

I put the gun under a pillow on the floor beside my bed. The gun that was required of me. Now it was a necessary part of my new life. As comfortably as Roland had pulled it from the back of his pants, or as automatically as my father picked up his briefcase every morning on his way out the door to work, I would pick up my gun, carry it in my purse, a signature of the path I was on.

Branches outside tapped my windows and the refrigerator made its creepy clicking noises. But I wasn't afraid. I lay there waiting for sleep to come with an oddly satisfied feeling that everything had changed for me, somehow for the better.

CHAPTER 10

In the morning, I dressed for work at the hospital in the pre-dawn dark. I put the gun in my purse understanding then in a new way its cold and bittersweet comfort, how carrying it would change me in ways that seemed as dark and cold as the gray morning.

The gun seemed to speak to me, murmuring on in my head from the moment of waking, while I brushed my teeth and drank my tea and on and on reminding me of its secret company, its lethal power, and the circumstances that required its presence in my life. Where the night before I had felt cocky and sure of my control, I now felt small and weak in its presence. When I parked my car in the echoing half-empty hospital lot, I reached inside my handbag, grasped the gun's cold no-slip grip, released the safety and readied myself for any kind of attack, for surely, if the rapist were going to choose a spot for his next victim, the shadowed and deserted corners of the parking lot would suit him perfectly.

The black night still hung beyond the circle of light from the street lamps, the air entirely still except for the movement of my breath disappearing in silent clouds. I felt so alone that even the appearance of my attacker might have brought relief from all the anticipation of whatever lay waiting for me in every shadow—each dark space full of indecipherable movement and silence, the lighted spaces empty with the hum of sodium lamps and the unforgiving return of concrete underfoot announcing my presence to the man waiting for me. Alone. Alone. Alone . . . my footsteps said, and my heartbeat another presence with its loud command to Run!

But I was afraid to run with the gun, clutching it concealed inside my bag, thinking that with the safety off the gun might fire somehow without even touching the trigger, no matter what Roland had said. And then I thought how the man with the stocking over his face might jump out at any moment and wrestle it from me, shoot me, or worse, force me into the shadows to rape me and then leave me dead. The gun offered nothing but its foreign sinister weight and I wanted to throw it away.

But then the distance between me and the brightly lit hospital entrance finally narrowed. There were people there, lots of them coming and going at change of shift time. In a few more steps I could hear all the sounds they made moving about, and the low hum of their voices. The sounds shielded me and made it seem impossible that anything bad could happen now. My fear began to settle and with it, the gun's murmurings abated, and I lightened with some of the confidence of the night before.

I nodded good morning to the security guard as I did every morning. To him, I was the same. I wore the same uniform, the same white nurse shoes, the same navy blue pea coat. I met his greeting with the same friendly wave as all the other mornings. I wondered if he could detect a change in me, any sign of the secret in my purse, of the other life that now defined me.

In the elevator, in the locker room where we changed into scrub uniforms, it was the same. I found I was able to act the part, smile, move about, change my clothes, speak to those around me without any awkwardness or any feeling at all that I might be harboring the events of the day before. And once I had on my mask and gown it was even easier. No one could tell that while I was arranging the scalpels on the mayo stand or threading sutures, that I was still in my apartment, with Roland and Devon and Sam, re-playing their visit of the night before, or worrying about Jo, or the gun that might somehow clatter accidentally to the floor when I opened my locker later that afternoon. I knew that no one could hear the acceleration of my heartbeat as I imagined getting caught at the end of the day, the police taking me away in handcuffs. But as no one could read my imaginings, I saw that I could hide too, and that all of my secrets had bonded me to Roland and Devon, Sam and Jo, and even to RoAnne, the bond pulling me away from my other life, the one I didn't feel a part of any more.

But when I came back to my apartment after work I couldn't stay there. It didn't feel like my home—just a hollow cell that would incarcerate me for the next eight hours until I fell asleep, if I slept at all. I didn't want to be alone, I didn't want to go anywhere alone, but I had to move. I decided to go for a drive, maybe to drive by the bookstore to see if anyone was there. To see if Roland was there—to be honest, that was all I really wanted. Nothing felt clear like the feeling of wanting Roland. Reckless, thoughtless, that desire was so big there wasn't room for anything else.

Sometimes coincidence is not at all surprising, is just destiny unfolding. And even though I felt a jolt seeing his unmistakable shape through the window of the bookstore, even though, alone as I was, I blushed with the feeling of being stripped and naked as if every minute of my fantasy of finding him there had been exposed and broadcast to him, still, I wasn't surprised that he was there, or surprised that he was alone.

He knows what you want, why you're here. You stand across

from one another, making small talk, small sounds that say nothing. Your eyes look everywhere but not into the fire—too bright, too hot. His chest rises with a deep breath. He puts his pencil behind one ear, pulls his hair back with a shyness you've never seen in him before. There are so many lines on his face, etched into his forehead, around his eyes—a map to study, to trace with care—at one turn, an open path; at the next, a dead end hemming you in with all your silly assumptions.

"I see you did a lot of work today." Your voice pulls back the bed-sheet.

Roland has put the room back together, a stranger would never know. There are even new posters on the walls. No soda spills. No broken bottle-necks. Just some papers and trash on the floor that still need to be picked up.

You don't go into the back room.

For a few minutes, you help him finish up. You work alongside him. Of all the possibilities of life on the globe, you are here with this man, intent on love with Roland. No other love will do. But not in this place. Not where the echoes of yesterday's attack come at you from every corner. This place is no place for love. As soon as you come in, there's a part of you that begins to find the quickest way to leave, with him or without him. Even with the work he's done, the room holds all the images of Jo that you've been pushing away and you begin to feel like you've made a wrong turn, like you're heading towards a dead end. You don't know why you came here at all.

But then he reminds you. He understands. When you've finished the last of the work, he reaches towards you and takes your hand. He puts his arm around your shoulder. You're allowed to lean on him for a moment, to cave into the leather smell, the so solid expanse of his chest. He says just what you want him to say. He says with his playful, kind, flirtatious voice, "Now that we're all finished here, why don't you let me drive you home in that sweet little car of yours."

You bring him to your room, the room of night-time spirits, the room of treetops and dancing light, dancing sprites that beckon, that permit and protect. You are safe. For this night you will be entirely safe. From the moment he pulls you to him, pulls off your shirt, pulls down your jeans, pulls your belly to his mouth—you open. You dive you rush into him you want every soft cell of his skin to be on you in you consume you swallow you swallow him swallow swallow until there is no more you, no more him. You are not shy—he wants you, wants you . . . you offer him everything, but not for absolution, not for forgiveness. There's no room for that, for thoughts, for thinking. You offer him everything because the more you offer the less of him there is that is separate from you, the more he disappears into you, and then there is no you at all . . . gone gone . . . blessed relief . . . no you at all.

But in the morning, waking brought us back into our separate spaces, back into the awareness of all we didn't know about one another. He was quick to dress, sitting next to me on the bed, so I pulled my clothes on too. He wasn't distant—not cold, like some, but he had work to do, that was the feeling I got.

I will never cling to him. Period.

"How long were you in jail?"

"Not jail . . . prison. Two years, and seventeen minutes."

He was already pulling on his boots, work boots he laced to the top. I knew he'd done almost the whole two years in solitary, two years for selling six dollars of marijuana. I ran my hand across his back, lightly, already not entirely sure if I still had permission to touch.

"And before that, how long in Vietnam?"

"I don't know. Forever. Longer. I don't talk much about that."

His head was still down fixing his boot so I couldn't see his expression, but the way he said it was a bit of a slap and I felt ashamed for asking, but then he sat up and kissed me, tasting like sex or love or both. I'd have made love again but I could tell he was getting ready to leave.

"I've been wondering about the bookstore," I asked. "What's going to happen to it now?"

"RoAnne wants to keep it open. She's going to keep working there."

"Alone?"

"Probably not. I think somebody's going to be there to help her out."

That somebody should be me. There was no question at all in my mind about that. Even if I never saw Roland again, keeping the bookstore open was the right thing to do, the best thing to do. It wasn't for Roland, or even about Roland anymore. It was much bigger than him, than all of us.

"I want to help her out."

"I'm sure she'd like the company, but that's up to you. Did you think about buying a gun? You should have one, and I'm going to need that other one back soon."

Now he was standing, fastening his belt, tucking his shirt in.

"Yeah, maybe I'll go today. Do you think they'll give me a hard time at the store . . . you know, buying one?"

He laughed outright at that. "Give you a hard time? I don't think so. You don't exactly look the part."

That stung a bit . . . I didn't know what he meant, if it was my clothes, my face, my haircut. Shit! What did he see that I couldn't?

"I'm going to make coffee. Do you want some?"

"Sure. But I have to meet Sam in a little bit. Can I put on some music?"

While I was in the kitchen I heard the first scratchy notes of Ravel's *Bolero*. I knew it before I even heard the first notes—I'd played it so many times I recognized the sound of the grooves on the record before the music began.

"How do you know this?" I handed him his coffee, sat at the table next to him, our knees brushing.

"My father liked it, and it was one of the only things we agreed on."

"You didn't get along with him?"

"Not always." By the way he answered I didn't ask for more.

I didn't know what to say, whether to tell him that my father liked this music too, that it was his record in fact, and that there were many things I liked about my father mixed in with the things that made it hard.

I took Flute out of her cage like I did every morning. She climbed onto my finger, grabbed hold with her weightless canary claws. The music was building slowly with my favorite part, the clarinets and the drums.

"Here . . . you want to hold her?"

I took his hand, moved his index finger slowly towards her, lined it up alongside mine. She fluttered her wings and I thought she might fly away, but then she tipped her head taking in whatever she saw with her little black eyes. She wasn't used to strangers but she moved over to him, first one foot, then the next, adjusting her weight back and forth between her two feet, getting used to the size of this new perch. He sat very still and stroked her back and wings with a light touch.

While he held her I got to study the tattoo on his upper arm, the clenched fist in dark blue, the red chain it clasped with links open on either end. To be a soldier, to be a prisoner, which would be worse? I used to think I knew something about what prison would be like, but now, being here with Roland I knew I didn't really know anything at all.

Bolero had the army gathered now, filling the room with its marching warriors, its freedom fighters. In another minute it was over and I put Flute back in her cage while Roland put the album back in its cover.

"I don't know when I'll see you next." Whatever regrets he had about leaving were only a moment's wistful shadow across his face, but they were there. He was preparing for whatever was outside the door, whatever came next - -back into his commitment to be first of all a warrior, a cadre of the freedom fight. Where was he going? Who was he going to be with now, lay with tonight? Whatever regrets I had about seeing him go I tucked into my own shadow, the place where nothing was expected and I didn't need anyone. *Do not lay claims on this man. Claims are like cages, like cells.*

"I know. Do you want to take the gun?"

"That would be best, as long as you're going to get one of your own."

I brought it to him from my bedside drawer.

We didn't kiss goodbye, but I held his gaze for a moment. I saw the distance he'd already traveled beyond our naked embraces. *You can come with me, his eyes said, but don't expect me to ask you. Don't expect anything at all, and if you do come, it's your choice . . . Remember that, it's your choice.*

CHAPTER 11

I had to shut down some part of myself, stuff it away, in order to carry my gun. My gun.

Did I ever really use those words to myself? When I took it out of its box for the first time and loaded it up chamber by chamber, sitting on my bed with the cotton green bedspread I'd had since I was a kid, with the afternoon sun warm on my back through the window glass, it still felt like it had to belong to someone else.

But I managed to load it smoothly enough, put the safety on the way I'd seen the man in the gun store do it, the way Roland had shown me with his own, and then I put it into my jeans, the nose end stuffed into my waistline in front, and then trying out the feel of it in my back the way I'd seen Roland do, and then I walked a few steps around my apartment, afraid with every step that the safety would release, that somehow the gun would go off.

"How big do you want to go?" the old man in the trading post who'd sold it to me only hours before had asked. I'd followed his slow rocking steps, wondering just that, past displays of hunting knives, arrows with razor tips, and then the handgun display, the four models to choose from waiting for me in the glass-covered display case. Two of them were out of the question; huge, black-handled, black barreled, bigger than the one Roland had loaned me. "357 Magnum" the sign read. 357's shot dum-dum bullets, the kind we'd been protesting at the Death Squad march because the police were carrying them routinely now. A dum-dum had a soft tip that allowed it to expand after impact, plowing through a body like a steel pipe. I didn't want one of those. The other two guns were smaller, closer to what I'd had before.

"I just need some home protection," I said, smiling at the man with an innocent look. I liked the sound of that—"home protection", like an insurance policy. It wasn't so hard after all to be this new person with a secret life, buying a gun from this friendly old man whose watery eyes twinkled at me, half flirtatious, half protective, like a grandfather.

"You get handy with this and it'll give you all the home protection you need." Then he showed me again everything I needed to know.

But I didn't feel "handy" with it, like he'd said. Back at my apartment, I sat on my bed and held it wondering if I'd been Jo and I'd had a gun, would I have shot at those men coming at me? How could I know? Part of me wanted to think I'd have pulled the trigger, that I'd be ready to defend myself or anybody else from an attack like that; to be clear the way Jo calls cops "pigs" and Sam vows to get the motherfuckers who did it. But then I see warm skin, red, hot blood—the way it feels inside the bodies I hold in the operating room, bodies alive and breathing with pink lungs, beating with slippery, jiggely hearts. And when the heart stops, how it lies there in a flaccid mass and nothing moves.

I didn't think I could do it.

In the days that followed, the thing I couldn't get used to, couldn't figure out, was where and when and how to take the gun with me when I left my apartment. Do you or don't you take it with you every day to the hospital? After a few days that felt too dangerous, too nerve-wracking to have it in my unlockable locker for anyone snooping around to find. So I braved the dark shadows in the parking lot without it. But then, do you or don't you take it with you to the grocery store? To your grandmother's house? To the beach when you go walking? All these rituals and places that I'd gone as the old "me" didn't seem to fit with the gun in my purse, the weight of it never something I could forget as it banged against my hip, or met me cold and hard to the touch when I reached my hand inside for my wallet.

At night I put it away in my sweater drawer, hidden as much from myself as anyone else; hiding it to escape the feeling that the gun had a life of its own, the feeling of never being quite certain what it would do. I'd put it away so I didn't have to watch it on the tabletop, or wonder if it would somehow just go off. It made me a little crazy that way.

RoAnne is glad to see me when I go back to the bookstore a few days later. She hugs me and I hug her back. If she knows about my night with Roland she doesn't show it in any way. Maybe I should feel as if I've betrayed her but I don't. Maybe I should have asked Roland if he was sleeping with RoAnne but I didn't. Honestly, I didn't care if she was. I don't have any more of a claim on him than she has. I know she would like to claim Roland for her own but that's her mistake. Somehow I believe that if Roland was really in love with her I'd have known it by now and then things between us wouldn't have unfolded as they did. For all of his everyday remove, I'm certain that Roland shared more than just sex with me the other night.

RoAnne said, "There's somebody I want you to meet," and took me lightly by the hand, steering me towards the back room of the bookstore. There was a man standing there—a big wild-looking man, dirty and disheveled with a beefy biker look, greasy hair in a kinky frizz around his face, and slits for eyes.

"This is Muck," she said with a grin that this wild bear returned; a toothless smile, an unaffected sweet smile, extending his blackened paw of a hand to me and gripping mine tightly in an altogether friendly shake.

"Just Muck," he said. "How doo you doo," he sort of lisps and laughs at the same time like he's shy or stoned or both.

That's the way he always sounds when he talks, I find out, which isn't very often, and I like him right away. RoAnne says he's here to "help us out", and in the days that follow I look forward to seeing him pop his head in the door only moments after we open up the store, like he's been waiting outside in the bushes somewhere.

"Do you ladies need my services today?"

By "services" he means just watching out for us, sitting in the back room listening to music and cleaning his gun or playing solitaire. I like knowing he's there every time the doorknob turns and we're not sure if this is the time they're coming for us again.

I don't know where he came from, who he knows, but I'm glad he's here. I don't feel scared when Muck's around. And I don't have to feel shy with him about what I don't know about guns. He's dying to show us everything—like a five-year old with the latest cap gun. Sometimes in the back room he practices his quick draws like an outlaw, only he doesn't wear a hip holster, he wears the over-the-shoulder kind that tucks the gun into your side. That's the kind I want if I ever get one.

Sometimes RoAnne and I take turns practicing along side him, aiming and pretending to shoot at a poster of Nelson Rockefeller. Muck laughs his big oafy laugh but I don't think he cares so much about sides, about politics, as much as just being useful and generous with his offering. He's an unlikely angel, but an angel nonetheless . . . that's how I think of him. It strikes me over and over how I have absolutely nothing in common with him except this odd circumstance, and yet he's showing up in a situation that could get him killed. I want to hug him for that, and I do, from time to time, and it makes him blush.

I'm even getting so that I don't think about the gun in my purse every minute when I'm carrying it. I'm getting used to it. Sometimes I even forget I have it for just a minute here and there until the heft and hard bulk of it reminds me.

Muck takes RoAnne and me target shooting out in the woods. He's taken us twice. The weather hasn't changed at all for more than a week, with the same brittle cold air and blinding bright sun, blue sky, and not a breath of wind. Muck leads the way and I follow RoAnne in her long black leather coat as we crunch through the ankle deep snow, past shining copper birch and spruce and balsam trees with their weighted snowy bows, everything frozen and still on the brink of spring.

I can name all the trees and the animal tracks along our path— mice and deer, rabbit and skunk, and I know whose little dark piles of scat belong to whom. I know this from last year's field-work in college, all the time I spent in the woods with Peterson guides and notebooks marking and mapping. But I didn't think RoAnne or Muck would be that interested. Besides, the woods have a silence sometimes you don't want to break with talking.

If I closed my eyes I could be following my father only three months before on Christmas Eve, the whole family weaving through the woods behind our weekend house in Vermont. Going to cut down the perfect Christmas tree in our annual ritual—the irony doesn't escape me.

We practice shooting for an hour or so. Muck is a good teacher— very patient, setting the cans up over and over and then trudging back through the snow to us to give us some pointers. The shots go off like ice cracks and echo in the silent woods. I'm not a bad shot as it turns out. I can put the bullet through the Coke can from thirty and then forty feet using the single action, cocking the trigger and then firing. RoAnne is good too, looking the part in her black coat with her straight-arm and spread-leg stance. Then Muck takes the can and pins it to a tree trunk the breadth of a man and we practice getting used to a double action shot, just grabbing the gun and firing two or three times in a row without taking careful aim, like there's someone coming at us. It's harder, but we're "naturals", Muck says. Pretty soon the can is shredded and we give each other high-five hand slaps all around.

Muck gets a new can all to himself. He wipes his nose on his sleeve and hocks and spits before he shoots. When the can goes flying off the tree stump he mutters something like "Got that motherfucker," or "Bingo! Right between the eyes" and smiles his toothless smile at us as if he's waiting for a pat on the back. Ro-Anne and I roll our eyes to one another or smile like that's just Muck and we're okay with it, but I know that I don't want to kill anybody ever and that's my secret.

I can feel the ties between RoAnne and me growing through all of this. I still don't know why she has the reputation for being "loose", untrustworthy in a careless way. Vinny and Jo have warned me, but except for her weakness for Roland, I think she is the stronger more fearless warrior between the two of us. We're still not entirely easy with one another, but the bond is growing anyway. I was thinking what if Muck was Roland teaching the two of us here in the woods, if it would be any different, the way it feels between us, and I don't think it would. Roland's not what's tying us together anymore. What it's really about is standing up for what's right in the face of terror, not letting the Ku Klux Klan, the police, and whoever else wants us to close the bookstore have their way. And too, it's a bond born of both being women who could be raped any time, any day, just like any other woman or girl in the world.

We have a poster in the bookstore that says that every ten seconds, somewhere in the U.S.A., a woman is assaulted by a man. There's a photo of a woman sitting by a window. Her arms are crossed in front of her chest and she has bruises and cuts on her face. Her dark eyes look directly at you with a distance that is both unreachable and eerily familiar. I know that look. I know her somehow though I don't know how. In that way I'm growing to love RoAnne, that we're taking this on together, not just for ourselves, but for all women. It's the kind of love that comes from the ground up, solid like a tree, not from some lightening bolt out of the clouds like the way I feel around Roland sometimes. "Sisterhood" is a good way to describe it, and it is "powerful", like they say.

Still, in the weeks that followed, after we'd finish shooting, we didn't hang out together. We didn't even get a cup of coffee. In the bookstore, we didn't talk about the attack, or speculate on where Jo and Sam had disappeared to, or where Roland had gone. Sam had said they'd be "lying low" while they looked for Jo's attackers, and Roland had all but said he'd moved underground to help in the search. But I couldn't help but wonder where RoAnne went, where she lived, if she was going to see Roland or Jo or any of the rest of them. I was afraid to ask because I took her silence as the authority on the subject since she'd known them all a lot longer than I had, since she'd been studying and working in the bookstore and organizing the prison group with Roland long before I'd arrived on the scene. I just had to wait and see.

CHAPTER 12

Vinny was the one who called me first.

"Do you know who this is? If you do, don't say my name. Just say yes."

"Yeah, I know who it is."

"I need to talk to you. We need to talk to you. Can I come over?"

"Sure . . . . of course. When will you get here?"

"Ten minutes."

When he'd gotten out of prison a month before, he hadn't come straight to my house. In fact, in no time at all it seemed as if he'd hooked up with this woman, Maureen, who I'd met once or twice. I'd seen them holding hands in the street, and another time making out in a bar I went to one night after the study group. I found out he was staying with her. That was okay with me. I knew I'd been a little impulsive offering to put him up at my place. Besides, my fantasies about Vinny had been crowded out by my night with Roland and all the rest of what was happening.

Still, I'd seen Vinny a few times at our study group meetings—at least up until the attack on the bookstore. During that time I'd witnessed how quickly he'd transformed after he'd been released. The ways he'd seemed so slight and tired and confused to me when he was inside, had been replaced by an air of authority. I admired the way his soft- toned voice had developed an insistent urgency. When he talked about how Che had managed to build a "cadre" of freedom fighters, about their discipline and sacrifice and dedication to freedom, I listened. He was on Roland's side of the table most of the time, supporting his side of the arguments that took place there. He couldn't say it in the group, he couldn't come right out and advocate guerrilla warfare anymore than Roland had, but I knew that's what he was thinking.

So it didn't surprise me that he was with them. I'd figured as much from the last conversation I'd had with him, sitting on the bench down by the fishing piers. That had been a few days before Jo had been raped. And then he was gone.

That day on the pier he'd told me he was going underground.

"Me and a few others. It's where I belong. It's where I can do the most good for the revolution." He was looking out at a fishing boat, men unloading their catch into tubs, stray fish flapping on the dock, loose on the deck. Since he'd gotten out he'd insist that we do most of our talking outside, steering clear of potential wiretaps and room bugs. In the late winter sun he looked pale, his features sharply contrasted against a cloudless horizon, dark circles under his eyes. Then he turned to me, looked at me head on.

"We need your support, however you want to give it, if you want to help. If you're not ready to go under right now, that's cool—everybody in their own time. But think about it. You could be like an aboveground liaison for us. We need that. The struggle needs you . . . solid sisters like you."

He went on to flesh it out a little, what it meant to be underground. I didn't really know . . . I still conjured pictures of some vast network of tunnels and subterranean lairs. He told me "bare essentials" to protect me from knowing more than I needed to. I was learning that there were things I couldn't ask, for my own safety, and for the others involved too—the less you knew the better. He said they had to establish "safe houses", and false identities, and get weapons together. I listened to him intently—snowed to be wanted like that—but even so I wondered if he should even be telling me. I wondered what Roland would say if he knew Vinny was talking like this. I wondered if Roland had asked him to talk to me.

"The struggle needs solid sisters like you," he'd said. I'd felt pleased that day to be included, some concrete validation that I had grown over the months as a revolutionary. And if I said yes, part of me could feel the relief, imagining a kind of welcomed amputation of everything that bound me to my world, a once-in-a-lifetime chance to re-create my life, overnight.

But I wasn't ready, not yet.

"I can't go with you Vinny. I want to help you out, I will help you out, but I'm not ready for that yet." I scanned his face for contempt, disdain. No matter what he said about it being okay to take my time, I was sure there'd be a kind of judgment there. "Above-grounders" were like Nick . . . weaker, softer, a little cowardly when it came down to it. And there was always the threat of being tagged an "armchair revolutionary", intellectuals who sat around advocating change without doing anything about it. At least as a "liaison" I could be a step closer to the hard core, the real heroes. They were soldiers ready to die for justice, the ones who laid their lives on the line.

I told him I'd have to think about it, I'd let him know what I could do, but that definitely he could count on me for some kind of support. I liked the idea of the "liaison" position. Maybe I could do that as a kind of break-in to help me make the harder decision about going underground all the way. I told him that.

That's the way we'd left it, though I secretly longed to be clear enough to turn myself over to such a straightforward destiny the way he had—to a struggle aligned with all that was essentially good in the world.

When Vinny got to my apartment I gave him a beer and we sat at the kitchen table, left the room dark except for the little lamp between us. The table seconded for a desk of sorts, mail and papers pushed to the sides. Vinny took the "Things to Do" pad my mother had put in my Christmas stocking last year and scribbled quickly *We need your gun. Can you help us?* He pushed the note towards me. I stared at the familiar script, the question mark with the circle dot on the bottom and I could feel his eyes boring into me for an answer.

Why my gun? I scribbled back. He got up and turned on the little TV on the counter, set it to an empty channel for some background static noise.

"We've got an opportunity right now, in the next few days, to hit something big," he whispered, leaning close to my face, his breath in my ear. "We'd make a lot of money, taking it from real pigs who are ripping off the people anyway. It's an easy job. We can do it. But we need another piece."

This was not a gun to be used in self-defense. This was a different kind of gun with a different kind of purpose. I could feel that in every cell of my body as I tried to reach inside and pull out the right response. Over the last weeks and months of study, and especially since the attack on Jo and the real possibility that the police were bedfellows with the local KKK, I'd come to believe that Amerikkka needed guerrilla fighters like Vinny and Roland to hold those in power responsible, to bring attention to the insidious ways they abused that power. It was in the particulars that I got confused.

This is how it's done, he's telling me. This is the beginning of all that we've been preparing for. He tells me if I give him the gun he'll file the serial numbers off of it so that it can never ever be traced to me.

I knew with the gun, my gun, and others that the group were probably gathering, that they planned to "do some jobs". Jobs that had been vaguely alluded to included bank robbery, theft of explosives, kidnapping of corporate criminals.

"We don't want to hurt anyone," he'd said to me once. "We have to protect innocent people at all costs. But this is a war. We are at war with the system, and in wars there can be civilian casualties." These were the kinds of particulars I got stuck on.

There was an edge of distraction about him that night that I hadn't seen before. His hands trembled slightly and his movements were on a kind of fast-forward. In the flash of his dark eyes, there was no reassurance that everything would be okay. In fact, some part of me knew that sooner or later it would be a mistake—to give him the gun, to file off the serial numbers, to let it go. But then here they were putting their words into action, putting their lives on the line. . . this small cell of freedom fighters ready to join others cells, ready to make the revolution more than words on a page. It felt like they had a lot more to lose than I did.

"OK," I said. "You can have it."

The easy part was giving him the gun. I wasn't sorry to see it go; it was one load off my mind not to have it around. He said they'd be in touch with me and hugged me good-bye. But at least some of my ominous premonitions were right.

The next time I heard from them, Roland was in jail, and Sam was too. They'd been picked up with a carload of guns and some armored car routes. And that wasn't all.

CHAPTER 13

"You sure you want to do this?" Jo asked me as soon as she opened my car door. She got into the front seat and hugged me quickly across the stick shift. It was as if she'd seen me yesterday, and the day before that, not a month ago with me kneeling beside her on the floor of the bookstore. It was the first time I'd seen her since then and I was looking right away for some evidence of the attack, something I should address, something I should say. I'd watched her walking towards the car, her determined, slightly bow-legged gait, her jaw thrust forward with the same stubborn, enduring edge. I hugged her across the gear shift as she settled into the passenger seat. I would have said something, something, but she pulled away before we could entertain a moment's collective thought about the last time we'd been together. Everything about her told me that we wouldn't be talking about what had happened—not then or later or maybe ever again. Now there were other more important concerns.

Devon slipped into the back seat. He had on dark glasses even though the sun was setting and a black knit hat pulled down low. I couldn't see his eyes at all but he patted my door as he got in like he'd have patted my shoulder if the window had been open. Two pats. And then he leaned forward from the back, his arms settled on the seat edge between us, his elbow just brushing my shoulder.

"This is okay with you right?" she asked again. I was glad to be driving so I didn't have to meet her inquiring eyes. Roland and Sam were being held in a prison outside of Boston. When she'd called me on the phone earlier she'd asked me for help, for bail money, and if I wanted to drive to Boston with her and Devon to talk to this bail bondsman they knew. "I know I'm putting you on the spot. You can hang up, forget I ever called," she'd said.

But I wouldn't, I couldn't do that. To hang up would be to cop out, to sit back in the armchair and wipe my hands of the trouble they were in. Hanging up would mean not showing up for a sister in need. Hanging up could mean never seeing any of them again. Hanging up would be to go back to wondering what I would do with the rest of my life, tossing about like a boat in irons with that ever-present feeling that whatever I did with those hours wouldn't measure up to much after all.

Jo lit a cigarette and put one foot up on the dashboard, hugging her knee. She wore a little pink lipstick that matched her soft wool hat and a white wool sweater under her corduroy coat—clean and pulled together. She didn't look the way I thought a revolutionary 'should' look, or a woman whose husband had just been locked up. She wasn't crying or shaking or in any apparent distress that I could tell, and all the ways her appearance and demeanor challenged my narrow pre-conceptions made me admire her all the more.

"So I guess you know by now," she said.

"Know what? Only what you told me on the phone."

I saw her glance back at Devon, biting her thumbnail. She shifted her body towards me in her seat. Then she told me in an even voice that Sam wasn't Sam at all, that his real name was Harlan King, and that he'd been a fugitive for seven years—but not just any fugitive. She said he'd been on the Ten Most Wanted list in connection with a bombing of a factory in Colorado that made missiles for the war in Vietnam.

"Nobody got hurt, but the bomb wrecked the place."

In spite of her non-plus, I thought I detected pride in her voice as she told me about Harlan and the life they'd been managing, and I felt it too, proud to be associated with the protest he'd been accused of, and then too, a rush of excitement and purpose—the Ten Most Wanted and my lover in jail! For a moment I didn't even hear her voice, I wasn't even in the car with all the thoughts whipping around me until Devon tapped my shoulder and told me I'd better slow down a little because I was going seventy in a fifty-five and we didn't want to get stopped.

"Jesus . . . sorry." It was almost dark and I hadn't even turned my lights on.

Jo was saying that Harlan would be extradited to Colorado to stand trial there, that we wouldn't be able to bail him out yet. "So we'll just have to work on springing Roland for the time being."

"Springing Roland." That's where I would come in. That's where my money would come in. Not my money—the 'people's' money. Money that I wanted to give back to the people—people like Roland who were leaders in the struggle. His power hadn't accumulated out of greed, entitlement, the 'old boys' network. It didn't wear expensive suits to work, had no office space, was not embraced by mainstream culture. Roland was a leader of the disenfranchised, of the poor and the oppressed. He was giving them a voice of absolute protest, making certain their life and death concerns would no longer be shoved under the rug of corporate greed. Money spent to free Roland would be money spent for the people. Dollar amounts could not be weighed against the value of a life dedicated to this work. I could feel his fierce eyes on me insisting that I do the right thing—not for him, but for the revolution. That was why I'd bail him out, no matter what the cost. For the revolution.

"So where are we going?" I asked Devon, and he leaned forward to tell me just how to get there.

* * *

Could a bail bondsman be a priest too in his off-hours and still pack a gun?

I wondered as much as I watched Karl, a short and stocky middle-aged man take off his overcoat and then remove a clerical collar from around his neck, and just as casually, take a revolver from his chest holster and slip them both in his desk drawer. I glanced at Jo and then at Devon to see if they looked surprised, but they didn't skip a beat in the small-talk conversation that was going on as we settled in, so I just hoped I'd figure it out on my own without making a fool of myself.

I was pretty certain that Karl was supposed to be an ally, but I didn't know for sure. Devon had just said in the car that he knew "this guy", that Karl had helped him out before, and that he was "solid". But did that mean he was a 'comrade', that he was politically sympathetic to our situation . . . that he supported other guerilla fighters in the struggle who needed his kind of services, whatever those "services" were? I couldn't tell if Jo and Devon had a clear take on this, though I figured my own discerning judgments wouldn't amount to much because how would I know anyway what to expect out of someone like him? How would I know if a bail bondsman's office was supposed to have an inch of smoke grime on everything, dust on the florescent lights, stains on the carpet? What did I expect—an office like my father's?

Karl was friendly enough, starting right in about what was going to happen now that Roland and Harlan had been "apprehended" as he said with a little twisted smile. I didn't know a lot of the other words he was throwing around—"remanding", "arraignment", "collateral fees"—and Jo didn't either, but of course she wouldn't hesitate to stop him and ask, laughing with her easy laugh, one hand covering her mouth to hide her teeth while the other reached out from time to time to touch Karl's sleeve.

I wondered how she could be as easy as that—close to flirtatious with this man, or with any man, after what she'd been through. Didn't she cringe at the thought of his heavy hands, their fingers covered with black hairs, touching her? Didn't she notice the bulge in the crotch of his tight fitting suit pants, stretched as they were with his legs spread apart in the chair? I didn't want to touch him, didn't want him touching me. I wondered at her composure, given the situation.

As Karl answered her questions though, I found him frequently looking at me—even staring at me—giving me this feeling that in fact I did have some kind of authority, some kind of power that I both did and didn't want. Somehow he knew I had the money and he was making it only too obvious by looking at me like that. It made me feel cheap, really, as if he could see even better than I could into my own poorly veiled greed for some kind of importance in the situation.

"I need four thousand dollars cash or certified check to get Roland out."

He didn't take his eyes off me.

That was ten percent of the total bond and he'd post the rest. He took a long drag of his cigarette, blowing the smoke out of his nose, and tipped the ash into his coffee cup.

"I can get you the money, but I guess we'll probably have to wait till Monday." I hadn't skipped a beat in my reply. Nothing would be open tomorrow, on a Saturday, so I had some time to figure it out.

I didn't know how I'd get all that cash, but I liked the decisive tone in my voice. I figured I'd just go to a bank and write a check. It seemed like a lot of money; more than I'd ever written a check for, but really nothing when you thought about how much I had in my account. Anyway, there wasn't much choice as I saw it. All these lives whirling around me like a bunch of low pressure systems coming together to make a hurricane of need for immediate cash, for my money, for me. That was more of the authority I both did and didn't want.

"Okay . . . I guess that settles it," Karl said, wiping his palms over his lapels. We'll talk over the weekend and I'll figure you'll get the money to me on Monday. You call me if you can't come up with the cash by then."

He was all chummy during our exit, putting his thick arm on my shoulder. For a moment, I let myself believe that he was genuinely interested in us, in our situation, and I let myself feel proud that we'd worked out such a smooth deal to help Roland out of jail.

But as we were walking out he whispered in my ear, "You know, Linda, these guys just reached into a bucket of shit and pulled out gold . . . you know that? You're the gold, kid . . . you're the gold."

For some reason, those words didn't feel like much of a prize coming from him. Why did I feel that what he was really saying was that I was no better than the shit in the bucket for the sucker I was, and that couldn't I see that I was just being used?

Was I? I didn't think so. Not in my heart. I trusted them more than that—both Jo and Roland. It had been my choice, my choice all along—and after all, I had my own selfish reasons, however counter-revolutionary, for much of my so-called generosity. I was glad when his arm left my shoulder and I could move away from him.

Was I being used? No. He was wrong about that.

"You can go fuck yourself, Karl."

That's what I wanted to say, what Jo would have said. But instead I thanked him for his help and we all waved good-bye like old friends.

*　　*　　*

We left Devon in Boston and Jo and I shared a room in a motel off the interstate. Early in the morning we were up and ready to drive to the prison for visiting day. It felt good to be with Jo again, pulling out onto the highway after stopping at Dunkin Donuts, getting tea and crullers and settling into that small car space together, licking the sticky sweetness off our fingers—sweetness like the early morning sun, the first spring warmth—all of it a new beginning for us, the two of us together. I could feel how alone I'd been in the two months since Jo had been attacked and the others had left, as if everything in my life had been frozen in a frame of great disarray waiting for one of them to call.

As we set off, I felt a surge of closeness to Jo, a wave of some kind of love, and though it seemed odd in a way to have such a strong feeling for her, our situation—being cast together as we were—left no time for a slow traverse across a long expanse of getting to know one another, but instead had thrown us off a cliff, possibly even holding hands, into a great river below. To be with her, to study her voice with the music of its inflections, the movements of her face as she spoke, and her thin pale hands as she sipped her tea and smoked a cigarette, and to feel her pleasure too in being with me as we drove into whatever was in front of us—it felt entirely where I wanted to be.

It felt, also, entirely, where I had to be. With Harlan and Roland in prison, and Jo's children staying with her mother outside of Portland, with Jo having no car or license because of her seizure disorder, or any means of coordinating visits between the two, as well as negotiating whatever legal maneuvers were imminent, it was clear that she needed someone to help her. She had asked me, and I had jumped in—the water deep but clear enough that I didn't hesitate to indulge my planning scheming thoughts about how I would leave my life in Portland to be with her, to help her. Wasn't that the right thing to do? Even my parents would have to agree. When I told them what I was doing, they would have to applaud my choice. Harlan and Roland would applaud my choice. Doing the "right thing" would keep me safe through all of it. Maybe not safe from guns and violence and law breaking, but safe from shame and criticism, and that, for me, was by far the more palpable danger. As long as I did the right thing, as long as I kept doing the right thing, there was nothing to lose. I'd be okay.

We were still on the interstate when Jo spotted the FBI following us.

"It's them all right. Two cars back. God, what do they think, that we can't see them or something?? You could spot their car a mile away! Switch lanes and we'll see if they're following us."

I saw the black town car, the silhouettes of the two men in the front seat, and while I hoped she was wrong, my racing heart didn't doubt her for a minute. I put my blinker on and switched lanes. The black car followed, and with no cars between us now, they inched closer.

"They're right behind us. Speed up a little." Her voice had its excited ring. It seemed that fear was not something in Jo's emotional vocabulary, or if it was, I didn't know her well enough to recognize it. I could only be certain that I was afraid, still light-headed with the initial rush of adrenalin that had bolted through me when I saw them follow us into the middle lane. I was already going sixty-five, with cars keeping pace all around me, and I felt suddenly sickeningly claustrophobic. There was no losing them, if that's what she had in mind, not in my red car that shone like a beacon, like a brand new fucking Christmas ornament, not that I wanted to try that. I was definitely not up for a high-speed chase. But what did they want with us? I wondered what I might have done wrong, what they might be after us for, but I knew that innocence didn't matter to the FBI, that they could run us off the road and say it was an accident, or stop us and plant a bag of heroin in the car, and no one would argue. Maybe if I just kept driving they'd leave us alone. Maybe they weren't really after us anyway.

I accelerated a little bit. The black car closed the space between us by another car-length. I could almost see their faces. They wore jackets and ties and dark glasses, just like in the movies. And it was exciting too, like the movies, as long as they kept their distance.

Then Jo turned around in her seat and stuck her tongue out, waved at them, laughing. "Assholes!" she shouted, and I thought that in some impossible way that they must have been able to hear her. I didn't like her doing that. I wanted to tell her to stop. I wanted to remind her that they could run us off the road. They could shoot out our tires or something. They could arrest us. It seemed stupid to taunt them, but then maybe I was being a coward. In light of the hundreds of evil plots they were guilty of and blatant infringements on people's liberties . . . the murders even that they had orchestrated of Black Panther activists that I'd learned about recently . . . calling them names hardly seemed so bad.

"Our exit's coming up. Should I get off? I'm going to get off."

"Yeah, get off. And don't get excited, they're just trying to scare us. Don't let them get to you." She kept waving to them off and on like I used to do as a kid in the rear-facing seat of my parents' station wagon trying to get a reaction, any reaction, from an adult in a car behind me.

When we pulled into the parking lot at the prison, they parked a few rows behind us, leaving empty rows between. They waited until we were out of the car heading towards the prison entrance before they got out, the two of them, only a few quick steps away from us. I felt sure we should have to run, shouldn't we? Or would that make it worse for us?

"We'd like to have a word with you ladies," one of them said as they closed their distance from us.

"Forget it!" Jo shot out and grabbed my arm, pulling me into a quicker pace towards the entrance.

"Are they following us?" I asked her, not daring but dying to look over my shoulder. I wasn't scared—not really—now that we were out of the car and past them, though I kept imagining that one of them would grab my other arm at any moment.

"I don't think so . . . no. Just keep walking and ignore them."

"So that's it? You just tell them to get lost and they go away?" I kept my voice low so they wouldn't overhear.

"Not likely. But you don't ever have to talk the Feds unless they arrest you . . . and even then, I'd rather eat shit and die!" She said those last words loud enough for them to hear. "If they're here when we come out, get a closer look at them. You might as well get used to this . . . we'll be seeing a lot of them!" She laughed as if it was fun, and in a way, now that we were almost at the prison entrance and they were far behind us, it was.

The visiting room in the prison was altogether different from the one at Thomaston. We entered a large open hall with high ceilings. Every sound had its own echo, every scrape and bang, murmur and shout filled the room with a hum of noise. There were tables and chairs filling up with visitors, no cubicles or booths, and the large barred windows, though dim with dirt, allowed the light of day to fill the room. Maybe we ought to have been depressed given the circumstances, but we were both excited to be there. I was pretty sure that Roland would be glad to see me again and was actually more nervous about seeing Harlan. As much authority as Roland had, Sam (now Harlan), Harlan had more, ever so slightly more. It was given to him by all of them, and I'd been able to tell before, with just a poorly defined hunch, and now that I knew who he was, Harlan King, Ten Most Wanted, longest fugitive run in the history of the FBI, I knew why. My own contributions to the struggle were just beginning and I was certain there'd be no way that this man, this icon of the revolution, wouldn't see into the depths of my soul, that he wouldn't pull out all the dirty contradictions that defined me and lay them on the table for all to judge—unless I proved myself, if I could, and I wanted to. I wanted to show them all that I could hold on, stay in the heat of it—that even if I wasn't forged from the same background, I was fed with the same fire to change the world.

Harlan appeared through the doors at the edge of the room and sauntered confidently toward our table, holding his own stern expression for only a few paces until he broke into a grin, smiling at us and making a beeline for Jo. He picked her right up when he got to our table. He winked at me over her shoulder as he held her, and I thought that was as good a beginning to our new relationship as any.

"Roland's on his way," he said to me,

I saw him then, poised at the entrance of the room. His gaze shot into every corner of the hall, skimming over us, locating our table without making direct eye contact. I thought he moved toward us as any great warrior would, still looking everywhere but at us, everywhere but at me, and sizing up the room as if he were one of the guards waiting to be jumped. Roland's face did not break into a smile; instead he seemed guarded, even aloof in his approach. I wondered if he'd actually seen me, and though I would have liked the unguarded greeting that Harlan had shared with Jo, I had no way of really knowing how he would be with me here in front of his friends, surrounded by prison guards, in prison once again.

Mostly, as it turned out, for at least half of the time we were allowed to visit, we kissed. It should have been humiliating really . . . infuriating that we had no privacy, that the prisoners, so hungry for touch, were only allowed as much as they could steal in front of the watchful guards. But if anything, that prohibition just turned the heat up for Roland and me. I saw women on men's laps with their skirts concealing whatever contact they could maneuver, couples maybe even coupling with a low groan, the slightest of hip movements. If you were caught, the visit was over, the man hurried away back to the cellblock, and a few were, but even so I wished I'd worn a skirt. I would have risked it and been brazen like that, because it was quickly torture, sitting on his lap, my legs straddled across his.

We did manage some conversation. Of course, first of all, beginning with how they'd been treated.

"They haven't messed with you have they?" I asked both of them. I didn't know who I meant by "they"—the guards, the other inmates—anyone who could corner them in a dark place and get away with it. But Harlan assured us they'd had "first class treatment" because of all the publicity. "It was front page of the papers today," he said. "Did you see it?"

We had, sitting in the car by a corner newsstand, our heads together reading the headlines of the New York Times, and then The Boston Globe. "SDS Fugitive Apprehended after Seven Year Search," and a picture of Harlan looking like Charles Manson.

"Some fucking picture, right? Leave it to the pig press," Jo had said, and I'd agreed, trying to imagine what my parents would be thinking, maybe at that very moment, sipping their coffee over breakfast when they saw that shot, with no clue at all that I was within a million miles of this very person.

Harlan told us he had a lawyer, the one who'd been assigned to his case until they sent him back to Colorado. "Then we'll have to pull out the big guns," he said in a staged whisper, taunting the guard nearby to eavesdrop.

Jo laughed, covering his mouth with her hand and shushing him. They were playful together and it made it easy to be there, to almost forget about the miles of cellblocks that surrounded us. I thought Harlan had a warm smile, his eyes closing into half-moons like clown eyes, his teeth white against his dark skin and black beard. If there was a mountain of trouble on the horizon for the two of them, neither showed it. In fact, for moments it felt like the four of us could have been hanging out together in a bar somewhere. Roland was slipping his hand down the back of my jeans, just an inch or so, running his fingers up and down the base of my spine. No one could see. It was all the privacy we were going to get, those few covered inches of spine and hand, but it was another conversation entirely.

"I've been thinking about who we should get for a lawyer," Harlan offered more seriously. "Call Bill Kunstler . . . he'll want to talk to us, and even if he can't do it he'll know who to get."

Jo agreed, not skipping a beat, and so matter of fact about it. But it gave me pause. Bill Kunstler was more famous than anyone I'd ever met, and a lion of a man. I'd read about him often enough in the paper, but I'd only seen him once on TV, watching the evening news one night with my mother.

"Ugg, he's so unattractive!" she'd said. But I thought just the opposite—his wild long hair punctuating his articulate remarks with every shake of his head. I thought he was eloquent and radical. I'd be daunted to meet him. But not Jo.

"And we're going to post bond for Roland as soon as it's set," Jo said. "Karl thought maybe even as early as Monday or Tuesday."

When Jo said "we", that we were going to post bond, I wanted to stop her; correct her. It wasn't "we" at all. It was me. I could feel that voice, that brat inside me that wanted all the credit in the most greedy kind of way. I wanted Roland to know how far I was willing to go for him—four thousand dollars cash, and then the money for the lawyer on top of that, whatever that was going to be. That was a lot, wasn't it? Or maybe it wasn't. After all, there was a lot more where that came from. I'd hardly be putting a dent in the stockpile, so to speak. Again, I had to remind myself it was money that belonged right back in the hands of the working class, those who'd made much of the money I was inheriting.

"Betcha' Million Flinn," is what my mother's grandmother told us they used to call her father, a robber baron in the steel industry. He'd gotten the reputation and the catchy nick-name she was proud to flaunt, by placing million dollar bets on which elevator would arrive first on the ground level of his office building. I wondered if he'd ever looked into the faces of his workers, many of them children as young as ten working twelve and fourteen hour shifts for starvation wages. When they went out on strike, the famous one in 1919, had he been the one to call in the Special Forces that tortured and terrorized them? How easy to make phone calls like that, like Rockefeller's in Attica, from the top floor, where everything is neat and polished and the city spreads out below you like your very own pacific kingdom.

It was payback time . . . time to give the money back however and wherever the opportunities presented themselves. Jo and Harlan and Roland, they were certainly "the people" as far as I was concerned. And whatever it cost to get Roland out was money well spent for the movement. Really, it was just as well that he hadn't acknowledged the money at all.

When we left, the FBI agents were waiting for us. This time, they moved quickly across the parking lot trying to intercept us before we reached my car. There wasn't even time to conspire with Jo before they reached us.

"Mrs. King! Ms. Coleman!" the shorter one called to us, animated like a news reporter. They were only about ten paces away. "Would you mind having a word with us?"

They split up then, the short one heading for Jo, while the tall one, the one I noticed to be somewhat familiar looking in a Waspy kind of way, came straight for me. I was walking as fast as I could without running to my side of the car and fumbling in my bag for my keys, but I knew he had me. I could feel him come up close behind me.

It must have been the suits, so much like my father's, that brought on the unruly feeling I had—the feeling that it wasn't the agent moving towards me as much as I was being pulled, sucked, drawn towards him. All that was familiar about him was like a deadly elixir, one that would lull me back to sleep, and by the delusional action of its contents I would wake at home, in my parents home, and they would be the way they could have been, and I would be safe and content as the daughter they'd really wanted me to be. I was in a panic of certainty that the agent would, by some kind of telepathy, read all of this in me, see the feeling that I somehow had more in common with him in some repugnant but enduring way than I did with Jo. And if I looked up into the face of the man next me, what I'd see might be my father's face, his head tipped slightly to one side, his expression wondering, perplexed, not quite yet able to entertain the sense of betrayal that would surely soon follow.

But I didn't look up. It was enough to see the large polished black executive shoes he wore, and the neatly tailored and pressed pant legs of his suit. I heard Jo on the other side of the car sing out strident and clear, "Get fucked, you pigs! I'll never talk to any of you. Leave us alone!"

I was embarrassed and proud of her at the same time. She was being awfully rude, wasn't she? That was one voice in me, wanting to tell the agent that I thought she was being a little unnecessarily provocative, while the other part of me was proud that she could be so fearless, and that just by association, they might see me as fearless too.

"Come on Linda," he said to me quietly in a little sphere of persuasive sound that only the two of us could hear. "This sort of behavior isn't like you. I know that. We all know that. You're in the wrong place. You just took a wrong turn. Why don't you get out before it's too late? Here—just take my card and give me a call sometime, whenever you're ready. You could really save yourself a lot of trouble. And your family. I know your family's worried about you."

I'd finally gotten the door open and slipped into the car. I unlocked Jo's side and she jumped in, slamming her door and giving them the finger with her free hand. I felt instantly bolstered by her presence and the clear car boundary that now held them on the outside. But his voice had rattled me, tapped a deeply familiar place in me. The "home" place where you never raised your voice and you got your mouth washed out with soap for cursing . . . but home nonetheless. I knew the rules there at least.

"Fuck you pig," I said and I knew he could hear it. But I didn't look up at him when I said it, and I didn't shout. It was almost an apology. When I drove away, there was his card lying in my lap.

CHAPTER 14

—◦—

Jo smokes Marlboros in a hard box and drinks her tea with half and half and two sugars. I do the same—now that I'm with her every minute of every day it's like I'm trying to slip inside her small body. I memorize her slightly bowlegged and certain stride, her ever-so-slightly concave slouch, the way she tucks her shirt in and pulls her belt buckle tight to the last notch. The thing about Jo is she always seems to have a plan—as if she's figured the world out in some way long ago, how to be in it with authority. It's not that she's bossy—we agree on things together, and I'm happy that she has a plan, moving us from destination to destination. It's not so important to me that I know where we'll end up. I can't pretend to know how to build the revolution, I'm only certain that I want the very changes advocated by all of them; and because they've lived in the proletariat trenches all their lives, I defer to their wisdom. I have an innate conviction about what's right, but I can fumble in the articulation. Jo never seems to fumble.

It's enough that I made the decisions I've made in the last week which are: to drop my job at the hospital, to drive Jo across country, to move out of my apartment. In the last week we've put a thousand miles on the car just going up and down the coast from Boston to Maine, out to the prison, and back again—driving, driving—with me at the wheel and Jo flipping tapes or radio stations. We play Linda Ronstadt singing "Willing" over and over. *I'm willing . . . to be movin'*, and the one where she's praying *Oh Lord, if you hear me, touch me and hold me, and keep me from blowin' away . . .*

We sing it out with everything we've got. The window's down, I'm thinking of Roland touching me again, wondering where we'll all land with so much unknown and miles to go before we sleep.

We're on our way to see the kids, and I'll be meeting Jo's mother Edna, and visit the home where Jo grew up. It's about an hour from Portland in a small rural town, somewhere along the winding forested road we've turned down. I asked her how her mother was handling all of this.

"She's solid. She'll do anything to help us out. You'll see. And she's always liked Harlan a lot."

"Did she know you were on the run all this time?"

"Nope . . . we never told her. The less you know the better, right?" She took a drag of her cigarette and blew it in my face laughing.

When we stopped to pick up a few presents for the kids, I got a box of cookies for Edna, the fancy variety pack. I wanted her to like me too. To have a mother stand by you in this situation—that must be some kind of love, some kind of loyalty I wasn't sure I'd get from my own parents.

We pulled into a narrow stone driveway, edged by old lilacs, and stopped in front of a small, one-story house with pale green clapboard siding. It was the kind of home I wished I'd grown up in—too small and close for the deep silence and chill of a house with many unused rooms. Jo reached over me and leaned on the horn as we pulled up, and her kids blasted out of the front door, in socks and underwear and T-shirts, stopping short of running through wet mud and leftover snow to the car.

"I'm coming! I'm coming," she called to them as they jumped up and down in unison, and then all over her as soon as she reached the first of the three brick front steps.

Edna stood in the doorway and reminded me of the nanny I'd grown up with, May, only taller and broader but with the same gray hair cut in a pageboy style, wearing the same shapeless housedress and baggy cardigan sweater, and when she hugged me hello it was the same combination of solid and soft. We all followed her through the living room, into the kitchen, into the thick aroma—a cottage mix of heating oil and mildew and something rich with meat and potatoes on the stove. I loved the tidy disarray inside, everything well worn, all the home-sweet-home bric-a brac. Edna was ready with teacups, Vienna Fingers, Cheez Whiz on Ritz crackers, and pushed aside the piles of bills and coupons and magazines that crowded the kitchen table to make room for our tea and snacks.

"Aren't you a dear," Edna said when I gave her the cookies and she opened them up and offered them first to the kids before she put the rest on a plate on the table. Jo showed me where the bathroom was, back through the living room, and I was glad to be left alone for a few minutes to take in the details of her home, to fit this place into the stories she'd told me of her early courtship with Harlan, how she'd met him here six years ago. It was a story that made any unlikely and fantastic love seem possible, and as I looked at the rooms more slowly, I took the few details she'd told me and filled in the blank spaces myself, the way I imagined it.

He shows up out of the blue—a fugitive already, he's passing through, needs a safe house for the night, and, through a friend, ends up here where Jo's waiting—waiting for the birth of her first child, the father long gone. She's in her eighth month, when Harlan appears. I imagine that moment when it begins, desire in the first eye contact. And how it grows strong between them so quickly, this unlikely wanting. She wants to run her hands down the length of his shining black ponytail. He wants to lie next to her, circle her belly with his hands and to feel that hopeful hot presence of the child thumping, knocking, rolling inside her. They're both surprised, startled at this force pulling them together. One day and it's hard not to touch when already the knowing is so insistent.

That night, with Edna asleep in her back room, asleep as always with the light on and the radio a low constant drone of talk shows in the background, they kiss on the old sitting room couch, laughing that there isn't room for all three of them to lie down— Jo and Harlan and the baby - so they tiptoe whispering over to the pullout bed in the dark corner where Harlan slept fitfully the night before. They lie down together, but holding back until he's told her everything about his situation, and she's explained about the baby, how entirely unattached she is to everything except the baby. Sometime before morning, they've decided to leave together.

Jo doesn't tell her mother that Harlan's a wanted man, only that she's going to leave with him for a few days, to visit friends in the city, she says, but the few days turn into months, and then they're getting married. Edna is their witness, proud to hold her new grandson, and she's happy for Jo, likes the sincere and caring way that Harlan adores her. She chooses not to probe for explanations of their sudden departures, their ever-changing addresses, nor to question outright why her daughter's always calling from street corners and Laundromats. She doesn't indulge her own expectations anymore. Mother of five, she's already raised a palsied son, has another in jail, and watched her husband die young from too much work, too much poverty, too many dreams that didn't pan out.

Mark and Lou are arguing about who will sit on Jo's lap. Lou, the two year old, has grabbed a fistful of Mark's long hair, wispy and shoulder length, and she's holding on and pulling fiercely while Jo tries to pry her fingers loose and hold Mark back from striking out at her. He's five, but small, all bones and pale white skin, with deep set and serious eyes that look more frightened than angry at his sister's assault.

"Why don't you give them those presents?" Jo says to me and at the mention of presents, the kids let go and follow me to the living room. I don't know who wants what, so I just dump the bag on the floor—a package of paper airplanes, a stuffed rabbit, a book, and a truck—and the three of us sit down on the floor to play. Mark goes for the truck and Lou picks up the book, and without hesitation, crawls into my lap to be read to. In moments, she has one thumb in her mouth and her head against my chest.

Though I've just met them, right away I have the feeling that they offer respite, an easy hiding place from my own harsh scrutiny of myself, and the scrutiny of others I so often feel certain awaits me.

I begin reading the story. It's about a turtle that's lost his shell, who's asking everyone he meets, all the animals in the forest that have their own homes, where he might have lost his. Mark crawls over and leans against my side to see the pictures, and it's silly, but I feel a lump in my throat, hear a crack in my voice at the sight of that turtle scurrying around in long underwear with a worried look on his turtle face, looking for his shell in all the wrong places.

I wish they were coming with us, their little bodies warm in my lap eager for the love that flows from some effortless source in me.

After the story, we go back to the kitchen. Jo is telling Edna about Harlan and the trial. This is not their first conversation since he's been caught, but I don't know the details of what she's been told, only that it's clear that what Jo doesn't tell is withheld out of con-

129

sideration, not out of fear of reprisals and judgment. Listening, Edna's eyes have a tired distance, like this is just one more river to cross and she's rowing right along with barely a pause—chafed hands, leaky boat, she does what needs to be done.

"But won't you have to get him a lawyer?" Edna asks.

"Of course, Ma. But there are some really big lawyers who want to take his case."

"Well, won't that cost a lot of money? Where will you get that?" Her freckled forearms are resting on the table, one hand slowly stirs her tea, and she looks at Jo with a worried frown.

"We're going to raise it. We're going to have a lot of publicity about it all and people who support him will send us money. We're going to start a defense fund." She is so definite about this that I'm certain for the moment that is exactly what will happen.

"And what about Mark and Lou? When will you be back for them?" Mark has crawled into her lap and she strokes his hair with a perfect gentleness, offering him a cookie from the box.

Jo tells her we're going to drive to Denver, find a place to stay, and then she'll be back for the kids. "You can handle it Ma, right? It'll only be a couple of weeks." The way she lays it out, with all the authority she has, it sounds like she's the mother.

Edna shrugs her shoulders. "Well sounds like you've got it all worked out, honey. You do what you have to do and God help you." She gets up to wash the teacups and I help her clear the table. She doesn't press us for more details, or fret, or show any real sign of disapproval, and I wonder about love like this, that allows anything, that "endures all things" like that letter in the Bible says, if it is the best kind of love or no love at all, if she's just too tired to care. I wonder if she's afraid of Jo a little bit, of her quick bite, the way I am, or has just given up trying to change her daughter's mind about anything.

When we leave, she kisses me too, her soft weathered cheek giving us all the permission in the world.

Touch me and hold me and keep me from blowin' away . . .

Driving. Driving.

Jo has no license because of her seizures and on our way back to my apartment that night she has one in the car, the first I've witnessed, its onset without warning *What the fuck is happening?* The thumping banging rocking bucking, the sucking sounds. I pull over onto the shoulder and reach out to hold her, to brace her head, to try to catch her somehow . . . what if she hits the window? breaks the glass? Chokes and swallows her tongue? What did she tell me the other day? *Put the tongue depressor in if you can, but otherwise just keep my head turned to the side so I don't choke on my saliva.*

But I can't catch her head. I don't have the tongue depressor. Fuck! The sucking sound is horrible, *horrible.* Her body heaving, jerking, heaving and jerking she's going to snap she must be choking she's going to snap . . . jerking . . . jerking . . . .jerking. It goes on and on and then it slows . . . and then it stops.

The next big heave is our car, the little dark box we're in, billowed by an eighteen-wheeler leaning on his horn whipping screaming past us. And I do have her head. I somehow miraculously do. It's resting in my hands. Her saliva is warm on my hands. Saliva or blood. I can't see. Something glistens in the oncoming headlights but they go by too fast to tell.

Is she breathing? I put my hand on her chest. It's not moving. But then she groans a little groan. Another oncoming car and I can see her eyelids flutter. Okay. She told me before, she warned me, there's nothing I can do. Just wait it out. Every time a car goes by, a deep shudder . . . me or the car or Jo? I cradle her head and wait.

"Jo? Are you okay?" She's groggy but she answers.

"Yeah . . . just a minute. Okay." And soon she starts to move, a dark silhouette come to life, and then she sits up, feels her head, her lip, and I wonder how she will look, how she might be crushed or broken, again, like the other time, but different. I hand her a napkin and she wipes her mouth.

"How long was that one?" Like I've seen this before.

"I don't know . . . maybe a minute, two minutes until it stopped and then a little more until you woke up."

"I bit my lip . . . Shit." She flips down the visor and looks in the vanity mirror. Her lip is fat on one side but the blood is already slowing. Otherwise she looks the same, back from the dead or wherever she was.

"Do you want to go get some ice or something?"

"No, let's just keep going. I'll put something on it when I get to your place. God, remind me next time not to look at the headlights. It does it to me every time."

*   *   *

Roland has not gotten out, will not get out at least for a couple of weeks, his arraignment delayed by legal details. The plan that unfolds, is unfolding, goes like this.

After I officially quit my job at the hospital and pack up and leave my apartment, I'll drive Jo to Denver. We'll find a place to rent for the duration of the trial, and once found, we'll drive back east to pick up Roland. Jo will get the kids and fly back out to Denver. Roland and I will drive out together. Harlan will have been transferred to Denver by then and hopefully we'll get him out on bail, hopefully. All along the way we'll be setting up Harlan King Defense Committees - in New York, Boston, Portland, and then in Denver, where our central office will be.

The hospital part was easy. I just put a letter in the mail to my supervisor that said, "Due to personal circumstances I will not be able to continue my training at this time. Thank you. Sincerely . . . " Jo told me what to write, me having never quit anything before. That was that. Signed, sealed, delivered. But then, to close the apartment up I had to bring all the furniture back to my grandmother's along with some explanation, and then I had to tell my parents too. There was no way around it.

I decided to write my parents, and then maybe I'd call them

after I left, to avoid getting tongue tied and swayed by their all too quick and cogent arguments about things; my mother's accusing tone, my father's quiet concern. Her *how could you do this to us?* His *are you sure you're doing the right thing? Are you going to be safe?*

I stayed up all one night writing everything I thought would help them understand—about the death squad, about working in the bookstore and in prison, about Jo being an epileptic mother with no money and no way of getting to Denver without me, whose husband would go on trial for bombing a missile factory at a time when our government was massacring innocent people in a war we never should have been in.

I didn't tell them anything about the attack on Jo and the store, about Roland, about the circumstances of his arrest, about the feeling I had that I might be stepping off a narrow ledge and falling willingly into the underground. That I might never come back.

In the end I wrote with an aching lump in my throat, listening to the birds waking and calling to each other, with Jo sleeping on the couch in the next room and all the boxes taped shut and ready to go all around me while I wrote the last part.

I want you to know that I love you both and that I know how hard this will be for you to understand—but if I accept a certain responsibility to be true to the values and morals I have set for myself, as you both have always encouraged me to do, regardless of the consequences, then my course becomes clear. "There's no turning back from awareness." George Jackson wrote that before he died. I'll send you his book when I get to Denver.

We spent the day taking my stuff to my grandmother's house. I got Scotty, her driver, to bring his truck and help me with the furniture, hauling it back up to the attic, into the very corners where I'd crouched in hide-and-seek as a kid, the smell of the place making me homesick, the way a house has its very own smell like a person, as intimate as that, and this one with its mixture of carnations and salt-must. It was a relief that Mammy, after all, was away visiting my uncle and that Scotty was his usual cheerful self and didn't ask questions.

Maybe because I hadn't slept, because my eyes were burning and everything had that tinny brittle clarity that comes from no sleep, but the day was dreamlike, suspended, with the wind blowing in off the bay in warm easy gusts. Every time I opened the back screen door with its particular squeak, carrying a box through the laundry to the attic stairs, it felt like it could have been any one of a hundred days in a lifetime of some other person I knew from long ago.

After the last load was done, Jo and I walked down to the point of land at the end of my grandmother's property between the bay and the cove and I showed her each of my favorite places. We straddled the great branches under the one hundred foot linden tree, walked down by the cove where the same old blue heron stood motionless in the green shallows, sat on the flat rocks warmed by the sun and threw skipping stones into water that was as clear and still as glass.

"God, can you imagine if this place was owned by the people?" Jo said, "If this were an orphanage or a home for battered women or a half-way house?" She was laying on the grass, looking up at the three story old Cape-style mansion with fourteen rooms where my great aunt lived alone with her housekeeper and her cook, a stone's throw, a fairy garden path from my grandmother's house. "It's so fucked up, having all this when most of the world's living in shacks or hungry or working three jobs like my father did to put food on the table. I wish the revolution would hurry up."

She was musing more than proselytizing, twirling a grass stem, but I still felt ashamed. It was fucked up, obscene in fact. But here, more than anywhere in the world, in my world, I didn't want it to change. It was beautiful—beauty made sacred by memory that wasn't like the rest, the other places where I'd grown up with their everyday silence and restriction and emptiness. Take those places away. Give them back to the people. But not this. This belonged to me and all my cousins, my brother and sisters—the twelve of us drawn together for a few weeks every August, our ever-changing constellations of bonding, always a friend somewhere, always a place to hide where you could be entirely free and unafraid—just the perfect amount of space and time together to make everything fit.

But these were bad thoughts. Counter-revolutionary. Selfish and entirely privileged. Of course she was right. So I told her stories of my grandmother's silliest excesses, "You won't believe this, but she pays ten thousand dollars a year just to have her trees pruned!" And of my great aunt's outside speaker system that allowed her to summon her gardener from her upstairs bedroom. I imitated and made ridiculous their elderly and distinguished voices, knowing all the while that I was betraying something altogether innocent and worthy about love.

The next morning we left for Denver. The apartment empty now, the walls bare again the way they'd thrilled me before, but bare without promises now of any kind of future there. The only thing left was a large pumpkin that had survived indoors since November, a Thanksgiving gift from Mammy.

Jo was on her way downstairs when I kicked it. Kicked it as hard as I could and split it open with a crack, spewing pulp and seeds across the empty floor. And then I closed the door, leaving the whole rotten mess behind. Let the landlord clean it up. Landlords were pigs, right? Now that I was heading west, he'd never find me.

CHAPTER 15

Once we hit Route 80 going west, I stopped thinking so much. Driving through Pennsylvania took us most of the first part of an interminable day. Then everything flattened out, my thoughts lulled by the wide horizons around me, the hum of the car in overdrive, the road that went on and on, water mirage after water mirage. I liked to think of the bird's eye view of the two of us, the tiny speck of red racing across the continent, keeping company with the big semi's that escorted us, blowing their diesel horns hello.

It was good to have a purpose, a destination, important work to attend to when we got to Denver—it allowed us this time to do nothing but keep going, flip radio stations, follow the road straight ahead.

We traveled well together. Good at driving late into the night, sleeping for a few hours in our seats in the little red station wagon. Good at living on truck stop coffee, eggs and hash browns, then waking up to the cold splash of water from the bathrooms where we'd brush our teeth, comb our hair, and put a little blush on. Jo always put a little blush on, so I did too. Not to copy, but to connect. Watching her every certain move was a way of locating myself. We'd gaze into the mirror—zombies, bug-eyed from lack of sleep, while the blush brush tickled our cheeks amidst all the comings and goings of the women around us, then the decisive snap of the compact when we were done, a small jolt to set us on our way again.

But often enough there were silences between us that went on too long, too long for me. Once I clocked a sixty mile stretch through Kansas when we didn't say a word, not even to wonder aloud at the oil rigs that appeared out of nowhere—armies of steel giants spread out on the plains, their rhythmic, never-ending reaming into the earth, or to marvel at the ocean of sweet grass that surrounded us, rippling in cross-currents of light and shadow.

I'd grope around for something to say, try to read her thoughts for how she was feeling towards me, if I was doing okay or getting on her nerves. Maybe Jo felt the same way, and I would have liked to reassure her, but sometimes the silence got as huge and ominous as the thunderheads that piled up and darkened out of nowhere, and I just had to wait for the first loud crack, or the sudden sheet of rain that would force us off the road, laughing a little nervously about the car getting washed away in a flash flood, waiting in the beautiful deafening sound of the downpour until it passed. At times like that I'd feel that whatever bound us was frayed and stretching, and every double beat of the road-dividers a quick uncertain heartbeat, my own dimensions mercurial like the road mirage, and Jo solid and impenetrable in the seat beside me.

Like my father, that's what it was like, that one time with him in that odd singular circumstance when we were alone together for the long car ride to our Vermont house. I was eight or nine, dwarfed in the front seat of the Chrysler where my mother always sat. I remember my excitement, ready with stage fright to take her place for the night. At our one gas stop at the beginning of the trip he bought me everything I wanted from the vending machines—a cup of scalding cocoa, M&M's, two six packs of Juicy Fruit that my mother never allowed. He bought cigarettes, two packs, something else my mother wouldn't allow, especially in the car, and as soon as we got going he opened the pack with two hands while he steadied the car with his thigh on the steering wheel, cracked the side window open, and lit up. He smiled at me, squeezed my knee in the way it tickled, and then, loosening his tie, slouched down, his weight against the door, and slipped away into his thoughts.

That dusk the sky was all the colors of fire, the trees delicate and naked. Did he see it? Did he wonder at the pulsing colors, how they changed every second? I wanted to ask but what I hated about these drives when my mother was there was how she'd try to shame him out of silence. "Old Stone Face" she'd call him. "Say something! Tell me about your day, about your partners, about the train ride—anything!" And you could watch him retreat as her tone would pick up a certain pitch of disdain—go deeper and deeper away from her. I'd think how she didn't understand him, how deep the hole he'd dug had become, how much he'd like to "snap out of it!" like she wanted, had even considered reaching for her hand to pull him up. But I knew even then . . . I knew exactly where he went. The hard-packed surfaces of the dirt walls too steep, too deep to get your foothold—such an effort to get out. And down there it was quiet at least. None of that relentless effort to watch where you stepped around her—all of those cleverly camouflaged traps she'd set. Lest you hurt her. Lest you disappoint her. Above ground, the sun was a single beam that followed her. Lest you steal it from her.

I would show him. In the dark car, just the two of us, my silence would speak to him. He wouldn't have to try. He could sink into his safe place wherever it was, and I would hold a vigil of understanding for the whole night drive. I'd be content to watch the red light of his cigarette in its triangular orbit, from the hand on the steering wheel, then the straight memorized line to the ashtray, and then to his lips, the way it glowed there, having found its home base, lighting up the mysterious profile of his face.

Still, I couldn't deny that I would have liked to hear his voice, to have him speak to me. "How's your cocoa, dearie?" he might have said, or even "How was school today?" But it wasn't important, not really, to speak, I told myself. Not when we were as close as we were. Not when we understood each other so well. I told myself that a lot.

We made it to Denver in forty-eight hours, crossing the city limits around midnight.

"I need a shower," Jo said.

"I need a shower and a bed. How much money do we have left?"

We dug up about fifty dollars between us. Tomorrow I'd have to go to a bank for more money, and meet with the lawyer Harlan had told us to look up as soon as we got here. Denver sprawled around us in all directions, strange and unknown, our first city since Boston.

"Let's just drive around 'till we find someplace we can afford."

Wherever we were was poor enough. Streets with Spanish names. Battered cars parked outside of small stucco apartment buildings with chain link fences. We passed a closed bodega, a few used car dealerships, the streets empty except for a few stray dogs digging in garbage cans. No one to ask. My head was pounding, my eyes on fire, and the taste of cigarettes and coffee a permanent sludge in my mouth. If we could just stop driving. I was getting ready to pull over into any dark lot and call it a day when we found the hotel, its neon lights promising enough in spite of the darkened "O" in Hotel, the missing "V" in Vacancy.

"Home sweet home!" I pulled into the cobblestone parking area in front of a three story old Spanish-type villa. There were people in the lobby, rock music over the drone of cicadas. We sat for a minute in the relief of the silence after the car engine died, feeling the warm air with its sweet dust smell. "I'll check it out."

The lobby was large and high-ceilinged, a chipped tile floor, stucco walls with fading painted scenes of Mexican dancers, peasants farming, caballeros with concertinas. Pretty cool, I thought, but odd that I was surrounded by men—men smoking by the marble staircase, men behind the mosaic counter. Dark, burnt-skinned men in muscle shirts, wearing gold chains. No women. The conversation silenced by my entrance.

I walked over to the counter, to the pock-marked man behind the desk.

"Buenos noches, Senor. Habla Ingles?"

"No." It might have been an English "no" but I wasn't certain. He was looking straight at me without a hint of a smile, an expression duplicated by his partner, who wore sunglasses and had his arms folded over his chest like a scary cliché. But I wasn't here to make assumptions about anything.

"Tienen un cama por el noche?" I thought I had it right. A room for the night, or was 'cama' a bed? My voice, however mild and mincing still echoed in the open room.

"Un cama. Si." He paused. He smiled. He smirked the slightest bit at his partner standing next to him. "Un cama. Si. Por la noche." He checked his watch. "En veinte minutos."

"In twenty minutes?" I asked in English, by accident.

"Si." He pointed to his watch. "Twenty minutes," he said, without an accent..

Okay. We'd wait twenty minutes. No problem. "Y cuanto es esto?"

"Cuarenta dolores."

Was cuarenta forty or sixty? I had to ask.

"Como? How much? Por favor, escribe me."

No one had resumed talking. Their silence was eating into my back, the presence of the men behind me closing in, and creeping closer. If I hadn't been so pumped up that my Spanish was carrying me it would have been worse, but I felt I was holding my own, making myself so clearly understood. Being so nice.

He wrote "$40" on a slip of paper, pushed it towards me and waited.

As soon as I handed him the money, I knew I'd made a mistake, the way he gave a slight shrug and raised his eyebrows like it was my choice, my crazy choice. And then too the way his friend cracked a smile from behind the dark glasses.

"I'll be back. Veinte minutos. Gracias." But I knew I wouldn't. I got it now. The twenty minute wait. All the men in the lobby. No women. Walking out, my heartbeat as loud as my flip-flops smacking notes in the silent hallway. A low voice in Spanish followed me, and then a laugh, and then I heard a catcall and a laugh and another called "Punta blanca" like he was calling his dog. Only I knew what a "punta" was, a punta blanca—a white cunt. They were making low kissing sounds, low like they didn't think I'd hear. Jesus. I got in the car and drove out of there.

It wasn't even funny. But then, it was funny. I started to laugh as I told Jo and then she did too—and we couldn't stop, the laughter gathering all the tension of the long drive and purging us of it. All of it. Everything so crazy you had to let go and that laughter blanketed us together, was its own kind of union. When we finally stretched our seats back to sleep in the Stop-n-Shop parking lot, I was glad for that moment to be with her, just the two of us, for one more night.

"Buenos noches punta," she said. "Jesus, this fucking car seat's horrible," pulling her sweater over her and stuffing some clothes behind her head for a pillow.

She loved me. I loved her.

"No, no chica, punta *blanca*," I reminded her. "Buenos noches." And then we were quiet again.

CHAPTER 16

In the morning we went to a bank in downtown Denver. There was no way to really clean up for it. There were no shirts I hadn't worn at least twice, no jeans without at least one coffee stain.

"Oh fuck them," Jo said tugging at her hair with a brush. "Come the revolution, anyone who works in a bank will get hung out to dry anyway."

Yeah . . . I guess.

We put on a little make-up, and I poured water on a paper towel and washed the black dirt off my feet as best I could.

There weren't any branches of the Bank of New York in Denver, the bank that held my account, so I figured I'd just pick a bank. Any big bank. High ceilings, marbled, hushed—banks were all more or less the same.

Jo and I were waiting to see a Ms. Holtz, one of the bank officers a teller had told us would be with us in a few minutes. Even Jo was whispering now.

"What if they don't let us cash a check?"

"I don't know. I'll think of something."

"Yeah, we'll have to rob the place!" Her laugh shook the silence of the big room.

A trim youngish woman approached us—clip, clip in her three-inch heels, her tan two-piece suit with the big bow-collared blouse—all that kind of chilly efficient ease.

"I'm Ms. Holtz. What can I do for you ladies?" I introduced Jo, and myself, and Ms. Holtz extended her hand to me with that kind of paid-for smile, with enough make-up on to hide any kind of expression beneath it. I noted her fingernails (something a nail-biter like myself never misses)—smooth, glossy red candies at the tips of her Noxzema hands.

"I need to withdraw $10,000 cash from my account in New York." I figured that amount would cover our deposit on an apartment rental, the retainer for Harlan's lawyer, and still leave some extra for travel expenses.

Her face didn't change expression, but her eyes looked disdainfully puzzled, not unlike the pimp's wondering gaze from the night before.

"I'm sorry," she said and you knew she wasn't sorry at all. "Do you have an account with our bank?" I was suddenly painfully aware of the little safety pin that held my glasses together and felt with a sinking certainty that she could somehow detect the nest of knots I hadn't been able to untangle from the back of my hair.

I explained as plaintively as I could that we were traveling, re-locating to the area for the summer at least, and that we'd run short on cash and needed the deposit for an apartment—*today*. I told her she could call a Mrs. Lee from the Bank of New York on Wall Street for verification. "There's definitely money in the account, I can assure you of that." I tried to sound definitive, even slightly directive, and needy at the same time. Jo wasn't saying a word for once, so it was all up to me.

"I see . . . " Ms. Holtz elongated the 'eee'. "Why don't you give me your account number and I'll see what I can do." But her cool brown eyes said nothing about helping us out. "This is quite an unusual request you know." Whether that was true or not, my first impulse was to apologize for the inconvenience, but with Jo there I held my tongue. Ms. Holtz brushed past me to get some paper and a pen. I could smell her perfume and I wondered for a shameful moment if she could smell that remnant ashtray smell that permeated all of my clothes. "Why don't you two have a seat while I see what I can do." She disappeared up some carpeted stairs, behind a balcony, and we waited for a long time.

"She's a prissy little thing, isn't she?" Jo snorted. "'Highly unusual request' my ass! If we were men in business suits she wouldn't have said that. All puffed up on her little power trip, isn't she?" She was right, of course. I felt sheepish about my apologetic impulses—glad I'd held them in check. She took a nail file from her purse and began to file away. She had pretty hands too, small and delicate with smooth nails that rounded off at the tip. "Oh I see . . . " she continued her mimic, "Like we're some kind of criminals or something." We shared a hushed laugh over that.

In a few minutes, Ms. Holtz re-appeared with no inkling of softening in her chilly reserve.

"Why don't you come with me, Ms. Coleman? Your friend can wait for you here."

I followed her feeling like a bad child, up the carpeted stairs to a windowless conference room furnished with a large mahogany table, more leather chairs, and a telephone with blinking lights there before me. "I have Mrs. Lee on the line. She wants to ask you a few questions."

I could see Mrs. Lee seated at her desk, a smaller version of this same table, in her office not unlike this very room, in her downtown Wall Street bank building. She would be sitting forward in her chair, compact, brilliant, and unshakably composed. Her red lipstick would be flawless; her dark eyes intelligent and unreadable.

We'd met once, last summer. Soon after my father presented

me with the stock portfolio, he'd brought me to her plush and carpeted office where I sat in uneasy confusion, while she and my father explained the terms of the account to me. I had absolutely no idea, no marker of how I was to act, what my relationship to her should be. Young enough to be her daughter, I was her 'client' she said, and she would be available to me whenever I "needed to discuss my financial concerns".

The stock portfolio lay on the desk before us with my undeserving name on it, and I wondered if I listened hard enough, scanned her face adeptly, if I could read or hear the judgments she certainly brewed about the inequities of inherited wealth. For all I knew, she might have worked her way out of a tenement in Chinatown to get to this pinnacle, a third-world woman vice-president of one of the oldest 'old boy' banks in New York. But that made her the enemy, didn't it? Her office no less than a bunker behind enemy lines, feeding the enemy machine by managing capitalist money. She and my father and I were all in it together. But the pleasant civility with which she kept the conversation flowing like a gentle brook, along with my father's paternal all-knowing concern for me, made it hard to focus on the moral compromise I was complicit in. In fact, I'd felt something maternally comforting about her. She smiled reassuringly at me over her gold-rimmed reading glasses without a hint of condescension. She double-clasped my hand firmly when we parted, and I thought for a moment that we might even hug good-bye.

I picked up the phone. "Hello, Mrs. Lee? This is Linda."

"Linda, hello! You're in Denver I gather." She sounded so convincingly glad to hear from me.

"Yes. I'm here for a little while I guess." I left an opening for her to inquire as to why I was in Denver, hoping suddenly that she would ask.

"I understand from Ms. Holtz that you need to have $10,000 cash wired to you today. I don't think there'll be any problem with this Linda, but I need to ask you a few questions to be certain of your identity."

Her voice was professional, respectful. She wasn't going to pry. But I wanted her to. I wanted her to ask me with sincere concern if I needed help and wouldn't I please talk to her a little about what was going on? She'd help me figure it out. She would be like the old sage from one of my childhood bedtime stories who pulls the boy up and out of the deep well he's fallen into. She'd pump the air into me and push the water out of me until I could breathe freely again.

But this was an adult conversation. An adult conversation about a bank transaction. She was paid to do as I wished without any invasion of my privacy. She wouldn't have my father on a third line. They wouldn't pry with parental concern and then offer guidance in a gently persuasive way. Of course not. My identity would be confirmed. The money would appear. It was frighteningly effortless, embarrassingly transparent to see the ease with which the money flowed to me because of my class background.

Ms. Holtz shuffled papers behind me. Mrs. Lee completed her questions:

my mother's maiden name; my father's mother's name; my social security number.

"One five nine—zero three - two nine. . ." That was all it took.

We said good-bye. We said we hoped we'd see each other again soon. And then I handed the phone back to Ms. Holtz.

CHAPTER 17

W e left the bank with a fat envelope of bills that looked like play money straight out of the five-and-dime. I'd watched Ms. Holtz count it out, licking her fingers to separate the new crispy bills accurately. I'd never seen $100 bills before, or a fifty for that matter, and when she asked me how I'd like it broken down, I realized I didn't know if they made bills any bigger than that. It seemed like she was counting and re-counting forever. Twenty twenty-dollar bills, forty fifty-dollar bills, thirty one hundred dollar bills, and the rest left in a checking account for later. She had to lick her fingers a lot, and wasn't any too pleased. I smiled apologetically from time to time. All in all it took us the whole morning.

Jo gave me a high five as we left the bank. "Wayda-go, sister!" and I felt grateful at least that she didn't blame me for the clearly privileged ease of the transaction, waltzing out the door with thousands of dollars, all because of the color of our skin and a phone call to the right person. But if Jo had made the connection, she didn't say, and I was glad not to have to unravel the contradictions of the event any further. Instead, I let myself join in her festive mood, as if we'd managed to pull off a great ruse and tricked them all into giving us this fortune like some kind of white-collar criminals, or some kind of revolutionaries.

It certainly didn't feel like money that belonged to me, and I wondered if I should give some of it to Jo, or all of it to her, if that would make everything balance out. Even though I thought that was a good idea, I still held on to most of it, giving her only a wad of twenties after we got in the car, the way my grandmother would have stuffed the same amount in my bag.

But the money didn't amount to much anyway. In less than a week it was mostly gone. First, the three thousand for the lawyer that Kunstler had lined up for us. He'd told Jo on the phone that this was the one we wanted, this David Harriman, that he was the best. "He'll take care of you. He'll be reasonable," is what Jo said he'd promised. But his office was lavishly pristine, spacious and air-conditioned, and I knew even before we sat on the other side of his immaculately polished desk the size of a Ping-Pong table that this wasn't going to be a "pro-bono" effort on his part. "Three thousand to start," he'd said, like he was doing us a favor and who was going to argue after he'd been nice enough to talk to us for an hour. It didn't seem to faze Jo in the slightest, so I just counted it out, licking my fingers the way Ms. Holtz had done a few hours before.

And then a couple of days after that, the apartment, which turned out to be a small house, cost us another fifteen hundred, what with the security deposit and the first month's rent. It was a steal, right? That's what Jo said, and it did seem like a pretty good deal to land on our first full day of looking—three bedrooms, a living room, kitchen, and two bathrooms with a fenced in yard for the kids. I knew right away what bothered me, even as the thoughts embarrassed me as they appeared. What bothered me was exactly what Jo seemed to like best about it—the wall-to-wall shag carpets, cheap enough but new and clean, the white painted wicker vanity set in the "master" bedroom, the flowery drapes and chenille style bedspreads. Jo was delighted, relieved we didn't have to live in a hole in the wall, and who could blame her.

"God, a house!" she whispered to me excitedly, as if the real-estate agent would hear her and jack the price up or something. "I haven't lived in a house for five years!" and she ran up and down the stairs one more time to look again. "This is perfect, don't you think? We should grab it." But I had to admit I was disappointed. We should be struggling, at least I should be. Honestly, I'd have paid as much for rug stains and windowless subterranean gloom just to keep myself on the right revolutionary track, and the fact that Jo loved the place with all its middle-class sheen made me lose just the tiniest bit of respect for her. I would have my own room, but even that felt strange and empty, missing as I did, the feeling of driving, the freedom and closeness of being together in the car, moving through all that endless landscape.

I counted out fifteen one hundred dollar bills and noticed how much thinner the envelope had gotten in just two days. The feeling I had, the tightness like a band around my head, the low rumble in my thoughts about spending the money was getting more familiar. I had to frequently remind myself why I was doing this. Did I want to be like every great-aunt and grandmother in my family with an attic full of antiques, stacked and packed and covered with sheets, worried about the rainy days to come? Maybe that kind of greed was genetic, passed on in the bloodline like all the other evils I felt imprisoned by in my history. I wanted that buck to stop right here. So when we got back in the car after signing a three month lease, I did give the rest of the cash to Jo, hoping to quell once and for all that gremlin inside me that was whining with increasing volume and frequency—whining that I was "giving away" too much.

And then there was our meeting with Harlan's mother Val, and his sister Suzanne the day after we got there. Harlan had grown up in Denver, I knew that, and we knew his sister still lived here and his mother somewhere nearby, and that Harlan had spoken to them both on the phone after he'd been arrested, his first contact with them since he'd gone underground.

Suzanne lived somewhere in the maze of the sprawling suburbs around Denver, but since Jo had never met her, we'd decided it would be better not to show up on her doorstep at midnight, at least that first night. We called her the next day though, after finishing up in the bank, Jo waving to me to join her in the pay-phone booth, sharing the phone with me so I could hear. Suzanne was "just thrilled" to hear from her. I could hear her high-pitched exclamations, that she most certainly was expecting us. And Val too, Harlan's mother, had come into town because she was expecting us, and they were so glad we'd gotten here safely. We should come right over. Plan to stay as long as we liked . . . they'd be waiting with some late lunch ready.

"Oh god. Here goes," Jo sighed when she hung up the pay phone. I knew she was a little nervous, not knowing what to expect. And maybe she had some of the same wistful feeling that I had, that our time alone together was about to end and would never be quite the same from now on.

"Well they sound pretty cool," she brightened as we got in the car. "You know, Harlan told me his Mom's pretty loaded. I guess she's always had money, but it sounds like now she has lots . . . I mean not that it matters. And he said that maybe his sister's rich too. They sell real estate together or something. Weird, don't you think?"

She turned on the radio, not apparently expecting an answer, which was just as well, because I didn't know what I'd have said, but I did think it was weird, uncomfortably surprisingly weird, that my underground hero might have this wealthy family behind him. I'd never considered that. It wasn't the way I'd imagined it to be, that I wanted it to be.

"But what I mean is," Jo said, lighting a cigarette while she spoke, "if they're rich maybe they'll help us with the bond money."

That would be good, wouldn't it, if Val helped us with the bond money. Harlan had told Jo his ballpark estimate of what he thought the judge would assign, and it was a lot, maybe a hundred grand or more. I'd been worrying since she'd told me that, wondering if they'd ask me to post it for them, and what I would say—should I just sell everything and hand it over? It would only be temporary, right? And even if I never got it back, I could do it—so should I?

As we wove our way through the endless suburban streets, watching the houses get bigger and the lawns become a bright Kelly-watered green in the middle of the desert, I could feel Jo's mood brighten, just as mine darkened, my heart sinking as we pulled into the neatly graveled driveway, parked behind someone's white BMW, and headed up the flagstone walkway towards the pillared doorway of Suzanne's entirely well-appointed ranch house.

But really they couldn't have been nicer. I could hear my mother saying that about Suzanne and Val because that's what she would have said. Their tans, their white teeth and knee-length flowered shorts, their toenails painted to match their lipstick—aside from their western accents, they could have been from my hometown.

They were friendly enough to me, hugging me hello, but they both fussed over Jo like she was the First Lady. Val held her at arms length, all dewy eyed. "I'm just so glad you're here," she must have said five times, and "I can't believe it's finally you!" until I had to wonder what she was really feeling behind all that enthusiasm. But before we even budged from where we stood on the driveway, Jo had pulled out pictures of Harlan and the kids to show them, and Val had to stop and wipe the real tears that trickled down her cheeks, blowing her nose into her mono-grammed handkerchief. There was nothing phony about it.

"C'mon everybody," Suzanne said, resting her hand on her mother's arm, "let's get inside out of this heat."

Suzanne had iced tea sweating in tall glasses complete with mint sprigs and lemon wedges waiting for us beside a plateful of crust-less triangular sandwiches and a fruit salad just as my mother might have served to any of her luncheon guests. We sat together in the air-conditioned room on leather couches with shades half-drawn to keep out the mid-day sun.

"Now tell me everything, "Val said as we sat down to lunch, putting her napkin in her lap and leaning forward in her chair with a grave expectancy. She had kind brown eyes, a weathered face. But who could summarize seven years on the run with an opening as wide as that, and even Jo didn't know where to begin. Val sensed her confusion.

"Oh I know all about the charges against him—I have a file a foot thick on that—about the bombing in '68 and everything around that time. But it's been so long since I've heard anything, anything." Her eyes welled up with tears again. "How is he?"

That's what she really meant, what she really wanted, so Jo gave her as much of that as she could—telling her how Harlan was just as strong as ever and ready to fight to make the trial a big expose of how the system was so one-sided in favor of the status quo, and what a farce we all thought the term "justice" was when the government wanted to cover up all the ways it had butchered people in this illegal war in Vietnam, let alone at home in our very own ghettos.

"Harlan's not going to give an inch when it comes to exposing who the real criminals are."

I wondered if that would be a relief to Val, or if she was hoping he'd grown out of all that, but her expression never lost its soft approval. "Well, good for him."

I could imagine my mother reacting the same way if her darling Charles, my older and only brother, had been gone for seven years. But that scenario was not easy to conjure since Charles had, in every way, stayed close to home, married the right girl, and followed in my father's footsteps, right down to Wall Street— Charles, her golden boy, her shining beacon of hope amidst the murkier accomplishments of her other, female, offspring. She and Val had something in common there, that fevered son worship. Maybe it explained why Suzanne seemed slightly less interested in the whole affair, orchestrating lunch, keeping our glasses full, but otherwise not taking much of a part in the conversation. It made me like her more, knowing as I do, what it was like living in the shadow of a glorified son.

I was altogether uncomfortably comfortable with the whole situation there. It was too much like being at home, and that was not at all the way I wanted it to be. An uneasy awareness had been growing since Jo had mentioned her mother-in-law's wealth— that Harlan and I might have things in common (as in class ties in common), when all along I'd been assuming that I was done with that, that I'd put it a million miles away from me in every way I could. It tainted the picture, the image I proudly held on to of our group, knowing its members to be righteously pure in their working class roots. It seemed that at every turn contradictions multiplied—gray areas that clouded a horizon I'd hoped would be clear and bright, and the way to travel fully apparent.

By late afternoon, everyone was talked out and Jo said she was ready for a hot shower and bed and that sounded good to me. Suzanne showed us to our bedroom, insisting it was ours for as long as we liked, the two twin beds looking untouchably neat and foreign after our cramped car, with matching spreads and two pillows apiece. Maybe Jo knew I was feeling uncomfortable because as soon as she closed the door she gave a sigh of relief like she was glad to be able to relax with me.

"This is too much. Check out these beds," and she flopped

down on one and threw her arms out. "Did you see Val's car? It's a BMW for Christ's sake! I guess she has money."

She said it like I wasn't like them, and she'd rather be with me. There was a record player and a few albums in the room and one of our favorites was there, on the top of the stack waiting for us, a Gladys Knight album. We'd listened to her song Midnight Train to Georgia a hundred times in the last few days of traveling and I put the song on now and sat on the twin bed opposite Jo. We sang out the part that goes I'd rather be in his world than live without him in mine like schoolgirls, smiling at each other because she knew I was thinking about Roland, and I knew she was thinking about Harlan, looking forward to tomorrow or the next day when he'd be transferred and she'd get to see him in the Denver jail. In the smile between us was the unspoken bond we had, part of what held us together, that we were women loving men, these particular two men who were in an honorable kind of trouble, and who we would be proud to admit it was our privilege to care for and defend.

But for me, even with all of my desire for Roland and my willing collusion in joining Jo in the romance of it all, even while I sang out the words, I wanted to qualify my intent, make it clear to Jo or anyone else that Roland was *not t*he reason I was in this unlikely place. I wasn't traveling in his world, not really. In my heart I knew I was on my own, my very own journey, and it was still about doing the right thing, traveling however far I had to go to figure out just what that meant. I was traveling to find out what it meant to be a revolutionary, a revolutionary woman, if I could be one who would give up everything to fight evil, to bring to reckoning the greatest evildoers in the world, to further the cause of peace and justice for all people.

As I crawled into bed, between the clean sheets, I wondered how my path had taken me here, into this room, with its familiar floral printed drapes and matching pillow shams, if I had taken a wrong turn, made a mistake. If anything, loving Roland was a distraction from my training as a revolutionary, but he was also my teacher, one of my teachers, in some ways the one I respected most, and I still had more to learn from him, *and* from Jo. Really, I had followed Jo here and certainly she was my teacher too, in a different way, as a woman like myself, but older and wiser and more traveled on the path. In her wake, I still felt like a girl by comparison, one who had yet to experience motherhood and marriage and what it meant to live the life of an underground revolutionary. But was she a revolutionary first, or a wife, or a mother? Could you be all three and still be as strong and powerful a leader as Roland or Harlan? Could a woman really be a great revolutionary leader? What about the thousands of women—nameless, faceless women all over the world who had picked up the gun to join the fight for freedom? In Vietnam, in China, in Latin America and Africa, in all the wars for liberation around the world women were fighting alongside men, and certainly there had to be great leaders among them.

I supposed that Jo could rightfully count herself a member of their ranks. Her slim shape was already motionless with near sleep in the bed next to mine. I thought that for all her strength and fierceness, her failings as a warrior would likely be ordinary ones like my own—feminine "failings" of attachment and love and physical weakness. If these could be embodied in a great leader of our movement, a woman who wouldn't shy away from the militancy and violence necessary to bring down capitalism, I hadn't met her yet. In truth, I couldn't imagine what she would be like, to encompass all of that, and if I met her face to face, would I shrink or rise to the occasion? Jo was fierce enough, intimidating enough, but I didn't think she was a revolutionary leader. She was a mother and a wife before she was a leader, but maybe it was that softness beneath the surface that allowed room for our friendship. Where did you put that softness when you aimed a gun? Was it just a luxury we couldn't afford to hold on to for now, a luxury that all of us, the women and men who chose to be warriors, would have to put aside until the revolution was over? In the name of love . . . in the name of peace and harmony? *But how could we do without it?*

It was still twilight outside and I had an old wistful memory of being put to bed in the summertime before dark; a small child, wide-eyed, restless, listening to the thrush notes of robins and the sounds of the older ones playing outdoors, resisting sleep with every fiber. But now my eyes were heavy, my body finally settled and I could stay awake no longer, and so I let the air-conditioner hum me to sleep, all the way through dinner and on and on until mid-morning the next day.

With the house chosen and paid for, ready for us on our return, we turned right around a few days later and drove back east. Harlan's transfer was delayed and this way Jo could pick up the kids and fly back in time to meet him there and I could pick up Roland and drive back with him. I didn't mind. Moving was the best of all, and it didn't feel right or comfortable being at Suzanne's house no matter how friendly she was or how comfortable the beds were. That just made it worse.

It only took us two days anyway driving straight through on Route 80 East this time to New York, cat napping here and there and feeling more and more like we belonged on the road, at the truck stop counters, part of a family of mud-eyed long haulers and underpaid waitresses who nodded to us like we were insiders as we took our seats at the counters.

On one long stretch we did get started on our publicity for the trial. We needed a flyer at least, or a pamphlet or a letter we could send out to raise funds about Harlan's situation. I'd been waiting, wondering anxiously when our work would begin, the "real" work of building a national defense campaign that seemed entirely in our hands. I didn't have much of an idea what the work would entail but it sounded important, legitimate—tame by comparison to joining an underground movement, but a contribution to the struggle nonetheless and an activity that would safely define my purpose to my parents, and, I'd have to admit, to myself. There was only so long that driving back and forth across country would suffice as a worthy revolutionary activity.

"Well, what have you been doing?" I could hear my mother ask in her accusing way.

Driving.

"And what are you accomplishing with all this driving?" I wasn't sure how I would answer that.

My parents would say that they hoped the world would be better in some small ways for the work they had done. But for me, small ways felt like the equivalent of nothing at all. I had no faith in little streams of effort, at least my effort, flowing into a bigger river, flowing into something unstoppably fierce and beautiful. *"One spark lights the prairie fire"* was the organizing motto of the Weather Underground, the underground group who I'd heard so often mentioned as real leaders of the revolution. I wanted to light that match, or at least be the bellows to the spreading fire. Of course I couldn't change the world single-handedly, make it all fair with a brushstroke, but that's as big as I wanted my actions to be. That seemed the only thing that would count.

I assumed that Jo had a plan for how to get started, but it was me who finally suggested we get down to writing the publicity piece. So while I drove, Jo wrote. She wanted me to tell her what to write, even though I thought it should be the other way round. She gave me a jump-start though with a block-faced FREE HARLAN KING!

at the top of the page and then looked over to me.

"Well you're the one with the fancy college education," she teased. "You can write better than me."

But I didn't know what to tell her to write. There had to be more than the bare details of information I'd heard repeated a hundred times already.

Former SDS organizer and war resister . . . accused of bombing a missile factory . . . fugitive for seven years . . .

I threw in all the over-used words and phrases that seemed to be required—like "oppression" and "Amerikkka" and "Power to the People". They seemed hollow already, over-used and a poor cover for my ignorance of what was needed to make a truly impassioned and convincing argument in Harlan's defense. While I was thinking of what to say, Jo sketched clenched fists with a broken chain between them in the margin, but I'd seen the image so many times during my few months working in the bookstore that I felt embarrassed for both of us. It seemed as if the language itself had us in chains. *Struggle, oppression, freedom, liberation . . .* each of those words profound and beautiful and unequalled and yet so flat on the page in front of us. I wanted to write a masterpiece that would convince even the most hard-hearted of the righteousness of our intent to defend this man who had risked everything to take a stand against a war that had so vividly and horribly, so ruthlessly and deceitfully torn apart or ended the lives of multitudes. It would be unbearable to be dismissed, to fail at this.

"Okay, what next?" She tapped her pencil against the pad. I wanted her to spell it out for me, what oppression meant to her, because she had lived it all . . . political oppression, economic oppression, sexual oppression . . . and though we shared the same conviction that there could be a better way, I was counting on her entitlement to the rewards of the revolution, and the justified outrage that fueled her experience, to bring whatever we wrote alive.

She had her feet propped up on the dash, her hair blowing out the window and for a moment I saw the two of us in this still frame, a still frame in the moving picture of us in the car on the highway and Jo looking at me with this half smile for the answer.

What I saw was that Jo didn't know any more than I did about how to build a national defense committee, or how to build a revolution either, not really. But did anyone really know? All that had already happened to put us in that particular moment together, and all that would continue to unfold going forward, seemed entirely bigger than I could ever fathom or comprehend, and yet I knew, deeply, that somehow our words mattered. That everything we did mattered terribly, each small step along the way. Maybe we would fail. Maybe there wouldn't be any network of defense committees, any thousands of letters of support for Harlan's cause, but we would try, and keep trying, and for a moment I purely loved us both for that.

As we approached New York City and passed the signs on the parkways that would direct me across a bridge or through a tunnel to my parent's home on Long Island, I felt an old stab of homesickness. The skyline of Manhattan cut the same awesome silhouette, and somewhere down by the World Trade Center Towers my father was at work, maybe even looking out his window in my direction. But we passed those exits and headed into upper Manhattan, into a neighborhood of tenements and projects on the west side. We'd been invited to spend the night with friends of Jo and Harlan's who were going to help with our defense work for Harlan. I'd never spent the night in Manhattan, other than as a child in my grandmother's east side apartment. Her building had a polished glass entrance, with a doorman and elevator man who both wore perfectly stiff uniforms and white gloves—the brownstones on the littered street where Jo and I parked looked nothing like that.

"There might be some people from the Weather Underground here," Jo said. She turned the rearview mirror in her direction to brush her hair and to put on some lipstick.

"Really?"

"I'm pretty sure. Some comrades who helped me and Harlan

out when we were on the run. There're a couple of friends I'm really hoping to see—two very solid sisters in particular. But they're really hot right now so I don't know—it might be too risky for them." She snapped her lipstick closed and turned the mirror back in my direction.

I worried that I should know more about the Weather Underground. They were the leaders of the underground movement after all, the ones who had been the first to organize active guerilla cells like Che had detailed for revolutionaries to follow. They'd carried out a lot of successful actions protesting our country's obliteration of Vietnam and its people—they'd bombed the U.S. Capitol, even the Pentagon, and then a few months ago the U.S. State Department, and all without injuring anyone . . . anyone, that is, except for the three comrades who had died a few years back when one of their bombs went off prematurely. Though I didn't know about it at the time it happened, it now seemed a tremendously radical demonstration of the group's commitment to the struggle to have continued after such a loss.

But even so, I'd learned there were "good" revolutionaries and "bad" ones on the Left, and sometimes, to hear Roland and Jo and some of the others talk, I couldn't tell where the Weathermen's reputation lay on that continuum. One minute they'd talk about them like they were great heroes of the struggle, and the next they were just a bunch of spoiled rich kids who got all their money from trust funds. That was the really interesting part to me—that they were "rich kids", that they had trust funds, that they were disaffected like me, but further along, further in. And still, even so, maybe not worthy of their radical status in the eyes of my working-class comrades.

Our group, the underground group that Roland and Vinny, Sarah and Devon, Harlan and Jo had formed, was going to be different. Our group would have solid working class roots, be closely connected to the prison movement and the Black Liberation Movement. Our funding would come from robbing establishment institutions who were ripping off the people, and sometimes from me, from my trust fund that was made up of companies who ripped off the people—but only when it was absolutely necessary, only to tide the group over when other sources were unavailable. I liked to believe that this was a strategy that had been discussed in the group before Harlan and Roland had been arrested, before anyone had asked me to help out. I liked to think they were making these decisions coherently, responsibly, as a group, writing down their strategies, their program to be implemented in steps, the way Mao had in his little cream-colored books.

As we walked down the block of a run-down neighborhood, the damp earthy scent of spring lurking behind the exhaust and subway smells, I thought about how Jo had said there might be women there who were friends, "really solid sisters" she hoped to see. And if they were really "hot" like she said, then it could be for anything . . . robbery, bombings. They could be the kind of women leaders I'd tried to imagine—beautifully self-actualized women, or would they be hardened intimidating warriors? What if Bernadine Dohrn was there? Maybe she was even one of the friends Jo had mentioned. I'd heard her name spoken with reverence more than once—a lawyer—a lawyer like my sister, my brother, my father, but one who'd turned radical. I'd liked what she'd said, something I'd read along the way, that the underground movement couldn't be just a bunch of white people who'd stand around and wring their hands when black people got murdered—people like Fred Hampton and Mark Clark, the two Black Panther leaders who'd been shot by FBI goons in their beds while they slept. If we meant what we said about protesting that kind of attack, sponsored by our very own government against its own people, then we had to amp it up—raise the stakes. I thought she was right, and I wanted to meet Bernadine and have her courage rub off on me. I imagined the relief of having a heart-to-heart conversation with her about class and money and how to manage all of the questions I turned over and over without resolve, questions that I could never speak about to Jo or the others. And then, I wanted to see if I could identify any part of myself in them, find something familiar that might even make me proud, for once, for just a moment, to be affiliated with that class background. I wasn't sure what I was looking for exactly, something like reassurance that they would smile at a stranger like me, and that what I would feel propelling them forward in their commitment and resolve would be love and good will and the very soft-heartedness I imagined was unacceptable for a guerrilla fighter to exhibit. Once I saw them, then I felt sure I would know.

The apartment was dimly lit, a spaciously cluttered room made comfortable by scarves over lampshades, frayed oriental rugs, and colorful sheets over the couches. The dozen or so people who were there all stopped talking when we walked in and then quickly descended on Jo in a flurry. She was hugged and hugged again, and someone handed me a glass of wine while others shook my hand, clapped me on the shoulder and warmly welcomed me. It was a party in Jo's honor. Someone had brought a cake with *Free Harlan!* on it, and one of the women, her name was Judy, linked arms with Jo and raised her glass to lead everyone in a toast. She apologized, saying of course, Harlan getting picked up wasn't any cause for celebration, but they knew he would understand, and would want them all to drink a toast to his freedom and to her, Jo, as a wish for strength from all of them for the ordeal she was going to have to go through with the trial and all.

"We're all with you, all the way. You know we'll all do whatever we can to help you out. *Free Harlan King!*" She held up her glass and we all drank to that.

I hoped I was right, that Judy was one of the women that Jo had spoken about, the way she radiated a strong goodness, with a singing laugh, and flushed cheeks and a round soft body. There was plenty of love in her, and confidence too. I wanted to be close to her, to have her resting her arm around my shoulder the way she now stood with Jo, laughing unaffectedly.

As we were eating our cake, the hum of conversation died when the doorbell rang. Everyone held their silence as one of the men went to open the door, and we waited while their footsteps neared the room. I was certain in an instant, from a few pictures I'd seen, that it was Bernadine, and that she was the other friend Jo had spoken about . . . the way her face lit up when she recognized Jo and hugged her. Graceful and dark-eyed, tall, with straight black hair and a strong intelligent face. And she did have the kind of power in her presence that Roland had, the kind that preceded her into the room and then dwarfed those around her. I could tell by the way everyone seemed to direct all their attention towards her, even as they continued in their own now slightly hushed conversations. There was more darkness in her face than in Judy's open expression, but it too drew me closer with a desire to hear her every word.

But I never heard her actually speak more than a few quiet greetings to people around her. She spoke to Jo off to the side for a few minutes and then to Judy in a back room, and on her way to the door before her exit, she brushed by me, looked into my eyes with a fierce and trusting gaze, and smiled. It was nothing really—a look, a smile, but I had seen enough to know that she was real, and that I wanted to be closer and to know more. If she'd beckoned, I might have followed to find out.

In the morning Judy came into the room where we were sleeping, shaking us awake. "Hey, look what's hot off the press! You two are just about the first ones to see this." She handed each of us a copy of a large paperback book with a Chinese red cover and bold black print on the front:

PRAIRIE FIRE: The Politics of Revolutionary Anti-Imperialism

The Political Statement of the Weather Underground.

I was awed and held it as if I'd been given a sacred text, the text that would illuminate the answers to all the questions that I stumbled upon. One hundred and fifty pages of the political ideology, the anti-imperialist strategy for revolution that would guide us—that would guide me. The three of us sat on the floor with coffee and feasted on its newsprint pages, its new book smell. I scanned the contents . . .

1. Arm the Spirit: Why Revolution is Necessary. I'd read that first—and then the chapter about Vietnam, and others on U.S. history, on racism and genocide and the women's movement . . . everything. With pictures in black and white scattered throughout of people—strong revolutionary people who had died for the struggle—like Sam Melville (murdered at Attica), and George Jackson (the Black Panther activist and writier gunned down in prison) and of people all over the world fighting for liberation. There was much to learn. So much in these pages that would give me the courage to make that ultimate choice to give my life to the underground—like Judy, like Bernadine, and like Jo, like all the freedom fighters in these pages. I wouldn't be alone. In this army there would be a family who would stand by me, just as I would defend and love them while we struggled against the dark forces of the world, bringing them into the light.

Prairie Fire is based on a belief that the duty of a revolutionary is to make the revolution. This is not an abstraction. It means that revolutionaries must make a profound commitment to the future of humanity, apply our limited knowledge and experience to understand an ever-changing situation, organize the masses of people and build the fight. It means that struggle and risk and hard work and adversity will become a way of life, that the only certainty will be constant change, that the only possibilities are victory or death.

That was the last paragraph of the introduction. Four people signed it, three of whom I didn't know, but the fourth was Bernadine Dohrn. Seeing her name there, while I sat drinking coffee with Judy and Jo, made everything possible. Maybe our leaflet about the trial wasn't so bad—I'd have another look at it. At least we were out there. At least we were trying to raise awareness about the truth of the evils that would consume us all if we didn't spread the word. In the end, my parents would see. They'd be proud of me.

CHAPTER 18

After I dropped Jo at her mother's, I drove to Boston to bail out Roland.

I had five thousand dollars cash in a bank envelope in my purse beside me, the results of another somewhat awkward conversation with Mrs. Lee from the Bank of New York. Four thousand for Karl, the bondsman, and one thousand for expenses I knew would present themselves sooner or later.

Karl was the last person I wanted to see, the last person I wanted to give money to, but once he was paid then Roland would be out, so I kept my sites on that. His office was grimier and gloomier by day, and there was somehow no question of exchanging even a hint of a smile in greeting or any small talk at all as he gave me the papers to sign.

"I hope you know what you're doing. The rest of this bond is on your back now. Sign on this line." I barely looked at the paper, and definitely did not read the fine print—not with him staring me down. Really, I didn't even know exactly what he was talking about. "Forty grand if he jumps. You got that?" I thought I knew what he meant, sort of.

He straightened up, putting one hand in his pants pocket, brushing aside his jacket as he did to flash the butt end of his gun tucked away in his shoulder holster. He did it on purpose, I was sure of that. Somehow, with him standing there in the flesh threatening me, his piggish face bulging out of his tight collar, and with the papers and desk between us, it didn't scare me. He didn't scare me. Nothing at all like the rapist who wouldn't show himself in the parking lot shadows.

With his other hand he slapped his index finger again on the line of the contract where I'd signed. "That's your signature, don't forget." He handed me my copy of the contract like I'd already done something wrong. Still, I was able to get some satisfaction from being able to look at him head on with a clearly fearless expression.

But when I left, as soon as I turned my back on him to walk out the door and across the street to my car, it was all I could do to keep from running, or from turning around to protect my back. If he was going to shoot me, I wanted to see it coming.

* * *

It had only really been three weeks since I'd seen Roland last, not even a month, but I could only hold on for so long—to the feel of him, the taste of his mouth, the taste of his desire for me—until it all began to slip away, to evaporate under the bright light of day leaving only the small hard kernels of my doubt: *Who was this man? What did he see in me?*

I didn't have much to re-assure me—one line in a letter that was waiting for me at Jo's mother's house. Jo had brought it to me, waving it in front of my face like ransom.

"My, my, my . . . .what do we have here?" She loved to tease me about Roland, to ride me, poke me, laughing when she knew I was thinking about him. She had a whole life planned out for us in fact—babies and all. I'd protest. I'd tell her she was wrong, it wasn't like that. It wasn't like anything, yet. But I couldn't completely hide my pleasure in her fantasies. Even his handwriting on the envelope alone brought a schoolgirl lump of relief to my throat. I'd been trying hard to stuff every ounce of expectation.

"I'll love you till the wings fly off at least, perhaps beyond. My love could burn you however, it runs hot and I have nearly half a millennium stored up. Mine is a perfect love, soft to the touch but it's so hot, hard, and dense at its center that its weight will soon offset this planet." That was what George Jackson had written in *Soledad Brother* to the woman he loved while he was in prison. That's what I was hoping Roland would write. I was certain Roland was as passionate as that, even if not about me.

It was a promisingly fat letter but I read its three pages impatiently looking for something that was not political theory and rhetoric, or what books were available in their poor excuse for a library. I didn't want to be picky. If he'd spent all this time writing to me then he must have been thinking about me. Be content with that. And I had to remind myself that the screws were reading it all over his shoulder and he'd never give them the satisfaction of reading a love letter. I couldn't blame him for that. Still, I looked for some coded touch—finally delivered in the last line: I imagine you know how I feel about you. Ha! I didn't know at all, but then I had a kind of deep unshakable knowing that we had connected beyond words or form, having everything and nothing to do with our politics or class differences. Still, I wouldn't assume anything, expect anything. And that would be okay. In some new cool remove inside myself, the place where the warrior put the needs of the revolution first, I could make it okay. As far as I was concerned, we'd never have to touch again.

But I want to.

From where I sit across from him in the diner booth I can take in the full length of the dragon tattoo down his right upper arm muscles, and the fist holding the broken chain on his left. Tendons in his forearms ripple as he tears his sugar package and shakes it into the coffee in front of him. Skin has never looked so good.

The diner has the door propped open to let in the balmy breeze. No one cares that it's just the parking area and then the highway that we we're looking at. The day has turned out to be summer warm, that fluke spring heat that makes any kind of love possible.

"That's your deltoid. That's your radius, your ulna. See how hard I've been studying?" I ran my fingers down his arm, to his wrist, found the artery and his pulse that was steady and full, while mine, I was sure, was what they'd call "thready" in medical jargon—a thin stream of galloping nerves. Really, it was more terrifying than waiting for Karl to shoot me in the back, touching him first like this. In the prison waiting room, when he'd come through the gate, we'd barely brushed lips, cheeks, did not touch on the way out to the car, or in the car—even in the car, where my heart began its dive, its plummet midair, a heart full of all the expectations I was certain I hadn't imagined this re-union to be.

We drove halfway to New York like that, talking and not touching. His body a taut million miles away when I'd been thinking I'd be inside it, wrapped around it by now. *I imagine you know how I feel about you.*

But then Roland was a man, not a boy like my lovers before him, boys with childish impulsive ways. Roland was older. In the creases in his forehead, beneath his eyes, in the darkness in his eyes, there was no boy left at all. He was a man with a life history of war and prison and violence I could only begin to imagine, and more important things on his mind than making love with me.

But with my hand on his wrist, he was smiling behind his coffee mug—like he was looking for permission to shout out a boyish whoop.

"Why are you way over there?" He tugged on my arm and I switched seats, slid close to him on the diner bench. We kissed as if he'd been waiting with all the expectations I'd been trying to bury. I wanted to straddle his lap like I had at the prison— or push the toast and eggs right off the table and lie down right there. I could be drunk on it in seconds and blind to everyone around us.

It would all be okay now between us, whatever came next.

On our way out of the restaurant, there was a photo booth, and he pulled me in, onto his lap on the single metal seat, and pulled the curtain closed. We were mouth to mouth for the first flash, cheek to cheek like old friends for the second. The third was a blur of laughing faces.

"The last one's for the feds," he said. "They'll probably get their hands on this someday." And so we went deadpan, as sinister as we could be, and I thought when I looked at the two of us in the photo, that we were handsome together, the angles of our faces matching, our eyes similar in their startled dark wildness.

* * *

"I thought he'd get a kick out of it." That was something else my mother might have said. I thought Roland would get a kick out of spending the night in my parents' home. They were away. It would just be the two of us, and May, my nanny from childhood and now my parents' housekeeper. She'd be there and she wouldn't mind as long as we slept in separate rooms, or pretended to. It was my idea to go there and I was showing off, wanting to flash the grandeur of this life at him to show him—what? All that I was willing to walk away from? Or, how righteous our revolutionary stance was given this perfect breathing example of unjustifiable extravagance? Or maybe to offer him all the ammunition I could find to aim at me, to hand over all my secrets to see if he'd punish me with them. And then again, maybe I just wanted to be disobedient—that being another of my mother's often used words—"disobedient", for one night, directly under their roof. Directly under their bedroom as it turned out.

"Don't leave me—I might get lost."

He was teasing me, willing to make a joke, to see the fun in this when it could as easily have soured everything to bring him here. I'd wondered, pulling in the driveway, at the point of no return, if I'd made a mistake.

The house wasn't that big. Yes it was—eight bedrooms, seven bathrooms, three stories of Georgian style brick and ivy. It was just as well we'd pulled up there in the dark. If I'd stopped to think about it, I might not have taken him inside—through the front door with the heavy brass knocker, into the spacious front hall with its polished black and white linoleum diamonds gleaming under the chandelier light.

I wanted to see it through his eyes to anticipate his judgments, or maybe his awe —the presence of all of this affording me some kind of power that I could steal for the night—like a jewel from my mother's drawer, I'd show it off tonight, and tomorrow deny I'd ever worn it.

"What's that . . . the stairway to heaven?" He was looking up the front staircase—wide and carpeted, the mahogany banister curving up to the height of the chandelier.

This was going to be fun after all.

"First, I want you to meet May," I told him as I led him towards the kitchen, through the dining room, the den, my fingers lightly electrically linked in his. "Without May, I never would have survived growing up here." I said it with a lift in my voice, a laugh, making light of the statement so he could toss it aside, at least the part about surviving, but still make a note of May's importance to me. What could I possibly know about hell?

As we walked through the house towards the kitchen I thought how Roland didn't see the same dining room table, the same silver candlesticks or upholstered chair or floral drapes that I did. And if he were to ask me what was so bad here that I'd barely "survived", I doubted I'd be able to tell him exactly, to describe the feeling I always had coming into this house—why its comfort held so much tension, and its beauty felt so superficial, so thin and easily shattered, how every return here was like coming home to a live being whose silence and judgment strangled me.

But I wanted him to meet May. May, my anchor of love and permission and the source of most of the real fun and comfort I'd had with adults when I was younger. It was her bed I would crawl into in the middle of the night, spooning close to her short plump body, her bedroom I'd retreat to when every other room in the three-story house was filled with the unreachable expectations of my parents. Wherever she was would be where I'd breathe most freely, where I was home. It was a feeling I wanted to share with Roland, that I was almost certain he'd understand just by meeting her, because that was how May made everyone feel, like they'd just come home.

She had dinner waiting for us. That was typical of her. "Just a bit of chicken," she said, but then there were mashed potatoes, green beans and gravy and warm rolls all neatly readied and warm on the stove.

I leaned down to hug her soft familiar shape. I'd been almost a foot taller than her for years, and even though she probably weighed close to my own weight, it was still almost effortless to pick her up for an extra squeeze and a little swing around. After I'd put her down I kept my arms around her.

I knew, sheepishly, that some part of me wanted to make sure Roland saw just how familiar May and I were, how deep our bond, because she was, after all, my most genuine link to the working class, a kind of proof that I didn't really belong on the firing line with my parents and other family members, that my true roots were with May—with May and all the other May's of the community I'd grown up with, the nannies that gathered for afternoon teas in rotating kitchens. It was there I'd learned to count to ten in Gaelic, Spanish, Polish, German, Italian and Yugoslavian, those smoky kitchens where we, the children, always held the spotlight and all the glory.

Roland towered over her but May pulled him down to her level for a kiss on the cheek hello and I could tell he didn't mind. In a way, they had the same kind of soft shy hearts, only Roland's was harder to find under the tough shell of trouble.

"You're a big fellow—Roland is it? That's a good strong name. Are you Irish?" she asked hopefully, peering up at him. She clasped his hand in both of her own and Roland's smile hadn't faded one bit.

He told her it was a French-Canadian name, that his family was from Quebec, that they came down from the north to work in the paper mills near Portland.

"Oh, like your uncle's family, Linda." May piped in and I nodded and busied myself with getting a few beers. No doubt, my uncle's family owned the mills that Roland's family died in.

"Let's eat." I offered.

Though May said she'd already eaten her own dinner, I enticed her to at least sit down with us, to have a glass of beer, and when I had it poured up and our dinner on the table I offered a toast to freedom, shooting a knowing look to Roland because of course May didn't know anything about his convict status. She crossed herself before she took a sip and said, "Christ died so we could be free," more to herself than to us, one of the small prayers of thanks she was prone to saying whenever she received anything.

I didn't know how Roland might take this and I felt a little anxious that she might go on, as she sometimes did, with a whole rosary of prayers under her breath. I had to admit, I didn't take May all that seriously where religion was concerned. I had when I was younger. I'd even thought I'd grow up to be a nun, or if I was lucky, a saint like the ones I'd learned about from her stories. But that was way before I'd caught on that everyone thought of God as male, a father, and Christ too, and all the apostles were men and the women were supposed to be sexless virgins if they wanted to be saints. I didn't know about God one way or the other now, except that I thought that people, people like May, used their religion to avoid the critical political issues that governed their lives. So I flashed a knowing, raised-eyebrow look at Roland that said that we both knew that religion was the opiate of the masses, and that May was drugged, but we'd let her stay high on it for the time being until the moment was right for her re-education.

May was smiling at us both, holding her glass up in a toast. There was a thin mustache of beer foam lining her upper lip. She knew more about love than I ever would. Shame on me. Sometimes I despised myself.

"Time for the grand tour."

As I led him around the house, I was able to imagine, at least for the time being, that we'd been together for much longer, that we were in fact comfortably close, even familiar as lovers, already beyond the stage of sudden inexplicable rejection. I felt giddy and brazen with him at my side, his body first brushing and then pressing against me when we would stop at the entrance to a room, his arms circling my waist and then, at the next room, slipping his hands beneath my shirt onto my belly, easily, comfortably, as if he'd been there many times before. And I was eager to respond, to find the soft heat of his skin, turning and kissing him with the feeling of almost no separation at all, just a pure euphoric desire to close the rest of the gap. But that would have to wait until later, until after May had closed her bedroom door for the night.

"The cell I was in would fit into this room fifteen times," he said in the living room after pacing it off. "I like this room."

In the dining room, he said the big mahogany table alone was twice the size of his cell, and I leaned against its edge to see if it would support our weight. Maybe here, later, with the chandelier dimmed above us. It was a possibility.

I took him down to the old wine cellar in the basement and up to the third floor, even into the attic where we pulled the dumbwaiter up on its rusty cables, ancient and unused except in our play as kids. I took him into all the bedrooms in-between. I hadn't spoken to my parents in almost a month, and their voices, which might otherwise have ricocheted off the walls in each of the perfectly appointed rooms, seemed far enough away to be of little consequence. Now it was like someone else's home that Roland and I could wander through and together ridicule for its excesses and bond over our disdain for it all.

But I didn't take him into my parents' room. I avoided opening that door with a rumbling wariness of what I might feel if I stood in the familiar light and current emptiness of that room—that I might open my father's closet to deplore the rows of expensive suits and ties and shiny shoes and end up with a lump in my throat instead of a laugh, or catch the scent of my mother's perfume and feel as I had as a child when she was away, that I'd better leave too, in a hurry, running hard to get as far away from her absence as I could. I'd do better to stay away from that part of the house—it could ruin everything.

I left Roland while he showered and went to have a cigarette with May in her room. It was the same room I'd smoke an occasional cigarette in when I was ten, sneaking them from her top bureau drawer, first alone, and then, later on, with her. It was exactly the same—the same worn sitting chair with the calico print, the same bed I often shared with her as a little girl, the same crucifix on the wall with last year's Easter palm fronds wedged behind.

"He's a lovely fellow, your Roland," May said with a small laugh, because we both knew that "lovely" might not be the first word that would come to mind to describe him, at least his appearance. "Do you think you'll marry him?" She was half-joking of course, but only half, indulging her own fantasy that I might marry someone my mother would sorely object to, my mother being possibly the only person in the world that May had a hard time loving.

"Well, who knows? Will you be my maid-of-honor if I do?" We laughed together at the double absurdity of this, the image of her being the maid-of-honor at the kind of wedding my parents would like me to have someday, and of me walking down the aisle of a big church to trumpet calls with my long-haired, tattooed, lover. Not likely. I doubted I would ever marry anyway—marriage being a tool of the oppressors used to keep women in bondage and the nuclear family intact. But I spared May that argument.

Later that night, I took Roland down to the living room. It seemed the most pristine, the least used, the most formal and forbidden. The French glass doors that separated it from the rest of the house were kept closed three hundred and sixty days of the year except for Christmas, Thanksgiving, Easter, and cocktail party nights. Over the fireplace in the center of the room was an oil-painted portrait of my brother as a young boy, sitting on the arm of a couch with a posture that foretold of his inheritance of all that was before him.

I spread the blankets beneath the portrait and then I turned the lights off.

I would have liked to see our naked bodies dimly lit, to see what I touched and kissed as we fell into each other at last, but there was something in the dark I needed more, this being only our second night together and almost two months between. In the dark I thought I'd be better able to turn myself entirely over to whatever forces had mysteriously brought us here, the two of us into this unlikely communion. I would let go completely, give myself entirely over to his hungry and confident attentions, attentions which seemed, moment after moment, to have less and less to do with the deep communication between us that I sought and more to do with finding the way to a climax, to our climax, if I could only allow that.

But I didn't. I couldn't. The further away I slipped from where he was traveling, the more I found myself caged by my own self-doubt. Roland would never be able to accept me really, not with all I'd revealed to him about my past. How foolish I was!

We weren't in a strangers' home - -he was! And every inch of this house pinned me down irrefutably to my history in this family.

His climax came quickly and after, in the dim light, I could make out the shadows of our bodies, Roland's shoulders and back now collapsed on top of me like the full weight of the failure I felt inside. I could see the shadows of my thighs still holding him, wanting the ending to be different. I had to move, to get out from under the weight of it.

"I have to go check on something," I said, moving quickly out from under him. It was a sudden pronouncement, too revealing of my distance, an abrupt tone that I wanted to soften. "I'll be right back. Can I get you anything?"

"No, I'm fine." He sounded groggy, relaxed, and already half-asleep anyway.

I covered him with the blanket, pulled the sheet around me, and left the room, pulling the doors closed quietly behind me. Once outside in the dark hall, I wasn't sure where I wanted to go, what would bring relief from the tension of the sudden wave of disgust I felt towards myself. Sex could be awful, painful that way, it seemed, highlighting the depths of an inner darkness and inhibition instead of showing off my freedom and liberated abilities. I'd wanted to please him with my own pleasure, be immersed and lost in the heat of sex the way it had been on our first night together. And now I just wanted to apologize.

I crept up the stairs without a clear destination in mind and down the long hallway towards May's door. There was no light shining from beneath the sill and I stood outside waiting until I could hear the slow whistling of her even breaths.

She would be lying on her side, her face resting on her folded palms. She would be wearing her faded nightgown and I remembered what a refuge it used to be to be spooned next to her, entirely safe and warm. If I stood there long enough, Roland would surely fall asleep, and then he wouldn't notice, would he, if I stayed here for a little while? If I crawled in bed next to May for just a little while—it would be okay.

But of course, it wouldn't be okay. I couldn't turn back that clock, not tonight, not ever again. I wasn't two, or twelve, I was twenty-one. There was no turning back. So I crept back down stairs, to our bed beneath the portrait, and curled close to Roland's back, to his long snoring indifference, determined to try again in the morning and make it all right.

CHAPTER 19

But by the time we hit Pennsylvania, I knew our little honeymoon was over. Whatever romantic notions I'd managed to carve out of the night at my parents' house were quickly being replaced by the starker realities of our situation. Though we were good-humored enough starting out, as the morning wore on it seemed that we were no longer driving away from the prison we'd only left yesterday, but instead driving towards all the complications that Roland was up against.

At least I think that's what he's thinking about . . . but he doesn't say much. His hand is not on my leg. He doesn't rub my neck now and then, or sing along to the music drumming his fingers in time on the dashboard. That was before.

I don't mind driving in silence. That's just the way of it—with Jo, with my father, with lots of people. But silence has its limits, and then it can grow like a third presence whispering all kinds of grief to me the way it did driving with Jo. Only with her we'd eventually find our way back together. With Roland, I lose faith more quickly. I want him to touch me. Just that. And though our shoulders are once again almost brushing in the small car space, I can't bring myself to reach way across the twelve inches to his hand.

He chews toothpicks, one after the other. When one's chewed down to a pulp he spits it out the window and then five minutes later he reaches for another. I can see the muscle in his jaw popping, boiling, from the corner of my eye. He'd like to drive but we can't take that chance, it's one of his bail restrictions. Or maybe it's that he's not allowed to cross state lines. I'd wondered for a moment about that, but I don't know the rules and I don't ask. He's warned me twice already to watch the speed limit—not in a mean way, just a somewhat anxious reminder—so I was being very careful, checking the speedometer every minute or so. I want to help him calm down. If I could reach through the wall of his tension I'd rest my hand on his leg to still the fine tremor of its constant motion. I'd rest it on the worn surface of his jeans, on the solid surface of his thigh, the one he'd wrapped around me this morning at dawn. This morning, it was fine between us, both of us moaning into pillows and skin so that May wouldn't hear.

I imagine he wants to know what's going to happen next, the anticipation being maybe worse than the event itself. His next court appearance is in two months so he'll have to make some heavy choices, choices I wouldn't presume to be able to help him with. And then he's probably thinking, he must be thinking, that every moment of freedom could be his last.

In the middle of Pennsylvania, around another bend, over another hill, out of the green ocean of trees swimming in another day of sultry heat, he took the toothpick out of his mouth and said, "Listen, I'm not going back to prison. They'll have to kill me first." When I looked over at him I could see perfect rows of little shiny sweat beads on his forehead. He bit his thumbnail, ran his hand through his hair, over the crown of his receding hairline.

"I'd get screwed at a trial. They'd throw away the key and that would be it for me. I'm not going to give them that opportunity. So you know what that means."

It was a statement, more than a question but I answered it anyway.

"You're not going to show for your next court appearance."

He didn't affirm this one way or the other. He looked away from me, out the passenger window. "I just thought you should know."

That was okay with me. Anything but a cage. Fuck the bail money. I didn't care. I wouldn't, couldn't weigh his life, his freedom, against a number like that—any number. I could almost touch him now, just squeeze his leg to let him know I was on his side, but Roland wouldn't want comfort or reassurance. He would never be sentimental like that.

"Karl might come after you for the money. But he might not . . . he might let it go. I think Devon might be able to persuade him."

I thought of the fine print I'd ignored before signing the papers with Karl and was still uncertain how much he'd come after me for. I hadn't even saved the copy he'd given me to check it out. I thought about Karl and his tight shiny suit, his jeweled fingers in my face, his gun. "I'm not worried about it."

I looked over and smiled at him and then he did put his hand on my neck, grabbed a fistful of my hair and gave it a friendly tug.

"Okay then." He left his arm extended across the seat back, his hand playing with my hair idly for a minute and then he took it away and reached for another toothpick, gathering himself. There was more. "There's something else you could help with if you want to . . . I need to buy a gun."

Another gun.

I was cool about it—cool enough to watch myself nod my

head like it was no big deal because it didn't shock me, Roland asking me for a gun. I felt older now since the last time I'd bought a gun, and we were going to talk about getting him a gun just about like we'd talk about buying him some new boots. I could say no, and that, in a way, is why I knew I'd say yes. Whatever Roland and I had, I believed he was beyond trying to coerce me, that he would never lower himself to that, would never allow himself to use me that way.

"I have the money, at least some of it, but I need you to buy it—for obvious reasons." He paused and I hoped he would say something more, something to push me gently forward to the edge before I took the step off into saying yes.

"Don't ever forget that I'm a revolutionary and I'm going to die a revolutionary." That bolstered me, gave me courage to be reminded that the gun was a tool for the revolution, for the higher good, the coming of the new liberated world. Judy would say yes. So would Bernadine or Jo or RoAnne. Any one of them had already committed themselves to more than I had.

"Where would we buy it?"

"Pennsylvania laws are pretty loose . . . like Maine. They won't ask you any questions. I know someplace close. It's not far from here."

I didn't ask him how he knew. I didn't need to know. You do what you can, and then you do a little more.

"Okay. Let's go."

The place I bought the gun was a lot bigger than the trading post in Maine—more like a department store with a huge selection of all kinds of rifles, shotguns, and dark rows of different handguns. And the gun Roland asked me to buy was bigger too,—one of the 357 Magnums I'd shied away from before when I was choosing my own, looking so menacing and overgrown. But Roland was definite about it, writing down exactly what I should ask for, and the skinny short man who brought it out for me didn't even bat an eye before he rang me up. The bag was heavy with the gun and the two hundred rounds I'd bought like he'd asked—twice the weight of the gun I'd bought before, twice the deadly force.

Can there be such a thing as a "good" gun? Remember, it's a war. In a war you need weapons. Roland knows all about weapons and war. I know nothing except that the war has to happen. Tell me again why it has to happen. Because all the power in the world is in the hands of corporate murderers who spit on any other life than their own and get fat on blood. They hire entire armies to murder and maim anyone who opposes their interests. That is why Roland needs a big gun. That is why you're buying it for him.

But carrying it out of the store it feels heavy enough to blow up the whole car if it goes off. When I give it to him, he takes it out of its box, loads it like he could do it in his sleep, and then rolls it in his jean jacket and stuffs it under our bags in the back seat. "Okay, let's go."

I don't know if it's legal to be carrying it, and that just adds to the tension that seems to hover over us, like we can't drive fast enough or far enough to get away from it. State after state we don't talk much. I wonder if he's thinking about me, about us at all, and now that we're traveling so far alone together, it feels like that's the only anchor I have in the world to hold on to, that Roland is the only one left who can give me a dimension, sketch me into the picture and color me in. How would he paint me? I don't know. What size? What does he see? I don't know. I can't do it myself.

The windows are down and the radio's telling us about pork belly prices on one station and the other about how the Lord is going to strike us down if we don't repent. The gun is wrapped in the jacket, tucked away under the bags. If we leave the car for a meal, even for coffee, he checks it when we come back. It feels like something's going to go off.

We drive and drive some more. I keep my eyes going in a triangular path—road ahead, rear view mirror, speedometer, road ahead. We haven't slept much more than an hour in the last thirty-six, and then it was at a road-side rest area dwarfed by the semis, one either side of us, their engines rumbling away and who knew who might looking in the window at us. Now the highway was straight and flat ahead of us, the heat mirages swimming on and on in front of my burning eyes, burning towards their wet, cool promise.

Road ahead. Rear view mirror. Speedometer. Road ahead. And then the siren.

Maybe I was even a little bit asleep when the trooper's siren blasted into my head like the war had begun. I know I started to swerve off the road, to run onto the shoulder because Roland grabbed the wheel to steady the car.

"Fucking A . . . take it easy." I knew he was pissed because he never curses. "How fast were you going?"

"I don't know."

"Shit . . . *shit!*"

When the State Trooper leaned down to check us out who knew what was coming. Between the shadow of his wide brimmed hat and the reflective black of his dark lenses, all I could see of his face was the thin accusing line of his mouth. "You in a hurry Ma'am?"

I leaned forward to hide Roland from his view. To hide his tattoos and long hair and those black eyebrows looking like he was always ready to take a swing at someone. I saw the trooper tip his head to the side to get a closer look. .

"I guess so. I mean . . . I didn't realize I was going so fast." If I was too nice maybe Roland would think I didn't have the guts to stand up to him. If I was rude, he might make us get out and search the car, find the gun. I smiled. I handed him everything he needed—license, registration, even the insurance cards I never kept track of. "How fast was I going officer?"

"Eighty-three in a seventy. You all wait right here for a few minutes."

"It's okay. Just be cool," Roland said, not like he wanted me dead or anything—more like he was re-assuring us both. It took years of waiting to see if the trooper was going to find something else on us in his radio contact. If he asked us to get out of the car I had this thought that Roland would grab the gun from the back and go for him. I saw the body falling, all this blood. I pushed the image away but it came back at me again.

He'd loaded the gun.

What hit me was that until that moment, I'd never thought of Roland as someone who'd actually hurt anyone. It was like mixing two colors, a red and a yellow, and getting green instead of what you thought you knew. What did I know? *Mix again. You must have made a mistake.*

Roland's not like that . . . . he has a gun . . . he loaded the gun . . . he's not like that . . . . you don't know . . .

So when he suddenly reached behind him for a pen from the book-bag he always carried, a pen to write down the trooper's plate number, I jumped in spite of myself, seeing the wrong color everywhere.

We got away though with just a ticket and a warning. We were free.

In the wave of relief that followed, we re-played the whole event, even laughed about me swerving off the road and the way I'd jumped when Roland had reached behind for the pen.

"You thought I was going for the gun didn't you?" he shook my arm playfully. "Didn't you?"

"Well, I don't know . . . would you have?"

"Jesus . . . no! But when he stuck his ugly mug in here and

looked me up and down . . . it was tempting." I was silent. "Jesus, I'm *kidding*!"

"Well have you?"

"What?"

"Killed anyone?"

"Yeah . . . haven't you ever counted all the notches on my belt?"

"No, I mean it . . . " I tried to find the answer in the cast of his eyes, his fading smile.

"No. The answer is no, I've never killed anyone. Not here. Not in Nam." I believed him. "I'm sure your parents will be glad to hear that." The humor had faded as quickly as it had arrived in the relief of our escape. But even with the edge in his voice I was relieved—relieved and shaking now that the adrenalin had worn off.

"We're both wasted . . . I know I am," he said. "Let's find someplace to sleep."

It wasn't close to dark, the sun still an hour from setting, so I couldn't help but think that we were stopping to celebrate our freedom. If we made love, it might smooth away the edge in his voice, bring him closer.

"I'll take the next exit."

We found a little motel on a street, with an ocean of cornrows filled with cicadas humming all around us. Roland brought the gun and its box inside, along with his nun-chuck sticks—two pieces of thick hardwood dowels about a foot long apiece attached by a chain. I'd seen him practicing once in a martial arts class, holding one piece and swinging the other around as a weapon. He was deft and coordinated with them, a graceful machine, with his black belt and his nun-chucks, a killing machine.

He laid both of them on the table between the two queen-sized beds, and then pulled all the curtains shut pitching the room into deep filtered shadows.

"Expecting company?"

"Always." He had his back to me, like a fortress again, I thought, the walls so hard to scale. I wanted to tell him I was just as alone as he was, and if he'd just turn around and look at me that maybe we could connect again the way we had that morning.

"I'm going to take a shower." I walked by him, pulling off my tee shirt, hoping that the sight of my bare breasts and back would entice him to follow me. He'd join me in the shower and we'd wash each other all over, wash away the separation under the hot running water and then fall into bed and make love until dark. But I took my time in the shower waiting for him, and when I came out he was asleep, stretched out diagonally on one of the beds, one arm over his face, fully dressed on top of the covers.

I moved over to the other bed in the shaded room and sat on its edge.

The air-conditioner droned on. I felt like that inside—that drone, this room, all of me shadowed and empty in the middle of nowhere. I thought of taking a walk—down the narrow road with the tall corn stalks on either side sealing out my longing for the rest of the world. To have sun on my back and all around me, illuminating everything in the rarefied twilight into its fullest most solid substance. Just to walk alone to the sound of my own footsteps.

I'd better not. I didn't want him to wake up. If he woke up I'd have to explain myself. I'd have to try not to say, "Could you just hold me?" And I would never, ever want him to see me cry. So what I did was to pull my clothes back on silently, and lay down, on my back, on top of the covers on the other bed. I stared at the ceiling—its white watery dimensions, its corners lost, the edges waving through tears like the heat mirages on the highway.

In the morning things were different. I was different. I could feel something cold in me, a cold space around my heart, maybe like the one Roland had. Now if I had to draw a picture of myself, at least I would draw that. A thick black circular wall. But inside the black circle it glowed. If I drew it, I wouldn't paint it red. It would be more like a star, like the first star at twilight, fierce and distantly burning.

All the other parts of me they can have. I'll give it all away. But I feel safer now knowing they can't get to my heart—not Roland, or Jo, or my parents or anyone.

CHAPTER 20

—•—

Jo and the kids beat us back to Denver by two days. When we pulled up to the house, the three of them were there to greet us, and when we went inside, it turned out that Harlan was there too.

"Surprise!" they all cheered and everybody hugged everybody. It was a surprise." How'd you get out?" I asked.

"My mother came through and posted the bond," Harlan said, lighting a cigarette, a filter-less Camel, his first inhalation as sharp as an exclamation point.

"Yeah, all $150,000 of it!" Jo chimed in. "She mortgaged all her real estate . . . I guess we lucked out again!" She smiled at me, but Harlan looked away, looked a little like he'd been found out. Frankly, I was relieved that it had all been decided before I'd gotten there and that I didn't have to be involved at all.

The house felt lived in already with toys on the floor, the TV on, Cheerios and milk on the counter. Mark and Lou had made a cake which they had to show us right away—chocolate with white icing and Fruit Loops scattered all over the top. Their excitement made it a celebration of sorts, even with the circumstances casting a shadow.

Inside, all the blinds were drawn, though it was still light outside. A few weeks before I might have thought this was to keep the sun and heat out, but by now I knew better.

"You want a beer?" Harlan asked me. The dark circles under his eyes were like smudges and his beard and mustache were longer and darker than I remembered, coming to a point below his chin that accentuated his broad high cheekbones. I thought he looked a little like the pictures I'd seen of Ho Chi Minh. I could feel my shyness towards him already tight in my throat and I wanted to swallow it away. Harlan King, Ten Most Wanted celebrity . . . royalty . . . no, just Harlan King . . . just Harlan.

"So how do you like the house?" I asked for something to say.

"Home sweet home!" His smile opened and closed quickly. If the wall-to-wall carpeting or the white wicker vanity sets made him uncomfortable he didn't say.

But when I took Roland up to our room he raised his eyebrows. "Wow, moving up in the world . . . middle class here I come!" I wanted to agree with him, to tell him it wasn't my idea to get such a place, but it seemed too complicated, so I let it go.

At dinner the kids were icebreakers. They both insisted on sitting on Harlan's lap, one on each knee, and they took turns feeding him spaghetti, one strand at a time, laughing in paroxysms when the strand disappeared with a quick suck and a small pop through his lips. He exaggerated the maneuver each time for their pleasure and kissed each of their heads from time to time. It was infectious, their child's laughter, and I could imagine, for a few minutes at least, that all the strangeness and discomfort of being there would be vanished for good just by their presence, their wide eyes and lispy baby talk, their silky bodies and sticky hands—but of course, it was only just beginning.

*　　*　　*

190

"Again," Lou says punctuated by the long sucking extraction of the bottle nipple from her mouth.

"Again?"

She turns her brown eyes to me, her buttery cheeks, and nodded, deadpan.

It's the third time we've gone through Goodnight Moon, picture by picture, line by line, giggling at the silly grandma, the cow jumping over the moon, finding the blue mouse hidden in every picture. It's only ten o'clock in the morning but I feel this weight on me, this heavy sleepiness like a drug. I could let my eyes close and drift off. Where would I go? I'd go somewhere green and humid, away from the stark brown dryness of the desert. Where would I go? Would I go home? Home is not home. It's not my house, but maybe I'd go there. I think about swimming alone in the pool at night in the balmy air, my skin milky white in the pool lights, everyone asleep in the dark house. Swimming underwater with breaststrokes to keep the silence intact.

"You know what?" I say, stroking her head, "We'd better go to the park before it gets too hot, okay?"

I have a day with the kids by myself, a gift.

Jo is with Harlan at the lawyer's office, and Roland's gone with them too. It's a relief to be away from the three of them, to be away from myself, the way I am with them, always watching myself watching them, waiting to fuck up. Harlan thinks the house is going to be raided by Feds any day. The day after we got there he got an extra set of locks for both the front and back doors. He reminds us to make sure we use them both whenever we leave, even if we're only going down the street for cigarettes, or around the block for a walk. When we're in the house, even in the daytime, the blinds stay drawn—no exceptions!

"We cannot afford to be loose about this!" he said on one of our first nights there, and when he uses his serious voice I'm certain I'll never be able to live up to his expectations. Even though we were all at the table, I could tell by his unwavering gaze that he was mostly talking to me—Roland and Jo being well trained in these routines already. I haven't messed up, but I think they all can tell that I don't anticipate feds at every turn the way they do, and that I don't have eyes in the back of my head to spot them. I'm trying to pay attention, to be attuned to these things, but frankly I'm more afraid of their judgments than I am of the feds. I can't believe the feds would shoot us—or maybe I just can't believe they'd shoot me.

Mark and Lou don't watch me in that way. Their occasional scrutiny of me is entirely curious with hardly a judgment at all. They play with me like I'm a big doll they can dress up, whose long hair they can brush and braid, a doll they favor, who they would just as soon take with them wherever they go. I like to turn myself over to their simple world, their seemingly effortless acceptance of me.

Lou runs to get her brother from the other room where he's watching cartoons. Jo says they need schedules, daily routines because of all the changes they've been going through. Breakfast, reading/TV time, walk to the park, lunch, nap, playtime, dinner, TV, bed. I admire the certainty of her wisdom, the parent in her that seems to know what they need and insists that they get it. I admire the way she seems to take charge and still flow with it all in spite of everything else she has to deal with. She seems to coast through these days that still don't seem to fit me all that well, like my jeans that are suddenly too tight, even with the button undone at the top.

"I've got Che!" Lou holds up the bear whose round saucer brown eyes match her own. She's chosen the name herself, and he is her constant companion, never more than an arm's length from her side.

"Okay, all ready then. Tell Mark not to forget his truck." As if he would ever leave the yellow plastic pay loader behind. These are the small ways they hold their world together. I think I'm like that now to them too, like the bear and the pay loader. I'm a precious fixture—a part of their routine, and a part of the landscape they hope will never ever change again.

But in spite of the relief I feel being with them, in spite of loving all of their unbridled sweetness, I feel suffocated by our routine—caged knowing exactly what will come next. For the last few weeks it's been the same. Roland and Harlan go downtown to meet with lawyers and to make contacts with other people in the community who are interested in supporting Harlan. A few times, Jo and I went with them, but it seemed like more trouble than it was worth, what with the stroller, the bottles of leaking juice, the diapers and change of clothes, and the heat, always the heat, no matter what we do, the sun burning our necks, our arms, baking them dry until it feels they'll crack open like the dried red mud in the arroyo we cross on the bridge near our house.

Aside from caring for Mark and Lou, our days revolve around meals, housework, and errands. How long will this go on? Jo got defensive when I asked the other day when she thought the trial might be.

"We don't know. How could we know? It could begin in a month, but maybe not for three or four, maybe longer. You know as much as I do."

She doesn't usually snap at me but I suppose the waiting is getting to her too. To me, it feels like I've just run off an escalator and the ground beneath my feet is pulling against this urgency I feel to keep up the pace of all that needs to be done in the world.

What are you accomplishing out there anyway? My mother's voice harps at me. I didn't speak to her last night on the phone when my father called. I should have, but that's what she would have asked me and I wouldn't have been able to tell her honestly about all the most important work I've been doing to rid the world of evil, that instead of driving across country, now I'm doing dishes, or watching cartoons, or pushing a couple of kids in swings at the park, back and forth, back and forth.

She would have asked me, in that accusing superior tone of hers, "Did you get our letters?" and then how could I have even begun to respond to the political essays they each wrote to me—my mother's typed five pages, my fathers eight, handwritten on a legal pad, their point by point rejections of the letter I'd sent them after I'd arrived here.

Lou climbs into the stroller singing her teensy-weensy spider song to her bear. Once we're on the street, Mark takes my place pushing her and we inch our way down the street, past the chain link fences that outline the small postage stamp yards, the identical houses, one . . . two . . . three . . . four . . . .four houses to the end of the block and we're there. We are the only ones there, as usual, but that's the way I like it.

We take off our sandals even though the grass is rough and prickly underfoot, but in most places it's been worn away and the dry, dry dirt is silky. In the one corner a big cottonwood shades the sandbox during the morning hours, and there the sand is watery cool and we cover our feet and our hands and our legs pretending it's a swimming pool.

I have their letters in my pocket. My father's voice from the phone call yesterday is still a clear echo.

Lou gets twenty pushes on the swing, and Mark ten revolutions on the round-a-bout, and then they settle in the sandbox to resume their daily game of truck and bear adventures. I have time now to re-read the letters.

The truth is I'd been waiting every day for their response. I thought, after I'd put many hours of effort and fore-thought into articulating what I believed were irrefutable contradictions in the way they lived their lives, that there was a chance that they'd understand. I even thought that maybe they'd agree. Like a dream that is entirely real enough to be a waking reality, I'd allowed myself to imagine them finding the errors of their ways—seriously agreeing to move out of their mansion, their racist community, and give their money away the way I'd decided to do. But now that they've definitively said that they won't, that they don't see or agree with my point of view, I wonder what we have left. How can I talk to them about anything important to me, or turn to them, or respect the choices they have made?

I don't know why I care so much, or even if I do. I used the word "desperate" in my letter to them. I said I was "desperate to convey the depth of my feelings about these matters". I crossed that out in disgust on the first re-write, there being moments, hours, stretches of days when I can't say I feel much of anything towards them, when they are so far away I can't even bring their faces to my memory. But then, on the second draft, I put it back in, that word "desperate", in one of those other moments when I had to try again to see if they could hear me. There is, after all, a family covenant to keep—the one that says that we are all very close, that we love each other very much, even when those words ring like so much small change tossed in a beggar's cup.

I opened my mother's letter first and it was just as hard to get beyond the first paragraph as it was when I'd read it the day before.

"I want to make it clear to you that I won't go on the defensive with you about how we live our lives. We enjoy our lives—our children, our work, our athletics and cultural activities . . . "

I looked up at Mark who was cradling the bear, feeding him an imaginary spoonful with gentle cooing sounds while Lou prepared a sand bed for nap time.

Harlan or Jo would die for them in a heartbeat.

It was that word "enjoy" that I gave up on; it's tepid love.

"Enjoyment" was not what you died for, what you risked your life to defend. And that was what I was talking about, what was desperate—this life and death matter of love.

> *"Obviously we see the inequities and injustices all around us, and we do what we can to alleviate some. We could do more—we could give up every waking hour and every red cent. You would say we should. Maybe so. But we're not going to. And we're not going through the rest of our lives riddled with guilt that we were lucky enough to be born more fortunate than most."*

There were pages of examples of how she has managed to do this, to put aside guilt in favor of happiness, her intelligent justifications. They come at me like her tennis returns in the blinding mid-summer sun—the way she would lob the ball back to me no matter how hard I'd try to put it away. "Stay on your toes! Always keep those feet moving!" she'd taunt me, run me back and forth across the court without so much as a side-step from her mid-court throne, without so much as a bead of perspiration above her carnation pink lip.

> *"Obviously, you must never 'turn your back on awareness' as you say. The trick is how to best utilize that awareness for the benefit of others, and at the same time keep your perspective and a sense of humor so that you will grow into a happy and fulfilled woman."*

Like me, she might have added. This happiness defined for me as being better, always better than I was, than I could ever be.

"That was such fun!" she'd say at the end of the game when I would be hating her, and myself a little more. "You see, I can still be happy when you are not," she might have added. "That is the real trick, darling." *Obviously.*

I put her letter aside and picked up my father's. I was wistful for the feeling I had when I first opened it, the weight of its many pages in my hand—like one of those crepe party balls you unravel with shiny trinkets inside.

This was my first real letter from him. Not just the perfunctory "Hope all's well. Love you, Dad" I was used to seeing scribbled on my mother's letters when I was away at school, but eight pages of his attention, of his nearly indecipherable script, and not a single word crossed out. I wondered if he'd written a first draft, if he'd struggled over every sentence the way I had in my letter to them, re-writing and re-writing, or if all of his thoughts and opinions, the arguments that defended how he has chosen to live his life, were so clear, so unshakably certain that they flowed from his hand, through his hand, onto the paper without so much as a pensive pause.

Really, there were no shiny trinkets inside.

> *"One point I think every idealist must face is that any individual must be humble enough to recognize that he or she is only one of many people, each of whom is also entitled to his or her beliefs, and that any civilized social structure must accord each individual the right to pursue his or her beliefs to the best of their ability within such rules as the society may impose to protect the rights of all individuals."*

And there were other points - rational, reasonable. Each one I'd raised in my letter had been addressed and argued like a legal treatise: *defense of the free market system*—check; *defense of political system*—check; *defense of foreign policy*—check; *of Watergate pardons, the prison system, misallocation of resources, private club membership*—check, check, check, check.

"I have never in my professional life done anything which troubled my conscience or which I felt treated someone unfairly."

But I have. Last night on the phone I treated them all unfairly.

Lou crawled into my lap to drink her bottle of apple juice. I held her close, even in the heat that made our skin stick together. I was thinking what a shit I'd been on the phone with my brother the night before, how I'd cut him off and insulted him and practically hung up on my father, wouldn't speak to my mother at all. Maybe if everyone on my end hadn't been listening to my side of the conversation. They weren't intentionally listening, but with only one phone, it happened anyway, even with the TV on. They couldn't hear my father's voice, it's halting monotone, the familiar way he always sounded as if he was reading something while he talked to me, like he didn't know how to talk to me. I knew my mother had put him up to it.

"Hi honey . . . Haven't heard your voice in a while . . . how's everything ?"

"I'm fine Dad." I couldn't really help him with the silence that followed, not with Jo and Harlan and Roland close enough to touch.

"I'm sitting here with your brother . . . He's got some great news he wants to tell you . . . Are you still there?"

I was still there, censoring every cell of expression, every hint of attachment, raising my eyebrows and making an exasperated face for Jo, who caught my eye and was laughing at me. My gatekeepers. Warrior not daughter, remember . . . it made it easier that way."Ya . . . I'm here . . . Put him on."

Charles, my older brother by three years, was named after my father with a "II" after his name. When we were much younger we'd been close for a time, I'd shadowed him everywhere I could until he was sent away to boarding school, and then I was sent away too, and then our paths had diverged quickly in many ways.

In the last few years we hadn't spoken much, but I knew his first child was expected any day.

"Hey, little sister, you there?"

"Ya.. I'm here. Hey..how are you? So what's the big news?" Like I didn't know.

"We had the baby . . . Well, Kathy had the baby. Two hours ago. It's a boy! I wanted you to be the first to know."

He wanted me to be the first to know. Really? I'd have to throw that away. It was a ploy to lure me in where I didn't want to be, couldn't be, not anymore. I didn't want to think about all of them sitting around that private hospital room with a million flowers and the view out the window, toasting the first grandchild, the next little golden boy, with $100 champagne . . . all relaxed now with the big work of their lives complete. A grandson . . . What a party.

"That's great!" I really tried for a moment to make my voice sing for him. "What's his name?"

"Well he's another Charles, only we're going to call him Chase."

I'm not there. I'm here. We're eating spaghetti with Ragu sauce. Roland has no shirt on . . . his "Break the Chains" tattoo almost within touching distance. Jo is smoking a cigarette, watching me, so I say . . .

"Wow—Chase . . . That's great. You could make his middle name 'Manhattan' . . . just like the bank . . . A chip off the old block, brother!" But my own words stung me, they sounded stupid, small and mean.

I heard his nervous laugh. "Yeah, right . . . that would be pretty funny . . . well I hope you get to see him soon . . . . He's really beautiful! I gotta go now . . . Here's Dad."

"Hi dearie, everything okay?" My father's voice was nervous too, a tone I didn't recognize, that made me feel like I really *had* changed, and become a stranger to them.

"Yeah, don't worry Dad. Everything's great here. Thanks for letting me know about the baby. I've gotta go though . . . "

"Your mother's right here. Just say a quick hello."

"No I can't Dad. Not right now. Just tell her I'm fine, okay? I'll call soon or something."

"Did you get our letters?"

"Yeah . . . thanks . . . Really . . . I'm going to write you back. We're just really busy here, getting ready for the trial and all."

"When *is* the trial? We're really in the dark about everything honey. You've got your mother worried sick . . . . we're all worried about you."

I will not cry. If I talk to her she'll make me cry.

"I'm not really sure yet but I'll let you know . . . I promise. Everything's okay, but I gotta go."

"Well you let us know as soon as you can. Bye dearie . . . we all love you."

I hung up the phone and it was like the snap of a towline, setting me adrift in a little dingy, dangerously rocking in the wake of the family ship that steamed away with whatever had been loyal and redeemable about me. I kept my back turned to Jo and the others, my gaze out the window on the rapidly gathering dusk, the concrete front path leading out to the aluminum heart-shaped front gate. I'd go to the park . . . right away. I'd go without looking at them, without seeing myself in them, smirking and smug and small—ready to joke about little baby Chase Manhattan and to put my whole family in a little box with a big "Pig" label.

"I'm going to walk to the park. I'll be back in a little while." Only Jo heard me.

"You okay? You want company?" She looked a little worried, not mean. I'd never left before.

"No thanks. I won't be long."

"Be careful."

Harlan had a big black book of bad guys, like a photo album, filled with pictures and write ups of all the real "killers" in the country—heads of corporations, bank presidents, senators—all the ones to blame for all the crimes of capitalism, the living foundation of the power structure. The book was like a thesis of sorts, years of work and careful research presented neatly in plastic covered pages, bound in a cover that had remained brand new looking, as if for years it had only been handled with the greatest care.

The night I was allowed to look through its pages was like an initiation ritual, another level of acceptance into the group. No one ever said so, but I imagined the book was a collection of targets for kidnapping or assassination . . . that someday in the future when the group got its shit together, they'd be able to really go to war with the system through attacks on this power elite.

I'd sat with Harlan under a light bulb glare as he'd placed the book on the table pushing it towards me with two hands, as if any sudden movement might damage the contents. He sat across from me, twirling his mustache, scrutinizing my face with his dark eyes as I flipped through the pages. I thought maybe I was sup-posed to oooh and aaah over some of them, show my disdain and disgust for these criminals who were so well protected by the system. I flipped the pages with reverence, trying to get hateful, to prove somehow that he hadn't been mistaken to take me into his confidence.

The problem was that the scenes and the faces were unnerv-ingly familiar.

There was the white-shingled house my friend had grown up in. There was the man in the Brooks Brothers suit sitting at his desk with the family photo behind him, all arms linked on the deck of the sailboat, just like the sailboat I'd been on last summer. In the bios I scanned there were places I knew—Greenwich, New Canaan, Oyster Bay, and schools whose alma-maters I'd suffered through singing every holiday meal at home—Yale, Princeton, Harvard. I hated all the smug, self-satisfied authority they assumed, all the entitlement to the power they abused. I hated how they hid out in their quiet well- protected communities, where nothing bad ever happened and where there was a uniformity to work and play that suffocated the life out of any rebellious spirit, anyone the slightest bit different.

Harlan was pointing out the particularly heinous executives, the ones responsible for casual massacres, the worst labor abuses, the most renowned war benefactors. I followed his callused finger with the roughly chewed nail as it slid across the pages. I had no trouble agreeing that not one of them deserved another minute of the power they abused. I nodded and made enough suitable comments to convince him, I hoped, that I was on his side. I *did* want it all to come crashing down. I was ready to sweat, dig ditches, work tirelessly to make it happen, but was this the first step I had to take? "Off" the pig on this page. On that page. In the name of love and tolerance and a better world.

I imagined my father's picture in it, the 8 x 10 black and white that sat on the table at home, the one where his smile looked almost relaxed for him; his sweater tied a little too neatly around his neck in what was meant to be an all-natural look, but actually was as controlled as everything else in his life. And my brother Charles and his wife could be there, in that book, and my mother. They'd each have their own page now, thanks to me, even little baby Chase Manhattan. Someday they might all be "war casualties" . . . wasn't that how they referred to the strategic necessity of "offing" certain high ranking members of the power elite? Is that what I wanted?

Back in its hidden spot, the book haunted me. The images from its pages were never far from my mind. I daydreamed of some of the people I knew being snatched off their front lawn—gagged and blindfolded, of there being some terrible mistake of identity. Though I never knew exactly where it was kept, I knew it was in the house with us—a cold commandment that if I stuck around, if I chose this course, I would someday have to measure up.

Chapter 21

Roland is leaving soon, maybe in a few days. There's not that much he can do out here and still maintain a low profile. He spends his days with Harlan, making contacts with other people working in the prison movement, making connections. Sometimes I go with him, help where I can, but in the daytime I keep my distance, act like an acquaintance, a friend who might by chance brush against him on the street, or be pressed against him in the car, but nothing more than that. I take my cues from him. I can see that I'm not foremost in his mind by a long shot, and that love is an extravagance he cannot afford, not at this juncture, where he must anticipate his next captors, must remain vigilant, disciplined in his every moment lest they catch him unaware.

I want to make him laugh, to play just a bit, to hear his low laugh that makes me hopeful. If I could find that again, then, under its blanket, any closeness would be possible. I know who he is beneath this hard distracted exterior, this temporary roadblock, the goodness that I believe in—honorable and kind. But I see how I am around him, like a silent mime, a shadow. I would be hard to find even if he was looking.

In the morning I usually wake early, before he does, and sometimes I lie there looking into his face that is deeply grooved, strangely foreign in its relaxed state. I wonder how I've landed in this bed, with this particular body, with its particularly mapped face, so close I can feel the warm breath of his exhalations on my cheek and still feel like we're deserts apart.

Really, I don't know if I love Roland or if it's just about craving something that always feels out of reach—his acceptance, approval, respect. Some kind of respect most of all. Whatever it is exhausts me with its tension and still I won't let go, because in spite of all that feels amiss between us, I know I would be giving up on some kind of greatness—his, or my own, or possibly something in the making that belongs to us both.

Sometimes I watch him out in the yard practicing his karate moves and swinging his nun-chuck sticks and I know he's preparing to leave for war, has already mostly left. The line of his mouth is like a line in the dirt I would never cross, and still, I want to be with him. I want to find the way in, the way across, to help keep his gentle heart alive.

* * *

Money is screwing everything up here. My money. It's like this force, this dark energy that lives with me that I'll never understand, that's so moody and demanding and mercurial I'll never get to see it in a full clear light for just what it is, whatever it is. I just wish it wasn't there, that I wasn't rich anymore. But as much as it feels like a blasphemy to be rich, it feels like just as much of one to even think that you don't want to be.

Every day it comes up somehow, my confusion about it. Like Jo and I will be in the grocery store and she'll be throwing all this stuff in the cart that I don't really think we need, or that I wouldn't have gotten anyway—like fresh asparagus at $2.50 a pound instead of broccoli at 79 cents a head. Or Bumble Bee tuna instead of the supermarket brand. She doesn't even take the coupons from the checkout person, and even my mother always took the coupons. I don't mind. I don't. It's really no big deal. But that's not the whole truth.

Why did I think Roland would understand? It was silly to indulge this fantasy that he would or could guide me around money. Or maybe I was just reaching out, one last time, to see if I could connect with him before he left. It wasn't a plan I had—it just happened, like an earthquake happens, with forewarnings available only if you have the right equipment.

We were in our room dressing before breakfast. He was running his hands through his hair, then quickly pulling it back into the ponytail the way he always wore it.

I was pulling on my jeans, my tee shirt, and then brushing my hair.

He said, "So, two days and I'm out of here, you know. I'm going back east to pull the group together."

If he asked me, would I go with him? I thought I could detect a faint light, a glimmer in his distant look. Come with me! Most likely, it was another mirage, my own romantic construction. But would I go with him? No. Yes. Maybe.

"I didn't think you'd be leaving so soon."

He was tucking his shirt into his pants, covering his body, the heat, the muscles skin and bones that continued to draw me to him no matter what degree of remove I read on his face. Behind him, in a note card propped in the mirror was the quote by George Jackson he'd put there, that I'd read so many times I knew it by heart.

"I have surrendered all hope of happiness for myself in this life to the prospect of effecting some improvement in our circumstances as a whole. I have a plan. I will give of myself until it proves our making or my end."

I could follow this man . . . live, love, die with him in this good struggle if I could only navigate the continent that already lay between us in this room.

"So," he said, "Do you want to keep in touch with us?"

Us he'd said, not *me*, I registered that. But were he and I warriors, fellow cadre, or lovers? I couldn't tell. If I reached over to him, who would I be reaching towards? A mate? A comrade?

"Yeah, I guess so. Of course I do." My ambivalence ricocheted off the walls.

"Well, if you're looking for ways to help us, you could always be our benefactor."

He said the word "benefactor" like it was supposed to make me laugh, and we both smiled half-heartedly. "That's one way you can help. It's not the only way, but it's pretty central right now. We're going to need money to set up a safe house, get our ID's together, and, I guess we'll have to eat." He laughed at that, trying to lighten the weight of the request, his discomfort in making it. He was standing across the room, leaning against the bureau, his legs crossed, his arms crossed over his chest. He wouldn't crowd me. He'd never asked me for a dime. It had been my choice to put up the money for his lawyer and give the bail to Karl. And he'd paid for the gun. Maybe he saw it like I did—like it wasn't my money anyway. It was the people's money. And this was one more way I could play my part in the reckoning of all those corporate gains that had been padding my existence.

"Yeah, well I do. I want to help you out. I just don't know how to put a dollar amount on what feels right. I mean, I've been spending all this money here, and on your bail, and I don't know what's enough. What's too much? Do you know what I mean?"

Roland's face could be like a darting shadow, hard to fix upon, to read unless he was smiling. But whatever light of a smile had been there a moment ago was gone now.

"No. Not really. 'What feels right?' What do you mean by

that? Sounds like maybe you want to minimize your losses, check the Dow Jones before you make up your mind."

There was no hiding the slap there and then I did want to reach out and pull him to me. Like a lifeline, I had to try to make him understand if I'd ever be able to crawl out of the crevasse I'd fallen in to. "That's not what I meant . . . I don't know what I mean . . . I guess I don't know how I should be spending the money . . . you know, maybe I should spread it around a little." But as I heard the words come out of my mouth I could feel the earth between us split open a little wider, the hole almost bottomless.

"Wow . . . you know, I think you've gone rich on me. That's what it feels like to me!" he spat out. "I guess I saw it coming. You can't really help it, can you, coming from where you come from?" He turned his back to get something out of the bureau drawer and I sat for an interminable moment in that kind of screaming silence that roars through you, that would be deafening except for the sounds of Roland shuffling papers in his drawer. But then he spun around, "You know what? Keep your money. We don't need it. When I'm in prison, you can send me oranges, okay? Just send me a dozen oranges." His voice was level, straight, sharp, perfectly aimed, and then he walked out of the room.

I stayed on the edge of the bed pinned and paralyzed with shame and stunned at the suddenness of the crater that had just separated us entirely.

I'd "gone rich" on him.

I was pretty sure I knew what he meant by that. That was hard enough. But the last line, the one about sending him oranges in prison—that was the one that stayed with me, that echoed over and over in my head because I didn't quite understand it—I just knew it was bad. I knew that with that line I'd been dumped into an entirely despicable group of wanna-be revolutionaries, or maybe armchair liberals, or like some Waspy member of the Junior League—a hypocritical do-gooder who would end up doing more harm than good and was better off staying at home and joining contests in flower arrangement.

I thought that was what he meant.

*   *   *

We didn't really talk again after that. We avoided each other during the day, and that night and the next I went to bed before him and he stayed up late watching TV and talking to Harlan. I wondered if they were talking about me, about what a fraud I was. I wondered if Harlan had said anything to Jo. I couldn't tell if they were acting particularly cool or if I was just entirely paranoid. I'd wake up when Roland got in bed, though I pretended not to, and he slept with his back to me while I lay there wondering if any touch of mine, any gesture or word at all could possibly redeem me.

When he left he hugged me the same way he hugged Harlan and Jo, briefly, dutifully, a soldier off to war, the three of us standing in a line by the bus he was going to take across country.

I held his arm an extra moment. "I'm sorry Roland. I hope we get another chance."

"Yeah, maybe we will. I guess we'll see what happens." But he wouldn't hold my gaze and he moved towards the bus without looking back.

I didn't know if I'd ever see him again and in my heart of hearts something whispered both rage and relief.

I wasn't any clearer at all about the money issue when Harlan asked me about a week later for the balance due to his lawyer. I wrote him out a check for forty thousand dollars, but if anything, after the conversation I had with him, I felt every bit as bad as I did after the one with Roland.

We were alone in the kitchen, sitting at the table and Harlan had the lawyer's contract in front of him, to show it to me. It was maybe the first time we'd ever been alone, and that wasn't helping me see my way to a clear resolve about how I felt one way or the other. I definitely felt uneasy about spending all that money on a lawyer, but I couldn't say 'no' either. I'd said I'd do it way before this so I couldn't pull out now. Maybe Harlan could tell I was all twisted up about it. And then too, I had no way of knowing what Roland had said to him.

"You sure you want to do this?"

"Ya . . . I can do it." He wanted me to look at him, but I couldn't get my eyes out of my teacup.

"But do you want to? Sometimes I get the feeling that you're pretty uncomfortable about spending all this money. It's really up to you, you know. I want you to remember that."

Roland must have said something for him to begin like that. God, he could sound so stern sometimes, like I was a child he was reprimanding. That certain tone of voice he used you'd better pay attention to. And I didn't like him leaning towards me in his chair, twirling his mustache the way he had a habit of doing when he was being intense about something.

My head was spinning with all the reasons why it was confusing to just haul off and write the check. I thought about how much I didn't want to call Mrs. Lee again to ask for more money, to imagine her raised-eyebrow alarm, the many silent judgments laden in her professional voice. And more than that there was the image of my father, slumped over his desk with this defeated expression, or possibly even an angry one, as he looked over my stock statement plummeting overnight, the one he'd made slow additions to year after working year.

But maybe my strongest confusion still arose from my apparently blasphemous thoughts that it might be my responsibility to put the money to "better use", i.e. towards other revolutionary causes. Even in the aftermath of Roland's reprimand I still wondered if I shouldn't "share the wealth" a little more, spread the money out to reach as many lives as possible, affect the most change. How did any one person affect global change anyway? Weren't we trying to start a revolution? Was giving forty thousand dollars to a lawyer a first and necessary political action to save one of our leaders? How could I value the outcome of Harlan's life, of Jo's and the kids' in a dollar amount that I controlled? Were these "correct" or misguided thoughts?

I had to ask someone and I didn't know who that could be.

"Yeah . . . I said I would. It's just hard giving it all to a lawyer, don't you think?"

I looked up from my tea mug hoping I'd see him nodding in agreement.

"Well, I know what you mean, but I get the feeling that with you that it's just hard, period, to let go of it . . . you've got some strings attached, and that makes me nervous. I don't really want to take any money from you if there're strings attached, if we're going to have to keep answering to you about what it's going to cost to get through this."

He wasn't yelling at me. His voice was very steady and calm.

"Yeah, I don't blame you."

He was certainly right. I did have strings attached. Ropes. What about the way I'd felt about renting the house and getting the groceries and even the toys for the kids? And then what about what I'd said to Roland?

When I'm in prison, just send me oranges.

"Listen, I really appreciate all you've done up to this point to help us. But if you want out, just say so. No one's faulting you or trying to push you around here or taking advantage of your money. It's your call."

All in all, this was about five times as much as Harlan had said to me the whole time I'd known him. I knew he was finished when he sat back, tipping the kitchen chair onto two legs, and tapped out a fresh cigarette from his pack on the table, waiting to hear what I had to say.

By then I felt like a war criminal myself. Really, like a bad child. Like the way I'd felt when my mother would lecture me, that creeping feeling of losing ground in the torrents that would flow from her like a spring river. Of course he was right. No one was forcing me. If I were just more evolved, more sophisticated in my political thinking, I never would have hesitated. I never would have hesitated with Roland either and then that might not have ended the way it had.

"Okay. I see what you're saying. I just hadn't thought about it like that before. Of course I'm in."

But even though I heard the resolve in my voice, to dig in and try harder, I knew I was holding something back. After I signed the check and he hugged me like a father would, I left the room, feeling more than ever like a child with a dark secret who has just realized her parents will never understand.

CHAPTER 22

—•—

It wasn't long after that conversation that I began to allow the idea of leaving Denver to gain a foothold in my thoughts. Once there, it spread like the chickweed I'd spent hours pulling up from my parents' lawn as a child; a weed that returned overnight to the very spot you'd pulled it from the day before, or, if not there, then somewhere nearby. For the next few weeks, I dug and pulled at these thoughts, afraid of the reactions I might encounter if I told Jo or Harlan; but as our days continued without any clear trial date in site, continued in what felt like a slow withering of my seemingly politically un-evolved and non-essential presence, these thoughts of leaving invaded most of my waking hours.

It seemed, really, that I'd been screwing up everything, disappointing everyone. Even my sudden departure from the hospital program haunted me; one day a student in good standing, carrying the family name (however ambivalently), with the head of surgery a friend of my grandmother's, and then suddenly I'd disappeared with only that rotting pumpkin meat kicked across the empty apartment floor as my parting note.

I'd go back to Portland. Maybe the hospital would take me

back. I'd make amends. And if Roland chose to contact me, maybe I'd be able to figure out a way to help him out, to make a contribution to the revolutionary underground and redeem myself from my Junior League status. He was still the one I believed had the most sincere conviction, the purest and most enduring commitment to "the struggle". Harlan had lost some of his hero status in my mind. While I didn't exactly blame him for taking the money from me for his lawyer, I'd had high hopes that he'd be better than me, stronger —a hero unwilling to compromise his values to buy a ticket out of jail, especially a ticket paid for by the very corporate scum he'd risked his life to oppose. I wished he'd insisted that I give it all to Caesar Chavez or to the Black Panthers or the United Mine Workers, that he'd decided to take his chances with a court appointed lawyer like every other poor and disenfranchised person in the system.

I'd gone to court hearings in Denver with him and Jo where I'd been quickly educated about how the system works. One white judge presided in a large room where the benches were lined with black and Latino people, where Harlan was the only white defendant in the room, the only one with private representation. The others had the best the system has to offer—overworked court-appointed lawyers and a judge who handed out his indeterminate sentences with a bored smack of his gavel. *One to ten. One to twenty. One to ten.* He might as well have been stamping blocks of meat with inspection stickers.

But Harlan's case was more hopeful. You could tell as soon as he stepped up to the bench with his well-known lawyer in tow that the judge perked up, paid attention. Harlan had a chance. His lawyer said he'd probably be able to get him off, and I was glad. Of course I wanted him to get off, but all the gray areas bled into what I'd thought was going to be entirely black and white. And, the truth was, I told myself, they didn't really need me there anymore.

"I have to leave, Jo."

I decided to tell her first because I hoped it would be easier than telling both of them together. After days of trying to get up the nerve, thinking about what I'd say, rehearsing it over and over in my head, and trying on explanations and justifications, the simplest one being that I'd decided to go back to the hospital program, in the end all I said was 'I have to leave'.

I let it hang there between us—the two of us at our old stations in the car, with the groceries in the back, me driving, Jo smoking a cigarette. That part of it felt familiar at least, even my worrying about her reaction, looking quickly at her to see if her small light eyes were squinting with displeasure the way I knew she did when she was angry. They weren't squinting yet. They were wide open in disbelief staring at me. I didn't know how hard she'd have to push to get me to change my mind; maybe just the slightest nudge would do it.

"You're what? You're *leaving*? For *good*? You're not even going to stay for the trial? After all we've been through?" Her voice did have that intimidating edge, the one that might throw something in my direction if I said the wrong thing,

"No . . . I can't stay that long." I told her about the hospital program, certain that she could tell that I didn't care all that much about it, that it was just a destination, a light on the far shore to point my boat towards.

"But what about the kids? They're going to flip when they hear this."

"The kids are okay. They're settled here now. I don't know how to explain it to you. I'm sorry . . . I just have to go."

"Jesus."

We drove the rest of the way in a silence that I wished I could fill with something soft, something light that would ease the heaviness between us, but I knew there was nothing to say unless I took it all back, and I didn't. I couldn't.

Jo told Harlan when we got back to the house, but his reaction was pretty matter-of-fact; he almost shrugged it off. He even smiled. "You gotta do what you gotta do. It's been great that you helped us out as much as you have . . . Really." I was relieved that he didn't lay it on any heavier than that, either wanting me to stay, or thanking me. Thanking me just made me squirm.

But Jo looked angry or sad or both, her eyes downcast, avoiding mine.

I wanted to touch her, to see if I could make it better like other times I'd touched her when I didn't have any words that would help. I still wasn't sure that she cared about me all that much. I still thought her judgments were the loudest of all, even if she'd never spoken one harsh word to me about my class or money, just about everyone else's. Or maybe *I* was the one with the cold heart and too many judgments, who couldn't feel anything but the steady hum of self-doubt these days, and fear that I was making a mess of everything in everyone's eyes. The only relief I could imagine was an open road, by myself.

"I can't believe you'd leave now," she said. "I just don't get it."

I didn't drag it out after that. Two days later, early in the morning, I was ready to leave. Lou watched my every move with her big watery eyes as I took my few loads to the car, and Mark parked himself behind the wheel, pretending to drive until I was ready to go. He seemed happy enough until I hugged him good-bye, and then he ran to Jo, letting out one long wail for all of us.

In all my life I've never been so alone. That's what I thought when I hit the highway, putting the car into overdrive and looking around as I left the suburbs behind and drove into the flat sea of desert. All the relief of being on my own with no one in the seat next to me filled the car, made me want to hoop aloud. But I didn't make a sound. I didn't because everywhere there was relief there was also a shadow of fear lurking in that empty space, in all the empty spaces—fear of the very same thing that gave me relief.

215

I drove all day, and as the light began to fade, the shadow that hung around the car with me, that hovered in the back seat, grew. I drove all through that night afraid to stop alone at a motel, afraid to stop at all. All the way through Kansas I kept the windows open to the comfort of the sweet grass scent of the night, and kept the music loud to keep me awake and to keep my solitude at a manageable distance.

Fear of falling asleep in the dark alone, of breaking down in the dark alone, or of being cornered by the truckers in the semi's that radioed back and forth, one of them following me for an entire tank of gas—the one with the bald head and the heavy face who pulled his reflective dark glasses up to leer at me whenever I could manage to pass him.

I bought candy bars from vending machines, coffee to go whenever I got gas, crossing the country in two hundred and fifty mile leaps. At the truck stops I felt certain that if I sat at a table that the bald trucker would magically appear. If not him, then any one of them might suddenly loom in front of my table, demanding something from me I'd be unable to refuse.

I wondered how long I would last before the straight painted lines on the road would begin to waver, before my eyes would shut without warning. In the middle of the second day, with the sun at its very hottest and brightest hour, I pulled over into a rest stop area, laid my jean jacket out on the patch of turf grass beside the curb, well in sight of as many travelers as possible, and slept.

I'm going to go home. First, I'm going to go home—then I'll go back to Portland.

I hadn't been planning on it, but after I woke up and got back in my car and saw pieces of my reflection in the rear-view mirror, the red ferning outlines of the grass and jacket folds on my left cheek, the right side of my face roasted red from the sun, the stray stems of grass in my hair, I wanted to be there and nowhere else.

I wouldn't call. I'd surprise them. That would be perfect.

Even with a thousand miles to go, the rest of the drive would be easy now that I had a purpose, the purpose being to get to someplace as fast as possible where absolutely everything would be familiar, whatever it was, good or bad, entirely familiar, a whole image of myself reflected back to me that I would recognize.

But it wasn't like that.

It was late, black and moonless when I arrived. I thought my parents might hear me pull in, and felt ambivalent about waking them, but no lights went on in their bedroom window. The key was there, behind the boxwood bush by the front door, and I felt clever finding it, letting myself in so soundlessly, only the smallest clicks echoing in the emptiness of the high-ceilinged front hallway. The smell of floor wax and wood polish assured me I was home.

I ducked into the 'powder room'. My mother always called it that, with its monogrammed linen yellow hand-towels, starched and ironed like sheets of parchment, and the perfectly shaped rose soaps in the porcelain soap dish. You don't ever use those. You don't leave them soggy and shapeless in the dish or a wrinkled hand towel on the rack. But I picked a bright pink bud and washed my face to erase the smell of cigarettes, dried it with toilet paper and wrapped the soap in the damp wads and put it all in my pocket to throw away later. I rubbed my finger over my teeth, clipped my hair back into a bun to hide its two-day old wind-blown road knots. My hands were shaking, my movements clumsy with caffeine and candy, fatigue and anticipation.

The hallway was still dark. Should I let them know I was home? It was required, had always been, to let them know I was home when I came in late when I was younger—I'd have to go in, tell them what time it was, kiss them goodnight. But I was not that young anymore. Still, I wanted to start out on the right foot, as my mother would say. If I went to May's room and they found me there, it would start out all wrong. And if I went straight to bed in my own room, there'd be no telling what I'd wake up to in the morning.

I climbed the stairs two at a time and slowly opened their bedroom door.

My mother's bed was first and as I leaned over her shadowed form to kiss her hello, just a small kiss on the cheek, my father's hand came bulleting through the dark, crashed into me, shoved me hard, harder, much harder than he'd ever touched me before.

"Goddammit! What are you doing? Be careful!" The man who never raised his voice, who never yelled, ever, at me.

But I don't understand. But then I do understand. I smell it, feel it right away, the heavy layers of drugged sleep, veiling the pain that hums in the room anyway. I know that smell. They should have told me. I should have known. I should have been able to tell.

"What's the matter? It's *me* Dad . . . Linda."

He was propped up on one arm, his body pitched over her—a shield, a cradle from harm, trying to see me through the dark. I wasn't sure which surprised me more—the force of his greeting, or seeing him leaning over her in such a deeply protective posture. It had never really occurred to me that he loved her like that, that he would protect her. Already the reflection I'd hoped to find had a big crack in it.

"Linda? What are you doing here? When did you get here? I'm sorry honey . . . you really surprised me."

My mother groaned, asleep, deeper than sleep.

"What's the matter with Mom?"

"It's another ruptured disk . . . . She can't move her neck."

In the last twenty years, my mother had had three operations on her lower back, two on her neck. I knew each of the incision lines, the older ones where she'd always ask me to rub at the knots in the muscles beneath, smoothing my thumbs over the silver white bloodless scars at the base of her spine, and the two at her neck—two red ladders, one in front, one in back, the way her skin felt loose and slippery over the bony ridges where only the lightest touch was soothing. After all, I'd grown up as her "little nurse", her favorite pair of healing hands. I'm the one she'd ask for whenever something hurt, the one who figured it out best of all, how to tiptoe around her, kneel by her bedside, blanket her, getting every pillow just right. "Just be careful!" they'd say, and I was.

He lay back and turned on his bedside light.

I could see my mother now with a thick white neck collar on, her face shining with face cream, her brow furrowed against the light or the pain or both, trying to surface.

Really I didn't want to look at her face, her neck brace. Not then. I didn't want her to wake up. I didn't like feeling that all of this had been happening without my knowing anything at all about it, that I hadn't done my part to help her like she'd expect. I'd have to pay for that now too, scramble and beg more or less, to paint myself back into the family fold, to hold on to whatever was left of my position in it. There was no end to the ways you could disappoint her and lately I had accumulated so many.

"I don't think she likes the light," I whispered.

He turned it off and lay back with a sigh. I could still see his profile in the waning moonlight.

"Well you're back . . . anyway, you're back. I've been so worried about you honey. Come give me a hug."

I was glad it was dark so he couldn't see my tears when I pressed my face into his familiar shoulder and held my breath deep inside to keep myself together. Everything the same and not the same at all—altogether entirely different. The clock, the lamp, the book just so, one hardcover on the bedside table I could just see now in the dark. That was the way I'd been hoping to find everything . . . exactly in its rightful place.

I wanted to get comfortable against his chest, but my position was awkward, sitting on the edge of his bed, leaning over, twisted from my waist. I waited for him to ask me again where I'd come from, why I was here, but already I heard the beginning of his breathing slipping into the deeper regular rhythm of sleep.

"You must be tired," he managed, but I knew that meant that he was tired, or just unable to deal with me one way or the other, so I sat up.

"Yeah . . . it's really late. I'm sorry I surprised you. Go back to sleep, I'll have breakfast with you in the morning."

"That'd be great honey. I'm so glad you're home." He found my hand in the dark and gave it a quick squeeze. "I missed you."

I knew his eyes were already closed.

"Me too Dad."

Then I left and went downstairs, found my way in the dark into the kitchen to make myself some tea, fixing it by just the blue light of the gas stove so I didn't have to look around and see what else had changed since I'd been gone.

"Well look who the cat dragged in . . . if it isn't my little Baba!" My mother is sitting up in her bed, in her lacy scoop-necked night-gown, her many pillows propped around her, her neck in the brace that forces her to pivot her entire upper body towards me as I come in the door with her breakfast tray. "Baba" has been her nickname for me since I was born. "*Little Baba*". I used to like it when I was younger—a name that fixed me in a special place of my own apart from all my siblings, a kind of embrace that I could sink into and have all to myself. But I didn't like it anymore. It assumed an intimacy with her that I didn't feel, that she had no right to. That embrace was a sham, a big empty pit with a trap door over it camouflaged to look like love. I would not be "little" with her, not if I could possibly help it. Not if I could keep her at arms length, be astute, aware, quick to see it coming—the many ways she had of working me back into being her little girl again.

Her smile has slipped to a wince, a wince that I knew well. A signal to begin.

The most important thing is to keep your attention on her at all times. To shower her with attention at all times. I present myself with a big smile, like I'm so glad to be home, finally, and that my time away has only been a fanciful vacation like one of her own worldly ones with my father, and I'm here to tell her "all about it". I know she will not let go until she feels that I've really told her all about it. I put the tray on my father's bed next to her and kiss her lightly on the cheek.

"Oh aren't you a dear. Let me look at you!"

Everything is white or light pastel-colored in the bedroom, the sheets and coverlets, the rug, the walls, my mother's light blonde hair and white nightgown, even the neck brace. Everything is bright and sunny and clean. I look away as she takes me in, scans me. I'm clean too, just showered, but my clothes are dark and baggy, my fingernails bitten to a ragged quick, and I've gained weight since she saw me last, something that has never ever happened to my mother.

"You look wonderful dear."

I help her settle the tray where she can pour her tea from the jade green china teapot, put jam on her toast from the matching miniature jam dish. I tell her she looks wonderful too, in spite of everything she's going through, and settle myself on the end of her bed, sitting sideways facing her, careful not to make any movements that might jar her. I ask her what the doctors have said this time, if they know what's wrong.

"Oh let's not talk about that . . . it's so boring. Let me hear about you. We've been so worried. I half think it's what brought this on." She adjusts her neck collar, wincing again, wincing in that way that is a small enough gesture to be denied, and large enough to jump out and accuse you of negligence if you don't acknowledge it. I put my hand on her leg, furrow my brow in concern—I am concerned, concerned and cautious.

"And your father . . . well he's just been a wreck about you. You can't imagine what he's been going through. Can't you tell me anything about what you've been doing out there?"

I watch her bring her teacup to her lips, aware of how every movement and aspect of her physical being has been imprinted on me, how I've studied, memorized, and can conjure at any moment with my eyes closed, in her immediate presence or away from it, the exact shape of each filed and polished fingernail, the way her mouth moves when she chews with the corners turned down in an ellipsis, the sound she makes when she swallows that I can hear above every other sound, as if there were no other sound, as if she'd silenced the room to make it heard.

It's not my intention to know these things, but I know them nonetheless—infinite mounds of details that I've stored to help me calculate, anticipate what's coming next.

I know already, for example, from the way she winced, from before that, from the moment she turned to me as I came in the door, that I'm supposed to take the blame for her current neck problem, for all of her current pain and immobility. She doesn't "half-think" I brought it on—she's convinced herself it's true. In some way we both know this.

"I don't know . . . we really didn't do that much. Met with lawyers, got the word out in the community about Harlan's trial. I told you Jo has two kids . . . I helped her take care of them."

I know it's futile, trying to deflect her; like trying to blow out a fire, it just makes the flames bigger. "We got William Kunstler to help us out." Maybe she'd have to take my position more seriously if she knew Kunstler was behind it, being that she's always so impressed by famous people.

"Ohh..God! I hate that man! He's such a troublemaker. And he's so . . . so . . . unattractive, such a slob! You don't really like him, do you?"

I avoid her eyes tugging me to look at her, look instead at the oil-painted Impressionist scene of French bathers by the sea that hangs above her bed.

"Oh I don't know . . . Ya, I like him a lot."

She lets out a deeply exaggerated, deeply disdainful sigh. "And did you find people out there who were willing to support this man Harlan and what he's done?"

"What he's allegedly done. Nothing's been proven yet, Mom. Don't you think he deserves a fair trail?"

"Of course. Of course he does. And where else in the world do you think he'd be able to get a fair trial? Where else in the world would a terrorist be able to get a fair trial?"

"It depends on what you mean by 'fair'. And besides, I don't think of him as a terrorist." I still can't look at her, not to really hold her gaze head on. I try, but it's too hard. There's a distinction between being a terrorist and being a freedom fighter, a guerrilla freedom fighter, that I have to defend, but I can't find the words to do it, not with her looking at me like this, staring me down, not with her sitting up in the white throne of her pillows. I want to tell her that we, our group, are not the aggressors, that we've been forced into a violent stance by the cold-blooded murderous actions and policies of our government. Doesn't she feel anything when she sees Vietnamese women and children trying to run away from the napalm burning on their backs, or the abject poverty that exists in the slums not five miles from the affluence of this neighborhood? If she'd been the one to find Jo after she'd been raped, and the notes from the Klan, and knew the police were in on it, wanted us dead and buried under asphalt, what would she have done?

"Well whatever you want to call him, he's a terrorist in my book. What do you think you're going to accomplish by blowing things up? By risking innocent people's lives? I gather it's what you believe in now too, isn't it?" She adjusts her neck brace with a strategic groan.

I'm actually proud that she's placed me firmly in the group and I don't want to argue against being there, to tell her anything about my own ambivalence about their strategies or about the tenuousness of my future with Roland, or if I'll even ever see any of them again. Whether or not I see myself as a guerrilla fighter at this moment is secondary to the importance of defending their right to exist, or maybe just my right to exist with beliefs that are different from her own.

"Well, in a way I guess I do . . . I mean I wouldn't advocate hurting anybody, but if he did bomb the plant then I guess I don't think it was so wrong given what the government was doing in Vietnam at the time."

My mother would have been a great actress. She's very theatrical and she loves an audience. I can imagine how she might spellbind thousands with the way she can gather herself into one small gesture like the lowering of a teacup, fitting it onto its saucer with a certain timing of great dramatic effect. But as her daughter, a witness to these postures a thousand times over, I have learned to steel myself against their manipulative intent.

Now when she does this, the way she does it, and when she says, "Oh, I just can't talk about this anymore . . . it's too upsetting. How could you do this to your father and me?" I know what's upsetting her most is how it will look to her audience to have a daughter who supports a "terrorist", who might even be a terrorist.

It's terrible to laugh, but these distances are somehow suddenly impossible to navigate any other way. I feel a smile, a laugh, creeping up uncontrollably, so fast I have to bite my cheek, hold my breath to keep it hidden.

"You think it's funny?"

"No! Really . . . . I don't."

"Then what are you smiling about?"

"I'm not smiling. Not really. I don't know."

"Honestly I don't know what's gotten into you. Really, sometimes I think I don't even know you anymore."

I'm thinking that she never has known me, that she's always taken up the whole stage, the full spotlight, with no place left for anyone at all. This is when I want to put my fingers in my ears like a five year old, to shut her up, to silence her. But instead, I'm the silenced one.

"Well, just so you know, just for the record," she says, her eyes sharp with disdain, "if you end up in jail, don't expect me to bail you out!"

And just as suddenly as the rogue smile appeared, I now feel my face burning, my eyes filling with tears. I want to run away from her forever for saying that—leave the room, the house—leave her in the middle of her next breath, in the middle of her demand that I account for myself—but not a muscle will move.

Don't cry! That's just what she wants, just what she's been waiting for.

But then she's leaning towards me. She's leaning towards me with her arms open. She's holding me. I'm such an idiot, a fool! This is exactly what she wanted, exactly, and I've let her have it.

"Oh sweetheart. That's my little Baba. Ohhh . . . that's it . . . cry . . . cry."

CHAPTER 23

Once I start to cry, I can't stop. I dig my fingers into my palm, I pinch my thigh to hold it back, to snap out of it, but instead I heave like a bellows and the tears run molten on my cheeks, as if their temperature is a measure of my distress, my rage too.

I hate my mother's arms around me, the way she strokes my hair, the way I worry even now that I'll break her with the weight of my head, the way I can't move away from her.

I let my nose run, my tears soak her lacy shoulder. Lightly, she runs her fingernails through the hair on my brow, tucks the long strands behind my ear. She wants me like this, to be the small sad girl that she needs me to be. I'm just the way I've always been, not changed at all, not strong and sure and certain about everything like she is, because there would be no place for me here if I was like that. This is the only way I can come home. It's another piece of the covenant.

"There . . . there," she coos at me like I'm a baby, like the girl that always wept without an explanation, inconsolable at the dinner table, in the car, in my bed at night. "*My little leaky faucet . . .*" she'd call me, she calls me now and I want to kill her, kill me.

I am not pathetic like that anymore!

But even after I manage to break away, to wash my face in her white marble bathroom sink, to finally leave her to her rest, it's the same. I don't stop crying. I cry just like I'm my younger self again. For two, three, four days I look everywhere for a place that will let me in, some piece of the house, the yard, the daily routines that will recognize me. Even though she's sick, I feel small and mean inside. I'm tired of her being the one in pain, the one whose pain shows the most. But no one would know I felt that way. I continue do all the things I'm supposed to do to convince her that I'm still "good". I bring her meals . . . I sit and talk when she wants me to . . . I let her lean on me to walk to the bathroom . . . and shuffle along with her, up and down the long upstairs hallway for exercise.

The day before I decide to leave, I can't sleep so I'm up at six to have coffee with Dad. He kisses me with his damp cheek, fresh from shaving, the Old Spice smell and Brylcreem. He sits in the same chair at the head of the kitchen table with his New York Times, his Brooks Brothers blue shirt, the water spots from his wet hair still dark on his collar, and this year's birthday bathrobe closed around him to keep his tie clean.

Two eggs, two strips of bacon. His skim milk blue and watery in the tall ship glass. Fifteen, twenty years of mornings like this . . . how can I not belong? But I don't want to belong, to be a fixture in his routine.

Down the road, across the field, my brother sits at his breakfast table, in his Brooks Brothers suit, getting ready to catch the same train. I should be dressed like that, dressed for success, not in sweatpants, a tee shirt. I should wear tortoise shell glasses, not wire rims. I should wear gold jewelry, not beads. If I did all of that would he pay more attention? Would he see me then?

I can tell he wants to read the Business Section but I'm here. And we haven't talked—not about "it". For two nights he's been home late, after supper, so tired . . . *Poor Dad* . . . that was the refrain we grew up with. I don't want to be a burden, but I do too.

"Are you feeling a little better today, honey?" he asks with his worried-for-the-moment brow. My heart cracks a little hair-thin crack, and something leaks out, trickles out—something that wants and wants an insatiable amount. All this tenderness for him I wish would leave me alone.

"Yeah, I'm okay."

"Your mother told me that you and she had a talk . . . . I just want to tell you again that I know you've been trying to do the right thing. You know we both respect you for that. You've put yourself in a very difficult situation."

I'm supposed to say something, but I'm embarrassed by his acknowledgement that I've been trying to be good (their "good" daughter), when in fact I want it to look like I'm smashing everything apart, that I'm not their daughter at all. I want to do both.

"It was smart of you to leave before the trial. Something like that could get dragged out for months . . . years. You're not going back are you?"

"No, I guess not. I'm going to go back to the hospital program in Portland."

"Well that's good. Stick to your work there. Those other people are just going to get you in a lot of trouble."

He puts one whole fried egg in his mouth and holds his left hand up to his chin, palm down, to catch the drips the way he's always done. He's being kind to me. Is it kindness? People say he's kind. They say, "Oh your father is the sweetest guy." What I'm thinking though is that he really wants to read the Business Section, that I'm getting in the way, and that any minute he's going to look at his watch.

The crack widens. The substance inside is heavy with the weight of all he doesn't know about me, about the last six months, will never know about me. But I suck it in, don't move, hold my breath. I'm holding it in, this feeling for him like mercury—

glimmering, vibrant. With the slightest movement it will slip through me, dash onto the floor in hundreds of tiny chaotic drops and everything I've defined as love until now will escape me, under the table and chairs, into the heating vents, the corner dust balls.

He doesn't look at his watch—not yet. Instead he sits back, his mouth a thin legal line, his eyes Brooks Brothers blue like his shirt. He looks at me with a serious no-nonsense expression. I think this is how he must look at his clients, his secretary. It's not a hard look. He's not unkind, never unkind—that's the hope of it.

"One thing I want to say, and I know you're not going to agree with me, but don't you think it's possible they could be using you for your money? Your mother and I are both worried about that."

I wonder again, this time in a bolt of panic, how much he knows about the money—if he's maybe actually seen the bank statements, the last one with the big $40,000 debit. I didn't think he'd have found out already. He wasn't supposed to know yet. I see the statement in its red envelope upstairs in my drawer hidden under my underwear, pages with the long typed list of stocks. After each one it says SOLD in bold, capital letters. Sold. Sold. Sold. Gone. Gone. Gone.

It's my money, right? He gave it to me. But I feel ashamed, guilty, horribly sorry.

He thinks they're using me. When he said that, everything good about each one of them—Roland, RoAnne, Harlan, Jo, the kids, even Muck, poured forth in a torrent of certainty. He's entirely wrong. So far wrong. I don't think for one fucking minute that he's on the right track. I'd never believe that. Never.

"You don't know them."

"I know. I know. You're absolutely right. I don't know them. I'm sure they're well intentioned, but these things get very complicated. I think it would be a big mistake to give them any more money."

When he said that was he thinking I'd given them a few thousand, or does he know about the forty? How would he know? Mrs. Lee could have told him. She probably tells him everything. She calls him up and says, "I just thought you should be aware of the fact that your daughter . . . " But she can't do that, can she? It's not allowed. Of course she can.

He takes a drink of milk, a half a glass in one gulp.

He must not know about the forty thousand or he wouldn't be so calm. But he's always calm. Not calm . . . reserved. I should ask him. I should tell him, but I don't have the courage. Let him bring it up. Let him find out when I'm not around. Maybe that was why Mom said she wouldn't bail me out of jail. I don't blame her. Good. Leave me there. It would all be so much easier.

I didn't want to give it all to some pig lawyer either, but what could I do?

It doesn't mean anything to me, all that money. But to him, it's everything. He'd say he's worked for it for me, to provide for all of us, but I'd say the money is more important than me, bigger than me, and he can't see how it controls him.

"They're not using me. You're wrong about that. Whatever I've given I've given entirely of my own free will because I thought it was the right thing to do." My voice doesn't waver one bit and I'm proud for the moment to be defending my actions in the face of his doubts.

"Well, I can't stop you. I wish I could but I can't. I think you should think about other causes you could support that would make a difference in the world. Look at all the work your mother does! She could help you find some good causes to get involved in. You don't have all that much money you know, when you come right down to it."

There it was again. Just a drop in the bucket, right? Oh please! Don't give me that, or that bullshit about getting Mom to help me sign up for the Junior League.

People say, "Oh you're so much like your father. You take after him." I liked to think so too. But right now he's looking at me like I'm from another planet, like I've landed at his breakfast table asking for directions and he doesn't have a clue which way is home for me. He wants to read the paper and now I've spoiled it. He's out of time. He can't miss his train.

All his movements are precise, timed. He finishes his coffee. Now he's going to look at his watch. He always looks at his watch after he finishes his coffee.

"Just think about it okay? I'm off . . . have to go. See you tonight I hope."

He stands up, pushes the chair back, and puts his napkin on his plate. Now, he'll tap me on the head with the newspaper all rolled up. He'll go brush his teeth, get his briefcase, his hat, his summer overcoat. He'll pull out of the driveway at 7:20 to catch his train.

Goodbye, Dad. He can't show me the way. What does he see when he looks at me? He can't see anyone outside of his world. I'm a ghost, a ghost daughter. He looks right through me.

But before he left for the train, he gave me back my book. It would have made a great movie scene, the two of us standing in the driveway in the early morning smoky light, dwarfed by the brick mansion behind us, the sounds of the gardeners busy with early morning lawnmowers. I'm wearing my purple Fight Back tee shirt with the picture of Ho Chi Minh on the front, and my father's in his gray suit and navy blue silk tie ready to jump into the Chrysler Imperialist (that's what I call it), and then at the last minute remembering the book in his briefcase. Snap, snap go the locks and there, sitting on top of his blue-back legal briefs in defense of Standard Oil or Morgan Guaranty Trust &Co. or one of his other corporate clients is Felix Greene's book, *The Enemy: What Every American Should Know About Imperialism.*

I chose this book for him above all the others because it's shy on rhetoric and packed with irrefutably well-researched facts and statistics, the kind I always forget when I'm trying to make my points with him. He seems to need those kinds of facts, but I've come to see that you can get lost in facts and figures and for me, all I have to do is drive by the country club down the block, take a look around at its Kelly-green grass tennis courts being rolled by the black help, at its golf course fairways without a dandelion in sight because of all the poisons they "fertilize" with, take a look at the yearly membership fee and requirements (no Jews, no blacks allowed), and that's the whole story in a nutshell, in a bombshell—as irrefutable a description of "the enemy" as anyone could ever need.

"This was very interesting sweetheart," he says and gives my shoulder a little squeeze and a look that's sincere but rushed, not exactly inviting a discourse about its contents, what with that train waiting.

Very interesting? I want to ask him all the big questions all over again, about how he can live with himself after he's read a book like this. I want to turn to the chapter on Farm Workers, the part where they detail the effects of the pesticides we dump on them, how their fingernails fall off and they can't breathe, and the kids who work in the fields vomit all the time and have diarrhea even though there's no running water or bathrooms where they live. Did you read that part? Is that an acceptable cost of free enterprise?

Or how about the *Foreign Aid Fraud* chapter that takes apart your holy Marshall Plan and shows it for what it was—not a beneficent outpouring to help the war ravaged poor and destitute rebuild their countries, but a shrewd scheme to dominate the European economy and put huge profits soundly in the pockets of U.S. corporate investors. How about that chapter?

But of course, standing there, taking the book from his outstretched hand, I'm speechless—empty of any response at all except for a wave of apology for all the trouble I've caused him. When he hugs me, I hug him back without an angry bone in my body, just more hot tears I can't quite manage to keep inside, so I turn away, reach down to pull a rogue weed from the driveway while he gets in his car.

"Maybe we'll get a chance to talk about it some more tonight, okay?" he says through the rolled-down window. He blows me a kiss and then he's gone.

CHAPTER 24

———

I wasn't sad to leave home. I was relieved. The next morning, once I pulled out of the driveway, my tears stopped—the floodgates clanked shut. On the way past the country club, past the early morning tennis players and golfers, I even floored it for a few moments, leaving a little smoky patch on their racist asses. It was easier to be on my own anyway, to get away from my parents' blinded material existence. They couldn't say I hadn't tried to help them understand why I was on this path, but it was clear they had too much to lose to really listen; their whole existence driven by their need to keep pace—cogs in the wheel of the capitalist machine. It was sad really that they couldn't see it at all, what prisoners they were, even at the top of the ladder. They'd never give it up, even half of what they had, even if it meant saving the fingernails on all the farm workers in California. I was glad I was going back to Portland, to a city where poor people lived, where I had friends who were trying to live accountable lives.

But then once I was out of town and heading north on the thruway I couldn't deny that my feelings were mixed about returning there. I couldn't wait to smell the salt air, even the paper mills, to be entirely on my own again, but other feelings lurked around the edges of my excitement. There was a constant steady stream of jumbled thoughts and images to contend with—of the bookstore and Jo, of RoAnne and Vinny and the others, and then, where would I live and what would I do when I got there? And of course, what would I do when and if Roland contacted me? I kept the music loud and drove fast to keep that roulette wheel turning, turning, to avoid coming to rest on any particular thought that might tip the scale of my ambivalence entirely in a dark direction.

My grandmother, Mammy, had invited me to stay with her while I looked for an apartment, but I was uncertain what my reception would be, given the possibility of her deep misgivings about my sudden departure last spring—how it might have been an embarrassment for her to try to explain to her friends, particularly Dr. Barker, the head of surgery at the hospital who had helped to place me in the operating room program. For all her kindness and generosity, I knew that Mammy was shrewd and fierce in her own way, a she-lion ready to flay anyone who might threaten her son's well-being or reputation.

And when I finally did pull over the hump on the last shadowy curve of her driveway, when I was hit with the familiar elixir of ocean air and pine trees, I wasn't thinking about how good it was to be back there the way I usually did. I was thinking instead that Roland could be watching me, could be staking out her home to see if I was there. Truth be told, since I'd hit the outskirts of Portland, I'd been looking for him everywhere, feeling his presence grow larger by the mile along with the push and pull of my feelings for him.

"You made it!" She hugs me long and hard, rocks me back and forth in her brown old-lady pumps, her summer wool skirt and jacket, her blond-rinsed hair just the same as always. Her cheeks are the same soft, the same smell of carnations. The air feels soft too and sweetly humid and for a moment I want to stay in her arms, to delay the inevitable barrage of questions I'm sure she has in line for me.

She holds me at arms length and says, "Let's have a look at you."

I wonder what she sees, how much she knows, what my parent's have told her about where I've been since she's seen me last. Her pale blue eyes dart about and I think I detect a false quality to her characteristic Mammy smile, a kind of thinly veiled displeasure. But then she pats my hand, gives it a little squeeze and says, "Isn't this wonderful?"

It's late afternoon and she bustles me through the house to the little guest cottage off the back where I'll stay, through rooms bathed in the thin September sun, everything fixed and neatly waiting, every chair and picture and lamp holding its breath in readiness for the next visitor. It's as if there are family ghosts milling around everywhere—my deceased grandfather at the bar fixing his mid-day martini, my aunts and uncles talking together on the patio, all of my cousins running around, each one looking for the next one older to tag along with.

"Now you go relax dear. The pool's all ready for you if you'd like a swim. That's a terrible drive! You must be exhausted."

But I'm not tired at all, just humming with the engine sounds still in my head and the edginess of feeling all these family spirits around me, particularly being assigned to the cottage where my parents usually stay. It's a privilege for any of us "kids" to stay here, in either one of the twin sleigh beds with their puffy floral quilts and cream white monogrammed sheets as soft as silk.

When Mammy leaves I sit on one of the beds and then lay back onto the two queen-size down pillows that exhale like a slow breath. I let myself go until I'm entirely cradled by their soft forgiving warmth in a nest around me.

But the room is too quiet and I have to sit up. In front of me, on the wall, there's a framed embroidered family crest—a spread-winged eagle with his head turned to the side to exaggerate the profile of his meat-shredding raptor beak. A perfect emblem of my heritage—imperious, ruthless predator that he is, all stitched in gold thread. Roland would love that.

When we talk over dinner, Mammy doesn't ask where I've been or why I left so suddenly. Certainly my parents have told her something. Instead, she starts right in with her plans to help me fix everything—to restore it all to the way it was before, only six months before—surely not that much could have changed since then. I tell her please not to bother. I tell her *really*, she doesn't need to help me any more than she already has, and anyway, I have some leads on apartments.

"We'll get you settled in no time, don't you worry dear." She pats my hand and then rings the turtle bell for dinner.

Over the next few days of being there I found that the voice of the revolutionary in me had grown even louder in the few months since my last visit. When I tallied things up it seemed like everything around me there was excessive, even the view from the plate glass living-room window that took in the huge sparkling bay, the dock, the seaweed-covered beach that was mine to walk alone. Excessive. Private. Should be shared and I couldn't find the feeling of home there that I'd had in the past. Now it had that air of silence, like my parent's home, the kind that belonged to someone else—where I was an intruder slinking around.

On my way into Portland from the rural suburb where Mammy lived, driving that new road where the Death Squad police were going to dispose of the bodies they'd planned to murder, I felt again that rush of hot disgust for the system that would so quickly, so blithely dismiss such calculated evil and lawlessness committed by the supposed protectors of those very laws. It seemed incredible, *impossible* that it could be so, and yet I'd read it myself—a small article in the back of the local paper that RoAnne had sent us while we were in Denver. The charges had been all but dropped—two of the policemen dismissed, the other two suspended for a few months. And it was that judge, Judge Albright, the friend of my family, who'd presided.

These thoughts put me right back into the other Portland I'd come to know as if I'd never left—the bookstore, the attack, guns, Muck, all of it, and with those memories more anger bubbled up—hot and sudden and clean with no wavering or qualifying thoughts to muddy that water, and for a perfect moment I knew I had the courage to fight back. I'd had my doubts about leaving Jo in Denver—had I bailed too soon? Had I let her down as a comrade? But I hadn't left Jo out of fear—I'd left Denver to be of more use in the struggle. My work was finished there, I felt sure of it, but here there was the unanswered question of just how deeply I could truly live my commitment to the revolutionary path. After all, what had I done to prove to myself that I had "what it took", that kind of courage like other Brothers and Sisters, some mythical, some real—those heroes and heroines that had set the bar high, very high, but perhaps within reach.

As the weeks trickled by, my isolation became like a bubble that protected me from finally having to choose my path, and yet I knew that my time was running out. I was certain they would know by now that I was back in town, and I knew in my bones that some day soon I would hear from them. What would I say if they contacted me? The question follows me everywhere—up and down the streets, in and out of the old buildings where I go looking for a new apartment. If I had speed—the diet pills I'd sometimes take in college, I'd take them now. I'd take them for that feeling that everything you did seemed entirely right, flying straight like the crow flies through a clear sky to your destination and you were way up high looking down so none of the detours, none of the dead ends got in the way.

Percoset. Valium. That's all I can find when I shuffle through my grandmother's medicine cabinet. In Denver, we drank soda, sometimes a few beers, never high or drunk ever because readiness is everything and what would you do if the FBI came barreling into your living room and you were all fucked up? Besides, it's not good revolutionary practice. But now I don't even think twice about stealing pills from her bathroom cabinet one afternoon after apartment hunting. I seek them out like I've been stealing pills forever, checking out the labels in the shortest possible time, screening the silence for footsteps on a carpet coming down the hall to her room. And even though there's nothing like speed to be found, I like the way these others take the nagging questions away for a few hours, the way I float through the day and then crash into sleep instead of lying awake listening to the late summer crickets turn off and on, off and on, hour after hour.

The next day, and the day after that, I steal a few more.

In my mind I see Roland everywhere I go—crossing the street, in phone booths, behind me, in front of me. I see the tails of his long black leather coat disappear around the corner. I see him walking, his whole demeanor of readiness, moving like there was no ground beneath him, moving with that unflinching determination to do the right thing for the people, to *serve the people*. But I also see his expression, the one of distance and disdain for me when we'd said goodbye at the bus station.

When I'm in prison you can send me oranges.

If he calls, if they call, I'm going to prove to them all that my commitment is real—not just a passing fancy, a whim. Just because I left Denver doesn't mean I don't care anymore, that I'm not committed. I want a chance to prove that, and at the same time I wish I'd never see any of them again.

* * *

They took me back into the hospital program and I was grateful to be inside that busy hive again, hearing the operator announcing doctors' names and codes and directives over the PA system. I craved the simplicity of its order and purpose: to help sick people. As clear as that. I was glad I'd found an apartment that was close by, within walking distance—one bedroom, a kitchen and a small living room on the second floor of a building much like my first place—the same shiny wood floors and old steam radiators, but smaller and darker. I kept it sparse—a mattress on the floor, a table and two chairs, a couch and my stereo. One window looked out at the brown brick walls of the hospital at the end of the street—I was that close.

I was also close, only a few blocks, from the bookstore—or from where the bookstore had been before. Down to the corner, turn right on Main Street and walk two blocks north. That's where it had been, but it was gone now. Roland had told me it wouldn't be there, that RoAnne had closed it a little while after I'd left for Denver. The storefront was the same, but the red star sign was gone and the windows were filled with small appliances—toasters and digital clocks and electric can-openers—another victory for the forces of repression.

After work, I have a routine. At night I steam vegetables, eat bread and butter, put away a half bottle of wine while I listen to all the music that Roland introduced me to—John Coltrane, Billie Holiday, Tom Paxton, Muddy Waters. All of it dark and heart-splitting in ways that force me to taste how alive and alone I am. Sometimes though, even with the music and the wine, my four walls close in on me and I should go out but I can't even get as far as putting a coat on. Where would I go anyway, and who would I go with? I save the heavy Muddy Waters blues for last when the wine has kicked in and then I turn it up loud to drown out any thoughts of being with Roland—of making love with him before it got too complicated to call it love at all.

Will it be a robbery or a bombing that they'll ask me to help them with? One or the other, I'm sure of it. If they contact me . . . when they contact me . . . all of it coming towards me again like a wave gathering far out in the ocean.

What if they don't call? What if they can't find me?

I go back and forth, wanting, not wanting, waiting. There's this feeling I carry around with me all the time, a slight tremor inside, a constant dread. I want to get away from it, but in its occasional lull I feel hollow again, like the most essentially alive part of me is missing. What if they leave me out and I'm never called to task again, never given the chance to commit to anything as fiercely meaningful and purposeful ever again? And still, when the phone rings, I pray it's not them.

Chapter 25

—•—

What I don't like my days off. Another one stretches endlessly in front of me, every minute ticks through me and I look at the clock and only ten minutes have passed. Two cups of coffee. Two cigarettes I didn't really want anyway. Over and over the same Joan Armatrading song . . . *If I could feel the sun on my eyes or the rain on my face* . . . It's a love song, but I don't feel love. I don't feel anything but the tightness of waiting in my stomach.

I drive down to a beach far out of town where the waves come up on a shoreline covered with loose stones. Together, they make a kind of music that washes things clean inside me, but today the sounds of the backwash could be footsteps behind me, and I feel stupidly nervous looking over my shoulder for the ghosts of strange men who I feel certain are following me.

And then I'm back in my room, the sun on the bed, its empty light. The book open on the pillow. More deep afternoon silence. Before the phone rings, the four walls are my prison, but after, I want to lock the doors and throw away the key.

"Do you know who this is?"

Now the sun is too bright . . . leaves me no place to hide.

I'm not turning back. I am not wishing it wasn't his voice on the phone. I'm glad. This is my chance.

"*We want to know if you'd like to help us out . . .* "

Here it is again, that crossroad, the point between. The time before and the time after. The time before the rape and the time after. The time before Roland and after. Before the guns, after the guns.

These things change you.

Already I know that I won't hang up, I can't hang up. There's no turning back. This is the beginning of what comes next.

"When do you want to get together?"

"The sooner the better. How about later this afternoon?"

"Okay. Where?"

"Meet me in the Holiday Inn in town. Look for me in the bar, in one of the booths. I'll be there by five."

Devon's the one who called. Not Roland. I think Roland must have told him to call so I wouldn't feel pressured or in any way obligated to him, but he might as well have been standing there in front of me, reminding me of the many ways I could fail them, fail myself, fail every oppressed person in the world.

"Five o'clock. I'll be there."

Devon was the handsome one, more than Roland or Harlan or any of the others. It was hard for me to ignore, this time even more than before, maybe because we were alone now, close together, face-to-face in the bar booth and the light was just dim enough. I took in all of his hardened street strength, the slow heavy hand that carried the cigarette to his mouth and away back to the ashtray, sultry slow, how his blue eyes had just enough of a dark shadow to them to make me look away.

"So, we're planning a job and we want to know if you're still interested in helping us out."

I thought maybe he meant money but I wasn't sure. "A job" wasn't clear enough, could be anything. But then, was there anything I would say 'no' to?

"What kind of job? Who's 'we'?"

He leaned forward slightly, got low over the table, without exaggerating any move at all. Even the look over his shoulder for potential eavesdroppers was smooth, almost unnoticeable. "We have a bank we're ready to hit, but we need another driver, either for the second getaway car or for the one that drives us to the job. Right now it's just me, Roland, Sarah and Vinny."

He was so close, his face a foot away, his lips smooth and naked beneath the edge of his mustache. A bank robbery, not a bombing—I was relieved about that. And they didn't want money. That was oddly part of the relief too—that I wasn't just a dollar sign. They trusted me enough now to ask me to help them with something like this.

"What do you think you're ready for?" He sat back and his voice was low and sweet, curling around each word like smoke.

I was glad I'd been offered at least that much of a choice—the first or the second car. I was glad they hadn't asked me to go into the bank with them. I wasn't ready for that, even though I might have implied at times that I was, almost, ready, I was not. It was one thing to shoot a gun at a target in the woods where everything was quiet and still, where you could hear woodpeckers after the sounds of the ricochet faded. But going into a bank, even if you had no intention of shooting . . . .they always swore they didn't want to hurt anyone, but things go wrong. Then what? But then I was a soldier, right? A guerilla fighter in training . . . I couldn't be a coward.

"I guess I'd rather drive the second car this time."

"Good . . . . that'd be great. That'd help us out a lot." He took another long drag off his cigarette and held my gaze through it. I looked away first. I couldn't help it. There was something so hungry about his look. Or was that me? It wasn't like Roland's gaze that was always a little cold and distant. It wasn't like Harlan's either with his superior, all-knowing edge.

"Do you think you can get your hands on a different car? Just in case they've been following you . . . they probably know your car by now."

My grandmother's car could work. She'd always said I could borrow it anytime. It was a plain kind of car, the kind old people drive . . . nothing fancy except for the vanity plates with her initials on them, but they wouldn't be looking for those. That car could work.

"Yeah . . . I think I can get hold of one."

"Good. Sarah'll drive the first car then."

Sarah. I hardly knew Sarah hardly at all. I knew her smile with her white teeth and perfectly smooth rosebud cheeks and her eyes that made half-moons when she laughed, a high girlish laugh. If she hadn't had the baby on her back when I'd met her I would have thought she was about fourteen. But she knew more than me. She must. I didn't know anything about this. But I was still glad she wasn't one of the ones going into the bank. Even though I knew we were always trying to be non-sexist about everything, I just had the feeling the men knew more. It was different for them. They'd had more experience. When Devon said to me *We've been casing the place every day and it should be really smooth . . . an easy job*, I believed him. He inspired confidence, like he was some kind of an expert. And I trusted Roland to be thorough, careful. I trusted Roland the most—but even he had gotten caught. Things could go wrong. I wouldn't think about that. Not right now anyway.

Devon told me the rest of how it would work. Basically, I wouldn't have to do much except wait for them at the safe house, and when they came back, I'd drive all of them to Boston and then Roland and I would continue on down to New York. I'd spend the night there, but then come back the next day. When Devon said this he smiled at me like it was no secret who I'd be spending the night with. I could feel the heat run up my neck and face and I wasn't sure if it was him or Roland that I wanted to be with.

They'd planned to do the job next Friday, late in the afternoon. I wouldn't even have to call in sick at work. I'd only have to wait for five days until then.

It would all go as planned. It would be an easy job, a smooth job. And with the money they'd get we'd be able to fund worthy grassroots causes. We would give the money back to the people who deserved it. We'd be like Robin Hood's Merry Men, robbing the rich and giving money back to the poor. It didn't sound so bad, like such a bad thing to do. It sounded necessary, the work that revolutionaries had to do. It sounded like we were good to our word, committed, worthy. Remember Che, Fred Hampton, George Jackson, Rosa Parks, Harriet Tubman . . . and all the others everywhere and since the dawn of civilization who'd given their lives to actualizing a world of freedom and equality for all people.

But I was glad Sarah would be staying in the car.

*   *   *

I'm waiting, a waiting machine. At the hospital, in my apartment, walking the streets. A machine that runs all day and night like a ticker-tape and never once stops hitting the same keys over and over: Friday at 4pm, 15 Bradford Street, Augusta, upstairs apartment. The bank closes at five. Between four and five I'll wait there for them in the apartment. For an hour. An hour. I'll watch the clock. I'll read a book. It won't be long.

If there's blood they think I'll know what to do with it. They think that just because I work in an operating room that I'll know how to fix a gunshot wound, that I'll be like the doctor taking the bullet out of Humphrey Bogart in Casablanca, only they're wrong. I wouldn't know what to do. They don't know how much blood there is in a person, how red it is . . . bright red and alive when it hits the air, when it first comes rushing out, how sometimes there's no stopping it, the way it gushes around the surgeons' gloved hands and the sponges and clamps and sutures, gurgling like a spring stream, overflowing a burst dam. They don't know about that.

I'll have my grandmother's car. I told her mine would be in the shop. As easy as that, I lied, right into her trusting, unsuspecting Mammy smile.

"Of course dear, you keep it as long as you want."

If she had two cars she'd lend them both to me. If I asked her for a hundred dollars for a toothbrush, she'd give it to me. That's when it's hard for me to see her as the enemy, an enemy of the people, the way I'm supposed to. I've decided there's no harm in using her car—a little bit of payback for the people after decades of pressing buzzers for servants, having the help sleep in the back room with the narrow day bed, the linoleum floor and hooked throw rug, when every morning she puts her bare feet down on her cushiony wool carpet and slips on a silk dressing gown. Fix this. Buy that. Go there. There's no harm in it, in using the car. Just the lie. There's harm in the lie but it's what I have to do.

The waiting time creeps along—Monday, Tuesday, Wednesday.

On Thursday I steal some morphine from the operating room just in case. In case of what? In case of gunshot wounds? That was part of it. The little one-inch glass bottles with bright orange caps like candies. Extra bottles, left over, always just lying there on the anesthesia table after the surgery. Everyone's busy cleaning up— their backs are turned. They're going to throw them away anyway. Just slip a few in your pocket. One milliliter, five milligrams in a bottle. Ten vials will do it if I have to. If I can't handle it. If I have to get away, disappear, be gone from all of it. Ten would put me to sleep, would put me out . . . .whisk me away poof like smoke. A syringe, a number twenty-two needle, a tourniquet. I steal those too, just in case.

On Friday, I'm at 15 Bradford Street at 4pm exactly. It's twilight, the sky pumpkin orange behind the many black tree branches, behind kids getting off the school bus on this side-street and neighbors turning lights on. Me climbing the outside stairs to number 24 like I've lived there forever, feeling nothing at all, nothing except the one breath I lose when Roland opens the door and nods to me. A half smile, a welcoming half-smile that puts our last hard parting behind us. There's no time anyway for more than that.

"Come in."

I don't have to do anything but watch. A witness to the packing of the sports bag—ski masks, three guns, a bag, gloves. Surgical gloves I've given them. I have to be there to send them on their way, to wish them well. To wish them good luck.

"Hope you get a lot of money." Did I say something as dumb as that?

"We'll be back at 5:00."

And if you don't come back? There was no space for those thoughts. In all the emptiness of those rooms, the clock-ticking silence after they've left, there was no space at all for any thoughts like that.

Do your part of the job well. Be where you say you'll be and don't fuck up. If they don't come back by 5:30, you know what you're supposed to do. Get in your car and drive home.

The hour passes, and then their footsteps are running up the stairs outside, a stampede of sound and all this commotion rushes into my waiting silence. I'm trying to suss out right away from the way they're moving, from whatever I can see on their faces that are all in a blur of movement, I'm trying to figure out what happened without saying a word. I don't want to assume that they'll tell me anything, or that I have the right to know. Maybe I don't want to know, and if I don't know then I can keep everything at a distance, like they're the actors and I'm the audience. If I don't ask then I won't find out if something went wrong.

Roland walks towards me, hands me a cotton drawstring sack, just like the one I took to sleep-away camp. "Now you're the one holding the bag," he says and he's smiling.

It must have gone okay for him to kid around.

"You and Sarah count it up, divide it in half, okay?"

It wasn't that heavy, not like I'd thought it would be.

So we dump the money in a big paper pile on the bed in the back room and begin to stack it by denominations. Sarah stacks. I count. Hundreds of twenties. Hundreds of tens and fives and ones. A smaller pile of fifties. A few one hundreds looking out of place at the end of the bed. All of it play money, like Monopoly money, only green and bigger and undeniably real except it has to be pretend because how else could I figure that I'd be there with this woman, this girl in braids laughing, both of us laughing under our breath so no one could hear us, with the craziness of being part of this, being part of this script, the movie that had us counting money into piles from a bank robbery.

Laughing is better than talking anyway because if I ask her anything she might tell me something I don't want to know, like if any guns had been fired, or if there'd been any kind of hitch or problem at all. But in the first concentrated lull, when it's quiet enough to hear the kids on the street calling out to one another, then I can't help myself. I can't not ask about it, because in some recess of the dream I'm in I have to know at least if anyone has been hurt.

"So everything went okay?"

"Totally cool. God, if they're all that easy we could get a ton of money for the revolution. How much do we have there so far?"

"About six thousand and counting. I think there'll be about

eight's my guess. Anybody fire any shots?" I slip it in, almost hoping she won't notice or won't hear me at all.

"No. No shots . . . Wow . . . eight grand!" She blows a low whistle, but I'm not sure if that's a lot or a little, if eight thousand was good or bad. It didn't seem like that much to me given what was at stake. Not enough to rent an apartment and buy food for more than a few months, and not even that long if there were other expenses. Not enough to give away all the extra to poor and working people and grassroots organizations like I thought we were going to do. But I made it good in my mind. I made it just the right amount so I wouldn't have to think about it one way or the other. I had to count, that was all. Count and then put each pile of bills into a shoebox and wrap it with birthday paper and ribbon and write the card in my own handwriting: *For Ellen from Bill. Love you honey. Happy Birthday.* And then we had to leave and I had to drive them out of there.

CHAPTER 26

Sarah and Devon got in the back seat. Roland slid next to me in the front.

"Do you know where you're going?" Our eyes met in a quick glance and he put his hand for a moment on my shoulder. It was supposed to be re-assuring, a gesture of camaraderie, of calm. Be cool. But to me that touch shot an electric bolt down my spine with shockwaves to my stomach and heart.

"Not really . . . I don't know Augusta that well."

"Take a left at the end of the street. There's no rush. Take it slow. No speeding tickets, okay?"

He squeezed my shoulder in a friendly way, maybe a friendly reminder of the nightmare stop on the road in Kansas. I hadn't expected him to be like this, nice like this, and the shockwaves from his touch continued to pulse.

Just do your job and don't fuck up.

I kept checking the rearview mirror like I was supposed to and followed Roland's directions and it was all going okay . . . more or less a Sunday drive, and once, when I glanced over my shoulder to change lanes, Devon caught my eye and winked. You're doing fine.

It was almost fully dark and the lights coming at me seemed brighter than usual, every one a high beam flashing towards me and the reds and yellows and greens of the stoplights inseparable from the flashing neon street-signs of the shops and taverns lining the main street. I wondered why we were headed into town instead of away from it, but we were moving along okay, until we came to a rise where the road went up a small incline and the traffic suddenly slowed, and then practically stopped altogether as it inched towards the streetlight that marked the top of the hill.

"What the hell . . . is this a roadblock? Can you see up ahead at all?" Now Devon was suddenly the jumpy one.

"It's nothing. It's rush hour. I think we forgot about rush hour." In spite of the directive clip in his voice, I thought Roland sounded like he was re-assuring himself as much as Devon, and I was sure we were all imagining the same trap that might be waiting for us on the other side of the hill. We hadn't heard any sirens, but they could be there, the cops, checking cars, looking for us, some missed detail, some unknown signature left behind. I couldn't imagine it, what I would do or say or what might happen if it was a trap. What I focused on was getting to the light without rear-ending the car in front of me and trying to glean the expression on Roland's face without directly looking at him.

"We should get around this." Devon's voice had an urgency I didn't like but Roland said, "No. There's no telling what the other roads are like. We decided together that this was the best route, remember? We're going to stick to our plan."

Devon kept quiet then but I knew he was tense, pissed off about it because in the rear-view mirror his eyes were sharp slits and two minutes later when we'd missed the green light for the third time I heard his "Fucking A . . . " under his breath.

I was glad in a way we were stuck in traffic, traffic being so normal and everyday instead of having to maneuver some high speed chase with me at the wheel, or having some accidental confrontation with the cops like I'd heard stories about with other robberies, stories that spread through the underground about things getting out of control and people shooting when they weren't supposed to and innocent people getting shot, or "pigs" getting shot and then the whole world was after you.

Still, the longer we were stuck there, the more I could feel the tension build in the car and I wondered how long Devon was going to last without flipping out. For all his usual calm demeanor and quiet voice, I'd heard about his temper. The way he and Jo joked about who was more dangerous once you got them going, herself or her brother, and Roland said he wouldn't want to be on the other side of a fight with either of them. If Roland said that it must be bad.

And then I heard the car door open, the rear door on Devon's side, and I thought for a moment that they'd found us, the cops in plain clothes coming up in our blind spot and nailing us, but it was Devon jumping out, standing on the side of the car to see if he could see over the hill ahead.

"Get back in the fucking car!" Roland had to say it twice without raising his voice too loud and he sounded like he was about to jump out and grab him, maybe shoot him himself, but Devon came back on his own. I made the car lurch then, jumping to fill up the space that had opened up in front of our car and Roland hissed, "Be cool. Would you all be cool? We're going to be out of this in a minute."

"Yeah well maybe, but maybe we're just going into it deeper," Devon spat back, and what I thought I saw in the rearview mirror then was Devon reaching deep inside his jacket and pulling out a gun . . . a big gun that glinted just enough in the surrounding light.

Roland saw it too, had turned around in his seat watching him." Put the gun away. No guns . . . that's what we agreed."

"You want to go into a trap with our thumbs up our asses?"

"Put it away. You're going to fuck everything up." And Sarah said the same thing to him, only she was pleading with him and Roland was ordering him and I didn't dare say anything for fear I'd tip the balance in the wrong way.

But he put it away and that seemed to put an end to it because then it was our turn to go over the hill, through the light and everything started to move again past the traffic cop who waved us around a stalled car and didn't even look at us as we passed close enough to touch him.

Straight ahead a few minutes later Roland told me to pull over into a mini-mall parking area and Devon and Sarah got out without a word and disappeared into the shadows at the far end of the parking lot.

"You can go now. It's okay. You don't have to wait for them."

"I thought we were giving them a ride to Boston."

"Plans change."

The two of us drove in silence then, except for his directions, but his voice had lost it's edge, sounding like a dull knife now instead of a sharp one, and I felt like he was relieved to have Devon out of the car and maybe even glad to have me there with him. I was trying to pay attention to everything around me, outside the car, but now that we were alone and the crisis with Devon was over, I was mostly aware of his proximity to me, and that in spite of the circumstances, I still felt my heart pounding over that. I couldn't forget that our last real conversation had been the one in Denver about the money, and that had left an imprint of aversion to him, to his judgments of me at least, that lay beside my desire for the touch I knew would absolve me. I wondered with some edge of bitterness if I'd managed to redeem myself in his esteem by helping out with this job. I wondered if I even wanted to be lovers again, to re-open myself to his scorn. What exactly did I want from him? No more shame. Forgiveness for my spoiled misguided errors, my counter-revolutionary mistakes, though I hoped I would stop myself from going belly up to him for that. Forgiveness seemed to be something I'd need to give myself, not get from him. And in spite of my resistance, he was still Roland, and that complex mysteriously intense desire for him had not vanished. On the contrary, it burned.

But he was tense, of course, and not because of me. He kept turning around to look behind us, and then trying to check out the people in all the cars that passed without looking too suspicious, without staring. In a way, I let him do all the worrying about that because I just couldn't focus on what would happen if we got stopped, or that we were driving away from the scene of a crime. Already it seemed like a long long time ago that we'd been at the apartment counting the money and I might not have believed it at all except that the box was there, on the back seat, all wrapped up with my hand-writing on the card.

When we got onto the turnpike without any trouble at all he lay his head back on the seat for a minute with a big exhale. "We should be okay now, just keep up the good driving." He put his hand on my knee and I caught the edge of a smile on his face.

His hand felt warm, even familiar, and solid where it lay and some of my fears of his former accusations began to subside. I'd forget, if he would, whatever had come between us. I'd forget, if he would, who I was—the one who had her own stash of thousands in another bank. Could we come together without asking why I'd let them risk their lives for the meager contents in the wrapped box, those hidden stacks of worn out ten's and twenties, when I could so easily have put the same amount there myself, could have walked into just about any bank and demanded crispy new bills, as big as they made them, and in moments they'd be delivered? Could we forget about that? But he wasn't asking me to go there. His hand was reaching out to me, and the job was done. I'd helped them with the work that guerilla fighters do, that they would have to do if there was no one around to fund them.

"It's good to see you." I reached over and rubbed his thigh.

"I was thinking that we deserve a little fun after such a hard day at the office. What do you think?"

I was ready for that. Everything that was bad about the idea of playing when we shouldn't, about laughing instead of seriously considering the consequences of what we'd just done . . . it was suddenly exactly where I wanted to be. There was still adrenalin pumping through me, and now that the immediate danger of being caught was over, I was high on relief, ready to take a head-long fall into the next scene of this unlikely script. We were the good outlaws, the Sundance Kid and Etta celebrating in Bolivia. "Hey," I said, "twist my arm."

He had a plan. He had a place already in mind, already picked out, and it wasn't some cheap bare mattress place on the Lower East Side like I'd expected, but the Chelsea Hotel, that icon of hip and groove with old chandeliers in the lobby and pictures of famous actors and musicians lining the walls of the hallways. It wasn't fancy, just exotic in a worn-out way. Just the sort of place that might house two good bank robbers for the night.

Roland named all the musicians in the lobby portraits with his arm around my waist, his lips on my ear. Louis Armstrong, Miles Davis, Etta James, Billie Holiday, John Coltrane—all of their dark beautifully travel-worn faces like his own in a way, the one I was high on loving again for one more night.

Our bedroom was painted in a deep rose color with heavy old gold-trimmed brocade drapes and slightly chipped stained-glass lamps. The bed had an ornate headboard, a chenille bedspread and layers of over-sized pillows. The instant the door locked behind us, Roland produced a bottle of Jack Daniels, and we passed it back and forth while we pulled at each other's clothes, laughing, finding hot skin and then the bed, kissing and pressing into all the weight we could crush against each other.

"Wait a minute." He paused, sitting up. "I've gotta do something first."

He pulled me up off the bed and reached for the box, pulling the wrapping paper off, pulling the bedspread down, the sheets apart, and then he shook the money all up and down the bed, spreading the bills like so many rose petals . . . for him, the spoils, the sweetness of his accomplishment, of his victory, to make love on, with me a little self-conscious under the spotlights, the camera crew, but never mind the cliché—I pushed all of that aside, to follow him into that sweet place where the money was ambrosia, was the forbidden elixir, rolling around on it, laughing about it sticking to all kinds of body parts, being swept away towards the same loud climax.

But another part of me lingered, wasn't on the bed at all, was sitting over on the chair, curled up in the chair, watching the whole thing and drinking big swigs of bourbon from the bottle, drinking to feel the burn in my stomach as much as the high, drinking to blur the reality of the money beneath us, the darkness of its origins and my uncertainties about the revolutionary coda that had driven us to steal it. And alongside all of that were the tendrils of an ugly superstition that maybe I was just a prop, an essential prop in this scene he'd created, and that whatever type of love I'd imagined between us was just part of my own silly construction, part of some story I told myself. I didn't know. With so much unspoken between us, I couldn't be sure, and that thought seemed as sullied as the money I pushed away, onto the floor, before I fell asleep.

In the morning, I woke before him—part of me wanting to reach out to him, but my stronger impulse was to steal away to the shower where I could wash off the money dirt, and along with it maybe some of last night's uncertainty about my purpose there. I showered, and when I came out, the money was all put away and Roland was sitting on the edge of the bed, his jeans on, but his chest still beautifully bare and his expression remote once again. I dried myself and pulled on my clothes feeling shy under his gaze, unable to read his thoughts.

I was buttoning my shirt when he said, "I bet you don't realize how much I think about you."

His voice had this tone, this soft stroke, and I didn't know what to say. It startled me to hear him sound like that, to hear he might care for me more than I'd imagined. I must have been wrong then, thinking that I'd been only a necessary fixture in the scene from the night before. But with Roland, the signposts that directed me to his true feelings were small and far between, almost illegibly worn. But certainly I was no better master of that, always waiting for his approval before I moved towards him, assuming he could read my mind and my heart. It seemed that we kept missing those signposts with one another, taking a wrong turn and looping back to cross the other's path, but always a few moments too late to intersect.

I thought how the room would look after we'd both left—the bed unmade, the curtains drawn, with not a single remnant of our presence. That's how it seemed it would have to be between us with this secret life, this work of being in the underground— leaving, always leaving with not a trace left behind. And at that moment, it was suddenly and certainly too hard to love him like that, our connection too laden with difference and distance and what was left unsaid. And so my heart closed to wanting it, to wanting him. I felt it close, a movement inside me that I could almost trace in it's imperceptible but unstoppable shift.

"No, I guess you're right," I said, "I don't."

There was nothing in my voice that would reassure him. I could hear the finality in the tone of it, a cold closure I hadn't predicted and had no way of knowing then if it would last. Of course he didn't pry or pull or dig any deeper into my feelings, and nothing more was said about it as we gathered our things, and Roland tied the money up in the box, put it in his knapsack and we left.

We kept to our plan. Parting on the street, we hugged briefly at the subway entrance and then he was gone, no trace, and I drove back to Portland.

CHAPTER 27

I keep the morphine bottles from the hospital hidden in a sock in the back of my top bureau drawer. I have eight. It's enough, and until now I've liked just knowing they're there, but now I have to get rid of them. News of the bank robbery is everywhere—on the radio, in the newspapers, and at the hospital everyone's talking about it. It was the first thing I saw when I opened the lobby door of my apartment building when I got back from New York. The front page of the paper from the previous day, left there on the foyer table like a message for me. It wasn't my paper, but I had to take it, the very act of stealing it like an admission of guilt to whoever was watching. No one was watching, but that's when it began, after that, the feeling of being watched everywhere I went. FBI eyes casing my apartment building, following me to work, staring in at me through the windows in my bedroom.

Police say they are looking for four suspects and possibly a fifth in yesterday's bank robbery in Augusta, Maine.

And possibly a fifth . . .

Why? Why any more than four? Even an eyewitness would

only have counted four—three in the bank, one in the car—four. *A total of four. And possibly a fifth.*

It said it again the next day, and the day after.

Police still report that they have no certain leads on the identities of the four, possibly five, suspects involved in last Thursday's bank robbery in Augusta, Maine . . .

No certain leads could mean they have some uncertain leads. Any leads at all could bring them knocking on my door. *We have a warrant for your arrest . . .* or . . . *We have a search warrant . . .*

When I thought about the search warrant, I thought about the morphine. If they couldn't tie me to the bank robbery, they'd get me on stolen narcotics and that might be worse. It seemed worse, in a way, the more direct crime. My hand that lifted them off the table. Not once. Not twice. Three, four times. Pre-meditated. *Thou shalt not steal . . . narcotics . . . from the hospital . . . where Dr. Barker works.* I didn't steal the money with my own hands. I know I'm still guilty by association, but in a way I think the hospital theft is the more direct and shameful transgression.

And why did you have this morphine, Miss Coleman?

It was there in case.

In case of what?

In case I couldn't take it anymore.

Take what? What do mean by "it"?

"It" was too much to explain.

I dumped the morphine in a dumpster, but still the fear was like metal in my mouth while I waited over the next days for that knock on the door. I'd tell myself this is nothing. *Get used to it. You're spoiled, soft, a baby blue-blood with too much fat, with too much protection from the way the world hurts most everybody else, the millions of lives of unrelenting fear and hardship. This is almost nothing at all.* I thought about Jo's six years on the run with her two kids and her courage. At night, I sought out stories of persecution in my books from the bookstore, re-read chapters on farm workers, stories of people who'd been framed and sent to prison because they were poor and not "white", testimonials of people who'd been maimed in one way or another and came back fighting. Then the fear abated some, was replaced by that other feeling, the burning insistence that someone, something had to come between this huge uncontainable bully and its victims.

I read and re-read the chapter on violence in *The Enemy*, the book I'd loaned to my father to read, highlighting much of the chapter.

"All class society, all exploitation of man by man is violence . . . the search for peace and non-violence is meaningless if it is not associated with and a part of the determination to overthrow capitalism and imperialism . . . To any thoughtful and humane person, even though it be against his own deep inclinations, there is really no choice left—he can only join with others to bring the present system to an end . . . or else be complicit with its violence."

. . . Even though it be against her own deep inclinations . . .

So maybe it wasn't that I was cowardly, entitled, soft. It wasn't just my inclinations that were being challenged to their core, my aversion to any, every kind of violence that obstructed my commitment to help bring this demon to its knees. It could be the same for all of them, for Roland and all the others, only I hadn't been looking closely enough. Instead, I'd been making assumptions that it was easier for them, more familiar ground for them, but maybe I was wrong. Again. Wrong. And along with that feeling came the desire for still another chance to prove that my commitment was real.

Alone and lonely, it was a relief when Vinny called to see if he could stay with me for a while. It had been a month or so since the bank job and it wasn't in the news anymore. He said, "Everything's cool," which I took to mean that there hadn't been any heat on him, so I thought it would be okay. Plus, I felt bonded to him through the secrets we shared.

His girlfriend, Shannon, who was about to have his baby, had just packed up and left him. Maybe not for good, but she went to her parents' home in Ohio to have the baby and then she'd said "she'll see". In the meantime she doesn't want to talk to Vinny. She told me before she left that as much as she loves him, she thought he'd been acting weird, "a little crazy," she said.

"Watch out for him. I think he's going to get himself locked up again."

I trusted her opinion because, even though I didn't know her very well, she seemed solid to me—all business, no nonsense, way more grounded than Vinny—or than me for that matter. She didn't want to elaborate because of the confidentiality thing, and I didn't even know if she knew about the bank job, but I figured she'd probably put two and two together by now since it had been in the news so much and she was no dummy.

I didn't see him during the day while I was at work, but at night we had something to eat and drank a few beers together while we sat on my floor pillows and listened to music. We talked politics some, but mostly we talked about his situation with Shannon, over and over. He was all messed up about it. We didn't talk about the bank job at all. It was nice having his company, his unassuming company, because he was always asking me if he could help clean up, or get me something more to drink—kind of the way I would. I've always felt we were a lot alike that way. It was easier sometimes just hanging around with Vinny than any of the others. He had a lot of opinions, but not about me. No criticisms of me at all.

The first couple of nights he slept on the couch, but then he started sleeping in my bed with me. I think I let him the first time because I felt sorry for him. He was almost crying over missing

Shannon, feeling like he'd maybe lost her and the baby forever, and since I couldn't re-assure him that that wasn't the case, I just went over to hold him, gave him a hug, but then he kissed me and because I kissed him back I didn't feel like I could say no to the rest of it. I asked him what Shannon would think but he was sure she wouldn't mind because they had an open relationship, no possessing anyone, and that seemed to be the way it was with everyone in the group except for the married couples, so I believed him.

As we started taking our clothes off I couldn't help but notice these red circles on his belly, deep and dark like bullet holes, like four bullet holes in the low light that marked an eerie kind of smile, two on either side of his belly button. I thought maybe they were bullet holes, and maybe I shouldn't have asked but I said "What's all that from? I mean, you don't have to tell me if you don't want to."

He said he didn't really want to talk about it in his softest whispery voice, "Maybe later, okay?" He was kneeling on my bed, my mattress on the floor, and looked so slight and sad again, the way he'd looked when I first met him in prison, looking at me so directly with his dark eyes, his long black hair cascading down around his shoulders, that I felt I'd do just about anything to make him feel better.

"Sure. Don't worry about it." I leaned over and turned off the light.

We made love, or we had sex, maybe that was more like it. I could hear the street sounds; I could watch our bodies in the half-light that came in from the window. I didn't need to know. It was enough to know that he'd suffered somehow for me to want to just be there for him, but he told me later in the dark that he'd had some bad times when he was inside. I thought maybe he was going to tell me that screws had done it to him but he said he did it to himself with cigarettes. "It felt better. I know it's weird, but it felt better, that kind of pain."

I knew exactly what he meant.

Even though I wasn't that into the sex, it made me feel like I might be healing something in him, that maybe he'd forget about those bad times even for just a few minutes. I made a point of kissing his belly, every one of the burn marks.

"Does that bother you?"

"No, it's nice. It feels good."

Maybe he was telling the truth, maybe he wasn't. Sometimes I lie about that kind of thing because otherwise it just gets too complicated, but I was hoping he could feel something even if I couldn't. I almost told him that I'd done the same thing to myself a few times—more than a few times lately, almost every day since I'd dumped the morphine bottles. Not with cigarettes though, with pins. I liked pins because they were so small. Nothing showed except one tiny drop of blood that I could wipe away and then you could hardly see anything at all. I know the relief he's talking about.

I guess I didn't tell him about the pins because I was afraid it might spoil it and then there'd be no relief at all.

But by the end of the week I knew what Shannon meant about him acting a little crazy. I think he does have a prison wish, like she said. That's another thing Vinny and I have in common. I know I have one too, right beneath the surface of my everyday mind, the tug to do time like the rest of them. Partly as a kind of penance for all my privilege, and partly because I just can't help thinking it would be another kind of relief in another sick kind of way to have everything so black and white, so clearly defined. "Screws" on the outside. "Prisoners" on the inside. The oppressor and the oppressed in high relief. And of course I'd be one of the "political prisoners", the truth seekers, the suffering champions of equality and true justice. I'm ashamed to say it, to even think it. I know it's not like that, that it wouldn't be anything like that fantasy, but it's the truth. Even so, I think my prison wish is more or less under control. I admit it to myself so I don't think it's driving me in an unconscious way. That's what separates Vinny and me. At least I know I have a prison wish, but I don't think Vinny does, and that makes him dangerous. When you don't know you have one it can make you do crazy things that jeopardize the safety and security of other people in the group. Even I know that.

The first thing he did that was really crazy was to rip off the mafia. At least he said he was pretty sure it was mafia. It didn't matter. What he did made somebody angry, made somebody want to find him and kill him, find him at my apartment. I knew he had some kind of plan the night before he pulled it off. He said he was maybe going to hit something big and he was going to do it by himself because he didn't know if it was going to work out. But Vinny's said that to me before, about hitting something big, and it hadn't happened. Frankly, I didn't always take him all that seriously. Maybe it was his slight air-boned body, just barely eye-level with me. Maybe it was because his voice was so soft-spoken and his expression always earnest in a sweet kind of way, but I didn't think of him as brave like that.

Climbing up the stairs to my apartment I could smell the stuff from down the hall, something wild and spicy. Something fresh-aired and familiar that I followed right to my door. All this commotion behind my door until I put the key in the lock and then it all stopped and I heard his voice saying, "Who's there?" And then "Linda, is that you?"

Inside, the entire place was filled, filled to bursting, with big green tightly stuffed thirty-gallon bags of marijuana. And in the room, men—strangers I'd never seen before. Maybe four others aside from Vinny himself were there separating and weighing and re-packaging the stuff. When I came in they all stopped, stunned and frozen, like me.

"Jesus Vinny. What the fuck?"

At first it made me laugh, laugh like this was some weird hallucination that would disappear when I turned my back or blinked my eyes but of course it all stayed fixed right where it was and no one moved or breathed. Bags piled so high they almost touched the ceiling in two or three corners and filled the room, only a narrow path of flooring shining from one end to the other. *Jesus.*

But he looked at me like I was going to be happy about this in just a second—as soon as he had a chance to explain I'd be as excited as he was. He told the others that it was cool, to just keep working and he pulled me into the kitchen where more bags crowded us into a corner by ourselves.

"I did it. I got them, those motherfuckers. I got them to give it all to me." Vinny doesn't smile much, and when he does it looks like his mouth isn't used to it, is nervous about it, but now he was high. Not stoned high, just hit-the-jackpot high and thinking, clearly, that I would be too.

"Got who? Where did it come from?" I said this even though I was pretty sure I didn't want to know. But he started right in and his voice began to pick up speed telling me how he'd intercepted the van at a stoplight and how he made them get out.

"I persuaded them, if you know what I mean," he said in a gangster imitation, how he made the two of them get out of the van at gunpoint. But when he said that, I definitely wanted to shut him up. I didn't want to hear what happened next, or how he'd scored, or how much money he was going to make for the revolution, or if he had that fucking stolen van parked outside around the corner.

There were a lot of things I wasn't clear about, but at that moment a crystal clear wellspring of panic rose up in me witnessing this invasion of my home along with a crystal clear realization that these three small rooms comprised the only space in my current world where I could pretend to feel safe, and I wanted that back. I had to have it back, right away, right then.

"You've got to get it out of here . . . all of it. And I mean, *right away*!" That was pretty directive for me . . . he heard the edge in my voice and he promised that it would be gone in a couple of hours.

"Hey, I'm really sorry . . . really. I didn't think the whole thing was going to come down the way it did . . . and that there'd be so much of it, jesus . . . fucking unreal . . . It was cool though . . . You wouldn't have believed how easy it was."

"Yeah you're right about that," I snapped. "I'm not going to hang around . . . just get rid of it, every fucking seed, okay?" If he did get it out of there in a couple of hours, then all I'd have to do would be to walk away—drive down to the ocean, read a book, take a walk. In a few hours it would be like it never happened.

"Seriously, it'll be gone . . . two hours tops." He leaned forward and gave me a kiss on the cheek I didn't want and then a fist salute as I backed out of the door. "You're a really solid sister."

After that he started staying somewhere else because he said there might be some heat on him, and he didn't want me to get wrapped up in it and that was okay with me. I never heard any more about the weed, didn't read about it in the paper, and there wasn't so much as a stray seed left in my apartment when I came back, so I more or less let the whole thing go.

I had to wonder about Vinny though, but not too much or it would be like a fine crack in a tea mug—the more wondering I poured into it, the bigger the crack would get, weakening the container of all my assumptions. Vinny was solid, right? Could be trusted, right? If Roland thought so then it must be okay that he was part of all this too. I covered the crack, held tight to the mug, and swallowed all those assumptions like some night-time elixir that might help me sleep. They'd call me again, contact me somehow, I was certain of that. After all, we'd only just begun, hadn't we? And in this expanse of waiting, in the space after the bank robbery had dropped out of the news and my fears of the

FBI showing up at my door had begun to fade, I fell into that familiar kind of numb anticipation waiting for whatever I'd be asked to do next.

Christmas came and went. I was supposed to spend it with my whole family at our home in Vermont but I feigned an excuse—the flu—at the last minute. It wasn't entirely a lie, I did get sick, but had the full truth been told, it would have included my fear of exposure to their probing radar into my unsettled mind. In their presence, I would have to maintain a secure impenetrable shell and yet not raise the suspicion of any one of my family members.

For all their materialism, my parents liked to keep Christmas simple, "like the olden days", as my mother would say, and it was seductive. In spite of my rejection of all the commercial hype in general, there was a promise, at Christmas, when all of us were together and away from the cold formalities of the other home on Long Island, that everything could be different here—that we did, in fact, love each other, or continued to try, and that was worth something. But that kind of softened atmosphere might erode the shell I'd have to maintain, leave it transparent, or even in places vulnerable to shatter. What if I drank too much wine and began to cry suddenly, uncontrollably, at the dinner table? What if I shared my secrets with a sister in a weak moment, or told my father in one of those awkward silences we often ran into on our walks deep into the woods? It was too much to risk. I didn't feel strong enough, shrewd enough to make it through a direct encounter with any of them and not forget the absolute confidences I had sworn to maintain.

It was hard enough on the phone.

"Have you heard from any of those people in Denver?" my father or my mother would ask regularly when we'd talk. And I could honestly say "No," because I hadn't, in truth, heard a word from Jo or Harlan in months. I knew, through a woman who'd worked with Jo and me sometimes in the bookstore, who I'd run into on the street a few months after my return, that the trial was dragging on, but that things looked good for an acquittal. "Oh, well that's good," I'd said, not wanting to get into any real conversation with her about it. But she went on anyway telling me that they were saying some bad stuff about me . . . that I'd left too soon, and that they were "disappointed in my commitment". She just thought I should know.

I remember blushing with shame or anger or both, that Jo had chosen to turn on me like that, yet somehow I didn't doubt that it was true, what she'd said. And maybe she was right. Maybe I had left too soon. Maybe my lack of commitment was "disappointing". But what would they say now if they knew?

Of course, I hadn't told my parents anything about that.

No, it was easier, safer to stay in Portland for Christmas, away from family. With "the flu" I even had an excuse not to visit my grandmother, and spent the day instead in bed, feeling older, companied by my newfound kind of aloneness, an adult aloneness that understands the ways that love can be a distraction, an escape from the more important work of maintaining a commitment to a higher purpose.

Somewhere towards the end of January, Vinny stopped by. He'd cut most of his hair off, trimmed his beard and long Fu Man Chou mustache. If he was trying to change his appearance, it had made some difference, making him look even younger and more innocent, like an adolescent who'd attached dark facial hair in a failed attempt to look older. I couldn't say I was glad to see him. It was like being forced awake, shaken and then surfacing too abruptly with that feeling of ominous alarm.

We took a walk around the block so that we could talk with assured privacy, but there was a fine, cold drizzle of rain turning to sleet that made us duck under the eves of a neighboring apartment building and there we had to whisper anyway.

Really, it was no surprise that he'd been in contact with them.

"We're going to have a meeting in a couple of days. You know, like a study meeting—to talk about tactics, and how to get the word out, decide who's going to write communiqués and stuff like that. Everyone wants you to come."

I remembered how he'd said something like that to me months before when we'd taken a different walk, down by the docks, how I'd been flattered when he'd asked me to go underground, flattered to be wanted that way. It had only been months, not the years that it seemed had passed since then, but I had to admit that if anything, my ambivalence about joining them had only grown— slowly, uncertainly. Ambivalence of a different character now, its contents focused not so much on my own inadequacies, my own lack of qualifications to be included—those were still loud enough, but now another voice whispered inside me—barely audible at all, another kind of doubt entirely.

Sarah and RoAnne were at the meeting too, along with Devon and Roland and Vinny and me. We met in a motel room off the highway near Brunswick, and it made me wonder, sitting on the wall-to-wall indoor–outdoor carpeting, leaning against the flimsy sheet rock wall, just who else might be staying down the hall, passing through for the night or for a meeting like we were having. Nobody at a meeting like we were having.

RoAnne and Roland are together now—a couple again. I can just tell by the same old way she watches his every move with her nervous flirtation while he sits on the opposite side of the room, avoiding even looking in her direction (or in mine, for that matter). But still I can feel all this energy between them popping and buzzing. She pulls, he resists, but to me it's immediately familiar, the same dance I've seen before, one that she somehow manages to lead in spite of his efforts to pull in the other direction. Had it always been this way between them? Roanne was one person at least who seemed to have some kind of power over Roland, someone who seemed maybe less disciplined, less confident than him, and yet capable of reeling him in nonetheless.

If RoAnne was jealous of me, I'd never felt it while we worked in the bookstore with Muck, though I anticipated at least a cool shoulder from her tonight, this being our first meeting since Roland and I had left for Denver. She was friendly enough though, smiling at me when Vinny and I came into the room, and after that, our energies were consumed by the task at hand. Anyway, I didn't mind that they were together. I was relieved that I didn't want to be with Roland, that I'd somehow been released from that heart-pounding puzzle of fear and desire. It was better this way—a clearer passage to seeing what revolutionary work needed to be done. From across the room where he sat I could see that he was the warrior still, in his worn jeans and black T-shirt, his dark expression tightly knit in concentration and his arms folded across his chest. At the same time that I was relieved not to be there as his lover, I recognized that without the far reaching discipline that he demanded of himself, I probably wouldn't have had the faith to be there at all.

"We need to decide what our next job's going to be and about a name. We need a name for the group." Devon brought it up, looking around the room at each of us with the same nononsense demeanor that Roland had about him. The Weather Underground—that's the name I really liked. The idea of there being wild and beautiful storms brewing underground was just right. Roland was clear he wanted to honor someone who'd died in the struggle, who'd been incarcerated for their political beliefs and died there because of them.

Nobody thinks of this country as officially killing off its radical elements, but now I know that it does. I've read some of the reports on COINTELPRO, the FBI's "Counterintelligence Program" that was run all through the 1960's—its stated goal to "eliminate" "radical" political opposition inside the U.S. using ongoing brutality against those they deemed "dangerous to our democratic foundations". The FBI was directly linked to the assassinations of the Black Panther leaders Mark Clark and Fred Hampton, machine-gunned while they slept in their beds, and George Jackson, shot in the back, and probably the deaths of all the other thirty-eight black male activists associated with the resistance movement during the last ten years, along with dozens of Native American activists as well. Maybe they'd even been behind the Death Squad in Portland, and the attack on the bookstore. You have to wonder what kind of "democratic foundations" they're out to protect, and who gives them the right to carry out such attacks?

It's the kind of thing my parents would dismiss as leftist propaganda, would simply turn the page, even a *New York Times* page, or change the channel, even the Walter Cronkite channel, or say something condescending and dismissive to me if I tried to show them proof. *Not in this country, dearie. Not with our system of checks and balances. Not here. We don't assassinate our citizens because of their political beliefs.*

If I managed to get them to read that list of the ones who'd been eliminated, the list of black men, I know what I'd see in their faces. They wouldn't be able to hide that uncensored moment of thought . . . *Oh well . . . them . . . What do you expect? They must have gone just a little too far.* They could dismiss anything—the violence against the entire Civil Rights movement, the millions of lives suffocating in ghettos, the abuses of prisoners, migrant workers, the genocide of Native peoples—dismissed with a sigh, with a shift of their gaze, a turn of the page, proud to live in a country that tolerated upheaval and managed to keep it out of their own perfectly manicured back yards.

So I think Roland's idea of memorializing George Jackson is a good one, but RoAnne brought up another point—that if we're going to have names in the title then there should be a woman's name too. She suggested Assata Shakur to be part of it, the black revolutionary woman who'd been framed on all kinds of charges and incarcerated for years. There was a pause then, an embarrassing pause. We couldn't have two black people in our name—we were all white, after all. And if we couldn't have two, then it made more sense, in a way, to have George Jackson, because who could deny that we probably wouldn't even be here without Roland's guidance and commitment and George was his particular hero . . . but then that would seem sexist, to just eliminate RoAnne's idea. It was instantly complicated, potentially divisive.

"How about just *Break the Chains*?" Vinny suggested that. It seemed like a possibility. We agreed to sit with it until the end of the meeting and then take a vote.

That's when we started talking about our tactics, our next action. About bombing someplace.

Bombing is okay, as long as no one gets hurt. It's easier for me to get behind the idea of bombing someplace than doing a bank robbery because in a bank you're just that much closer to people that could get hurt even if it's not your intention.

Bombing feels supremely bad, and harmless at the same time. More than once I've thought how I'd like to level my parent's home, blow it's silence sky high and dance under the rainfall of all the shards of antiques that always felt more precious than me. In the reading I'd done, the discussions we'd had, I'd never flinch when we'd talk about bombing as a tactic, bombing an empty building.

I don't care about things, inside places, rooms. They're just symbols to get lost in, that cover up life, that close doors. And if you're a true revolutionary, you have to blow things up in every way, figuratively and actually. Like Marx said, you have to do anything you can to de-stabilize the system, because the very upset promotes increased awareness among the people, allows them to see more clearly the true nature of the beast, the beast that would sooner maim its own children as upset the balance of power. It says the same thing right in the first chapter of *Prairie Fire*, the political statement of the Weather Underground.

We had the book with us and Vinny read off the long list of targets they'd already hit, twenty in all—courthouses, Departments of Correction, police precincts, draft recruitment centers, even the Pentagon after the U.S. bombing of Hanoi, and each action had been planned in direct retaliation for some brutality of war or aggression against the people. When he put the book down there was a reverent silence.

"Those brothers and sisters have got their shit together!" Ro-Anne said, and I felt the same way. It was hard to believe that it was a group like our own, that they had accomplished all of that in less than four years.

Somebody pays attention when a bomb goes off . . . has to look up from their morning coffee, put down their business section, stop their golf game.

But then Vinny said that maybe we ought to also be considering other tactics too, like he'd been thinking about kidnapping this guy who's the head of the Maine Power Company because they'd jacked the rates up so high and were pocketing millions of the people's money. "We could pick him up and demand ransom for the people . . . and then if he doesn't deliver . . . Pow!"

The "pow" came out flat and matter-of-fact like the rest of the thought. He'd cocked his hand like a gun and held it to his temple. His voice was measured, as always, and I could almost have let the words float by—I wanted to let them float by and disappear—but they hung, they hovered, and filled up all the empty spaces between us.

He's crazy, isn't he? I'm praying—it's a kind of prayer, for anyone else to please please think he's crazy too. But he doesn't look crazy. He looks like Vinny, small and earnest and well-intentioned with his brow furrowed and his dark eyes pleading for some kind of understanding. His hand lingers for a moment, cocked by his temple and, it's the first time I see it in him, that he'd just as soon pull the trigger there, into his own head, as anywhere, only he doesn't know that yet, and I don't want to believe it. I turn my gaze away, fix it onto the little brown and black squares on the rug, don't move a muscle or breathe, waiting. I know, I know he's crazy, but I doubt myself. I can't get up and walk out of this room because I'm not sure about equations, if there is an equation for justice. If, in a war like ours, murderous corporate greed is a sin punishable by death.

I'm not sure. I want to be right—that horrible paralyzing need to be sure—I want to find that path. In my head all I hear is the sound of the gun going off. Not the explosion, just the click. I hear the man's last punched-out breath like a grunt, and I'm looking into his eyes, into all of the contradictions that make him ultimately not all that different from me, or Vinny, or anyone. You'd have to look into his eyes once the blindfold is off. You couldn't escape the eyes. The eyes would find you and then you'd see . . . what would you see? I think we'd see how far wrong we'd gone. I wish I had the courage to say that but I don't.

I'm waiting for Roland to say something, to lead us away from the kidnapping plan, but it's RoAnne who jumps in and says it's a fucked up idea and she doesn't want any part of it. Her face is all red and she crushes her cigarette out in the ashtray so hard it slides halfway across the table, the butt still smoking.

Vinny and RoAnne don't like each other. I didn't know that until recently. Vinny told me he thinks RoAnne's "loose", not careful enough to be trustworthy. If that isn't the pot calling the kettle black. But even so, it's not the first time I've heard the rumor and maybe that's why I don't jump right in and support her. I should . . . but I'm like the smoke still spiraling up out of the ashtray, blowing this way, that way.

She said a bombing was hard enough for people to sympathize with. Forget about a kidnapping . . . that would just turn everybody off. I agreed with her, but the way she said it contained all this subtext of whatever else was going on between them, all this contempt. I could see Vinny getting his back up, his expression fixed in a hard frown, and maybe just because it was RoAnne who'd said it. It gave me this sickening feeling that really all our arguments in our earlier study groups, all our discussions about tactics and who would take which side, that they were all muddy like this one, never just about what I could see in the one inch of clear water on the surface, but always stirred up by what I couldn't discern in the murk beneath, the rotting leftovers of some past misunderstanding.

"Yeah, well it's a better way to draw attention to the cause," Vinny spat back at her, "and what good has bombing an empty building ever accomplished? You can't barter much in exchange for an empty building. But an *executive officer*, his *life*—that'll make the pigs stand up and pay attention!"

I waited for someone else to say something. I wouldn't be that surprised if Devon agreed with Vinny—not after our ride out of town in the car a few weeks ago—and I wouldn't hold my breath waiting for Sarah to take a stand. I didn't want to say anything either. It felt like it would take way more courage to take a stand at this juncture than it had taken to drive away from the bank, or even than it would have taken to go into the bank—that's how much I didn't want to speak. But then Roland made the decision for me. "What do you think, Linda?" he said, and everyone looked in my direction.

No one had ever asked for my opinion about strategy before. I'd always been the student, the revolutionary apprentice to all of them who knew more than me, just from their life experience, more than I think I will ever know. What did I know about what it felt like to suffer from rate hikes, for instance? To not be able to put food on my table, to feed my children, to have the heat or the electricity cut off in the middle of a sub-zero night?

But even if Vinny wasn't crazy, I was losing confidence in his

277

judgment. He might be a hero in everybody eyes but RoAnne's, he might be counting on my support, but I didn't want to step foot into his muddy water.

Why did Roland ask me? Maybe because he was stuck between his girlfriend and his comrade? What did I think? I had to find my own opinion about this. Not Roland's.

"I agree with RoAnne. I don't think kidnapping's a good idea either."

"What about bombing?" He looked right at me. He wanted to know what I thought. He really did.

"An empty building?"

"An empty building."

"That's okay. I just don't want anyone to get hurt."

That's where we left it that night. Our theoretical discussion way at the end of a fuse waiting to be lit, and I knew it was only a matter of time before someone, one of us, struck the match.

CHAPTER 28

A few weeks after the meeting in the motel Vinny called. He wanted me to meet this new guy, Eddy, who'd just gotten out of Thomaston prison and was staying at his house.

"He's cool. He's one of us now," he said on the phone. By that, I guessed he meant that he was part of "our" group, but I had to wonder for just a split second, and later, after I hung up and got in the car to drive over there, for longer than that, who made the decision to let Eddy in. The image that hadn't let me alone was the one from our meeting when Vinny cocked his finger like a gun to his head, like an assassin's gun, seeming so detached from the terror of it. Maybe people would have to die in the revolution. They certainly had and continued to die by the thousands all over the world in resistance struggles. And it was our government who killed, or helped to kill, most of them. Maybe there was some justification for that kind of retaliation, that kind of tactic to bring the bully to its knees, to win the struggle for a less violent and unjust world order, but I was uneasy, increasingly uncertain that this could be the right way, at least for me. And even then I had to wonder, I always had to wonder if my perspective was just clouded by the veil of privilege I saw through, the veil that made my perceptions as questionable as any that Vinny might have.

In addition to that, their acceptance of me into their inner fold, so evident on the night of our last meeting, made it harder to decipher where to question and doubt the decisions of the group. They trusted me now, and it wasn't just about money either. I could join them, an equal warrior. I could go with them now as far as I wanted to, or had the courage to, or the commitment. It was only up to me to decide.

It was another gray day—salty, raw and cold from the ocean, and it was gray inside Vinny's apartment because that was all the light that came in through the little domino shaped windows—that, and a dull yellow glow from a table lamp in the corner by the couch on the other side of the smoky room. Eddy stood just behind Vinny when he opened the door and I thought right away that he looked awfully young to be an ex-con, to have been inside for six years. Maybe it was his freckles, which were sprayed across his round face like paint, or his reddish hair that kinked across his crown in rows of boyish waves, and his voice hardly sounding grown at all when he said hello. He was no taller than Vinny, a little shorter than me.

We opened beers and Vinny and I sat on the couch, covered with a faded paisley sheet, and Eddy took one of the crates they used for chairs and offered me a cigarette before he lit one for himself.

"So how's it going?" I asked, more to Vinny than to Eddy, but I glanced at them both.

"Things are going good, sister. Really good." He nodded his head slowly, his eyes opened wide with emphasis. "Wouldn't you say so, Eddy?"

"Fucking great!" He had a high-pitched brittle laugh, a boy's laugh that made me think of my brother and his friends when they'd gather to pick on something smaller than themselves.

"We've been very, very busy," Vinny said. I knew by the way he said "busy" that he was going to tell me something and this something was going to be the reason for the visit.

"You remember what we were talking about at the meeting?"

I was confused about how to respond because for one, Eddy was there and I didn't want to be loose, and for two, there were a lot of things we'd talked about so I couldn't be certain which he was referring to.

"Yeah, I guess so."

"Listen, don't worry about Eddy. He's cool. He knows what we're into. He's already helped us out big time."

I noticed that when Eddy wasn't taking big swigs of his beer, he was biting his fingernails, one after the other, and watching me—his eyes shifting back and forth between me and the nail he was working on. I told myself that he seemed nice enough, as if "nice" was a revolutionary qualification, but some part of me knew that I was just telling myself that because I thought I had to like any ex-con they introduced me to and right away I wasn't so sure about Eddy. I wondered if Roland and Devon had even met him.

"Well, we scored some," Vinny said in a lowered voice. "We got some dynamite . . . We got a lot actually. Do you want to see it?"

"You've got it *here*?" It had to be wrong to have it here and it had to be wrong to want to show it to me. Maybe not wrong, but "loose" in some juvenile way. It wasn't what Roland or Devon or Harlan would do.

He patted the tabletop that was in front of the couch that had my beer and an ashtray on it. It was just a plywood board covering a wooden box about three feet square. I didn't really want to see it, didn't need to see it, but Vinny was already moving the table top off the box and there it was—twenty, thirty or more long fat sticks wrapped in the same red paper as the miniature ones my brother used to light off in our backyard. Maybe that's why they didn't seem all that real.

"Is that a lot? I mean, I don't know anything about the stuff."

"That'll take down a building for us."

Take down a building for us? For us, he'd said.

"It'll fucking do the fucking job, that's for sure," Eddy said in a low voice with a little half-smile to no one in particular.

"Roland wants us to bring it to the safe house this weekend. We were thinking . . . I mean, Roland suggested that maybe you'd be willing to drive since your record's clean if we got stopped." He was giving me the look that says I'm a solid sister and he can count on me.

Of course I said yes because I couldn't think of a reason fast enough to say no. I wanted to say no, that was my first thought. *No! No! No!*

And the 'no' followed by all the heaviness of all these decisions about what role I was going to play and wishing again for all of it to go away—the box of dynamite, the revolution, poverty and injustice and which side are you on?

And so I said yes . . . sure, . . . I'll do it, and they smiled. They were glad. They knew they could count on me, Vinny said, and even though I wanted to tell him it wasn't like that, that maybe they shouldn't really count on me at all, even so I could feel the rush of the heat of the decision—that hot wave that seemed to follow these decisions—a heat that made my hands tremble, that made me start to bite my nails like Eddy, and reach for the beer to cool me down, for the cigarette to steady me, I met that rush, that fire wall that slammed into me even as the three of us continued to talk over the details of the trip.

Now I'm all jagged up, driving home—alert, aware of what feels like every cell in the universe coursing through me, around me, and I'm high—I've never been so alive, so much a part of the world. I drive fast with the windows down, the air cold and raw on my face and I can taste every drop of the sea's wetness and the salt that it contains and I'm aware of my every breath, my every heart beat.

I'm going to move the dynamite.

Knowing this puts me close to the heart of things, of action that might possibly liberate, could release whatever binds us, resisting the oppressor, making him in some small way accountable—the dropper of napalm, the Nestles' men gathered at their polished tables. Who will stop them if we don't? I'm part of it, proud to be part of this fierce and terrible *NO!* Maybe not central, like some of the others—maybe not at its heart—but close by. Maybe not striking the match that lights the prairie fire, but close by—a gatherer of matches, a hand holder, one who could help to steady the hand that lights the match that lights the fuse that starts the prairie fire that will free the world.

The Weather Underground had done it—already fourteen targets and nobody hurt. The Pentagon—they'd even hit the Pentagon.

I rounded the corner where the view opened up to the bay and then the ocean beyond. Far out on the horizon, beyond the barrier islands, the sun had broken through the clouds, fiercely lighting a stretch of water. I had to smile, for if I believed in signs from higher powers, this would be one—this momentary distant blaze. It was validation of a sort I allowed for the moment, even if only as a measure of the infinite revolutionary possibilities that we might achieve.

But when I got back to my apartment, that rush of certainty was gone again. I could barely stand to close the door behind me. I could barely stand the sound of my own footsteps, the water running into the teapot, the spoon hitting the sides of the mug. I couldn't escape Vinny's expression showing off the dynamite, or Eddy's high-pitched laugh and his shifty eyes.

What if we were wrong?

I didn't' know if moving the dynamite was the same as using the dynamite to blow something up, but I make a distinction, I draw a line that I haven't crossed . . . not yet. Only the line isn't something I can see looking head on. Looking head on it shimmers like a mirage, and disappears as I move closer, squinting. Where is it? The line that will tell me what is right and what is wrong and what to do. I can only catch a glimpse of it from a side-glance. The line is about life, allowing life to breathe. About breath. Creating more space for breath and life for everyone who suffocates under the weight of all the fat ones on top.

Using the dynamite could be part of the problem, or it could be part of the solution. It could open up more space or it could take it away. Beneath rubble, nothing breathes, nothing moves, but all around there is new blue sky and space.

But if there is someone, anyone, beneath the rubble—suffocating there, injured there, dead there—then nothing is saved. Nothing is opened up. The whole sky falls in.

I don't want to hurt anyone or any living thing.

Maybe I'm a coward. Not a soldier at all. I'd surrender before the first shot's been fired. I'd tell everything before the first fist hit my face.

I still had time. I still had time to decide about these things.

Moving it from one place to another just kept my options open. Didn't decide anything. I was just the driver.

I can't sit still here. I'd as soon run a hundred miles, lift a thousand pounds with the energy that's pumping through me, so I take the stairs at a run to get to the street, and then I head towards the pier and the fishing docks as if police dogs are after me. But I can't last long at that pace, what with the burn in my chest, and then the questions that have been chasing me, corner me.

I don't like the idea of Vinny and Eddy deciding how it should be used. We'll have to decide together. Vinny and me and Devon, Sarah, RoAnne and Roland. And now maybe Eddy too. But it seems I have nothing to offer that isn't wrapped in all of these questions none of them can afford to answer, not if they're going to go forward, take action. Even I can see that there will never be enough time to understand exactly how to proceed. To do nothing is to sleep your life away drugged by the enemy's potions of lies and propaganda and to become the enemy in the lethargy of your own passivity.

And so Roland's question was there again—are you on the side of what's right or what's easy? It was odd, but when I thought of him lately, it wasn't as a lover, not often like that. Instead it was more of a complicated collage of all that he is with his eyes asking me that question. The eyes are not accusing me, not condemning me, but they have no time to wait, no time to waste with indecision. In the next second his eyes will turn away. There is no one else in the group that I trust as much as I trust Roland to make these decisions about life and death, killing and not killing. Not any of the rest of them or myself either.

It's dark as I head home, and I was chilled in my damp clothes, with only occasional streetlights to look to for direction. No streaming sun through a cloud break. No certainty at all and in my ever-near paranoia of being followed, I began to feel that creeping suspicion of the shadows.

I don't know anything about dynamite. Somebody told me once that one stick could blow up a car. There'll be thirty sticks in our trunk on the way to the safe house.

* * *

Vinny has to show me the dynamite again the morning that I meet him and Eddy to drive the stuff north. We're not going in my car, or my grandmother's, and I'm relieved about that. One of them has borrowed a four-door sedan from a friend. It's missing one rear fender. The dark blue paint has been patched with rust stopper in several places and there's a coat hanger for a radio antenna. He opens the trunk to show me how the dynamite is all packed in, padded with blankets and towels. Is the padding just to disguise it or to keep it from getting banged around? Do you always have to light it to make it explode or can it just go off? If you hit a big bump? If you get in an accident? I don't ask.

We're not alone. We're on his street with every neighbor watching out of every window. That's how it feels, like the whole street could be watching our every move and still he has to show me.

"Let's get going okay?" I said.

Eddy's in the drivers seat. I thought the whole point was that I was supposed to do the driving, but Vinny says I can have the front passenger seat and Eddy'll take the first driving shift. "It's a real long way you know. It's going to take us about eight hours. You might get tired doing it all yourself."

I guess he's right but I'd rather do it all myself anyway. Eddy swings the car out into the street with one hand on the wheel and his cigarette hanging from the corner of his mouth. I don't like the way the car's muffler sounds and there's enough cigarette smoke in my eyes to make them sting and water. I crack the window and since it's sunny and a January thaw day, even the streets smell like snowmelt and the mud that's loosening underground. As the car picks up speed I look out to the road, to the houses going by, to the houses with people with everyday lives just getting up, turning on the TV, living lives with smaller questions.

When we get out onto the highway and there are no other cars around, just a straight road ahead with dense pine forest closing in on either side, I hear Vinny pop a can open and he hands a beer forward to Eddy. Eddy takes it and says with his high-pitched laugh, "Good breakfast." He chugs about half of it in one swallow and then belches.

Vinny offers one to me. It's only ten o'clock. No thanks. And then I hear him click a lighter and since I know he doesn't smoke cigarettes I turn around just when I get the first sharp scent of the grass from the joint he's just lit. He's holding it out to me but I don't want any of that either—I know before he even reaches for it that Eddy does.

He takes a deep hit and holds his breath until his lungs explode in a spasm of coughing.

"This shit is strong," he says, his eyes half shut against the smoke and the cough, but he squeezes in another little hit before he hands it back to Vinny.

It's bad—Eddy at the wheel with the dynamite in the car. I don't like it at all and I'd like to protest but maybe I'm a little high too from all the smoke in the car because I don't say anything. I let myself slip into that stoned zone of attention to every little thing around me where the big picture is just too big to grasp. I keep my thoughts away from the big picture—the dynamite in the back, the old car, Eddy drinking and getting high. I let it go, choose instead to listen to the rhythmic double bumps of the tires crossing the breaks in the blacktop, letting the rhythm of it lull me away from the knot in my stomach. Eddy fools with the radio but all we get is static. I notice every time we come to a rise that the sun on the tops of the pine trees makes the green needles iridescent and sparkle like water. The forest spreads out in front of us—just the trees' surface lit, and the understory a dark ocean that we are in, swimming through like fish, on and on.

"Do you want one of these?"

Eddy is well into his second beer when Vinny offers him a pill, white and round like the ones I stole from my grandmother, the ones that would make me sleepy and dizzy and feel like nothing in the world mattered.

"What is it?"

"Uppers, downers . . . who cares?" They both laugh at this. They get going and can't stop laughing. Eddy puts his hand back to get the pill from Vinny and the car swerves all the way to the other lane before he gets it steady again. I'm not feeling stoned anymore.

"Come on man," Vinny says in protest, "you're fucking crazy. What the hell."

Finally I can say that it's my turn to drive and Eddy doesn't mind anyway. He just keeps on laughing, but he pulls the car over to the shoulder and lays a little patch as he stops.

"Okay, okay," Eddy says, "Man, I got to take a piss anyway."

Fucking asshole—that's what I thought. And what was Vinny trying to do? I didn't like him either, not right then. I wanted to yell at them both—but then I don't yell, do I? I don't get angry. I guess I'd rather get blown to pieces than offend anyone. *Jesus.*

As soon as we got going again and I was behind the wheel I felt a little better. I could stay focused on driving and they could just get high and pass out and leave me alone, which is what they did. I didn't want to think about my situation, but then I had to. I had to think about it and what I was going to do. Alone with my thoughts I couldn't ignore my conclusions that Eddy was shifty, sleazy, and Vinny, for all his sweetness and good intentions, was fucked up, acting way more than crazy, and that I had turned my life over to the two of them.

My life. I viewed its thready pulse as if from a great distance.

My life. No greater than the sum of the moral decisions and actions that defined me, all of them now entirely conflicted—a life drained of clarity and vision. It wasn't death that frightened me. The thought of that oblivion from all of this beckoned me. But if I was going to die, at least I wanted to be clear that I'd chosen the right course, the course of dying for what was right, not at the hands of someone else's suicide. As much as I wanted the revolution, I couldn't escape my unwelcome doubts that we were somehow on the wrong road. Or maybe just that I was on the wrong road, driving farther and farther into the forest away from shore.

I had to think about what I was going to do.

CHAPTER 29

I want to live in a farmhouse. In an old farmhouse in the country, somewhere at the end of a deeply wooded dirt driveway, opening up to a meadow with a brook and a barn and gently rolling hills in the background. I want to have animals in the barn—horses, chickens, goats, sheep. I want to do chores in the morning before sunrise, dig in the garden, make useful objects and read in the late afternoon by a wood stove. Some part of me knows absolutely, unquestionably that I have been made for this sort of life—that I belong either to another place and time, or in another family altogether. Not the one that drives up from New York to spend weekends in the newly built ski chalet, bulldozed into the woods leaving great scars everywhere. Not that one

When Eddy and Vinny and I pull up the dirt-road driveway of the safe-house, I can see it's just the kind of place I dream about. It's just that kind of house, a farmhouse, looking like it's grown perfectly seeded in this spot, fed for decades by the white meadow of snow that surrounds it. This house has never left scars, belongs to the field, could be home.

The dusk light is quiet and pink and swallows the sounds of

our car doors slamming. RoAnne and Roland and Devon come out to greet us, and for a moment, it's like we're old friends up for the weekend. We are older than I've ever felt, like grown-ups. Just the smallest bit like when my parents would have guests for the weekend when everyone greeted with backslaps and hand-shakes, talking all at once. But here, Roland and RoAnne have their long black leather outlaw coats on, and I think I see the strap of a shoulder holster inside Devon's army coat, so the similarities don't go very far.

Roland gives me a small hug, brushes my cheek with his lips, and for a fleeting moment I'd like to linger on their warmth, I'd like to lean against him, but the feeling only surfaces for an instant and then dives down again. RoAnne is just behind him—I scan her face for any bad feelings she might be having about my being there, about being greeted by Roland with a kiss, even a small kiss, but her smile to me is open. She calls me "sister" and she hugs me too.

Our boots crunch under the snow and RoAnne's coat makes loud leather noises as she and I follow Roland and Vinny out behind the house to the barn. Roland's carrying the box, and even though it's not that heavy, he slides on the snow in his leather boots and lurches once when he breaks through the crust. I hear Vinny murmur a "Whoa . . . " under his breath and I realize I have been holding my own. I wonder again what kind of impact it would take to explode, and try to imagine the crater it would leave if it did, how we would disappear, all of us, into little pieces—our remnants red and then pink on the white snow.

The barn is falling apart, the roof caved in, but I can imagine the roof standing, I can smell the remnants of horses and hay, imagine their steamy breath and heat from the stalls that are empty and dark. Vinny and Roland look around for a dry safe spot. Roland is serious, intent. He moves about, pushing loose boards out of the way, kicking at junk on the ground with his particular insistence of mission—the kind that has or shows no fear or hesitation at all. Vinny follows suit—splinters a baseboard with a kick of his heel.

"This place is fucking falling down," he says.

"It'll be fine. It'll work for now," Roland says with his calm authority. He pushes on a supporting beam in one corner and it seems solid, steady, even while small flecks of dirt or shingles or both rain down. "This'll be good over here." He checks the dirt beneath for moisture, but I don't see him check the roof—the small specks of dimming light I can see overhead.

He lifts the box, lowers it carefully into its dark corner.

RoAnne and I watch them and I want to ask her what she's thinking—if she sees the horses in the stalls, if she flinches the way I do when these men kick cans and splinter boards, what she thinks about the box that Roland almost dropped in the snow. To me, it has all this darkness about it, all this death that I don't want to be near. But then it's like Roland kicking the junk around—I can't entirely tell if I'm more drawn or repelled, more afraid or excited by its danger. I wonder if RoAnne feels the same way.

We're standing side by side, not saying anything, watching as they lay an old tarp over the box and then re-arrange boards and hay around it so it's well hidden. The last of the sun is on her face and there's a slight smile there that's her very own. I know it from when we'd target shoot with Muck and she'd be just about to pull the trigger, and from the way she'd talk to customers in the bookstore, or listen to Etta James while she smoked a cigarette. Mostly, I know it from the way she always looks at Roland with a singular attention that sees nothing else of what's happening around her.

I'm surprised when she notices me shivering and links my arm. "You're cold. Come on. Let's go make some tea."

She stays close to me as we walk back towards the house. For a moment, for a few steps while we're walking in the snow in the dusk to the house with the smoke drifting out of the chimney, I feel safe. Or I want to feel safe and I can almost imagine trusting her with what I've been thinking about. I want to tell her about how Vinny and Eddy got high in the car, how Eddy swerved and almost went off the road and how that began to change everything for me, to put everything in a different focus. I have the feeling she might understand, but then I think of the way she looks at Roland and how wanting him keeps her on this path no matter what, and so I don't say anything.

"I'm glad you're here," she says. "If you hadn't come it would have been just me and the guys."

I believe her. I think she means it. And I'm glad she's here too—for a moment thinking that she might be a kind of anchor for me, the same way that I felt for a moment that the house could be home.

Devon and Eddy are chopping wood for the stove and we stop to load up with armloads of split pine. Devon has stripped down to layers of flannel, has wood chips and an icicle in his reddish beard. His good looks make me look away. He loads me up and when I tell him I can carry more, he raises his eyebrows, puts one more big piece on and then pats me on the back. "You're strong," he says with a wink. I think he's flirting with me, or I'm flirting with him, and I'm suddenly embarrassed to be wanting his attention like that.

Like RoAnne, I bang my boots off at the doorstep before we enter through the wave of firewarmth, into the aromas of tomatoes and garlic cooking. RoAnne shows me where to stack the wood in the wood box and then makes me tea from the kettle already boiling on the wood stove. She moves around the kitchen, getting the sugar and milk like she's lived here for a long time, like this is her home, and I envy her that even though I know that since she went underground with Roland, she's been moving every few months. Still, she seems settled, less nervous and shy than I feel almost every second. While we sip our tea, I stir the sauce on the stove and she sets the table, puts the pasta water on and some blues on the stereo. The others trickle in, set up around the table for dinner.

What's odd is that there's nothing odd here, on the surface. On the surface, we're friends sharing a communal meal, passing salt and pepper, spooning pasta, talking about cold fronts and snowfall and the family of skunks that lives under the doorstep. I'm sitting next to RoAnne, across from Roland, and if I don't let my eyes or my thoughts rest in any one spot for too long, it's all fine.

But what's odd is that right beneath the surface of the small-talk are the reasons we're together, the shared secrets and danger and this mission that sets us apart from the world, even though it's for the rest of the world that we're here. Of course we can't talk about it all the time, of course we can't chat about blowing up buildings, about the dynamite in the barn, but for me the presence of these matters is so huge, so loud, that I can barely hear what anyone is saying.

I want to come right out and tell them all about the secret I'm holding onto. It's like a stone in my pocket I won't let go of, feeling its shape and weight, deciding whether to save it or throw it away. The secret is the letter I started composing in the car while Vinny and Eddy slept. In the letter I'm going to tell them I want out.

All the way out? Most of the way out? I'm not sure. I can't decide until it's written, until I have the words in front of me. But I already know it won't be the whole truth, that I won't be able to tell them about how I'm more and more certain that motives are complicating the mission. About how I know now that Vinny and Eddy would just as soon die stoned and high in a car crash as on the front lines of the revolution, and how RoAnne would do almost anything at all to be with Roland, or how Devon is a powder keg looking for a lit fuse.

And my own motives? They're as muddy as the rest of them.

One minute I'm thinking about how justified we are to be wanting to turn the system upside down, to be fighting in this way for a new world order, and the next I'm thinking about my grandmother's smile when she can't quite hear what I'm saying, or I'm following my father across a meadow, just like the one outside, to find a Christmas tree, and then everything I'm doing seems like some kind of blasphemy, and then thinking about my family in a sentimental way seems like a blasphemy too.

The only thing I can say for sure is that I'm not sure, and that is not something I can say at all. Not here. Not to them. It seems like the weakest place of all, like a vacuum of shameful gray that I'll disappear in forever, no substance at all. I'm not as solid as a stick of dynamite, and if it's come to using dynamite then I'd better be solid like that and I'm not.

In the meantime I feel like even more of an imposter than usual—eating food and making small talk like I belong, like I'm part of the family when I'm not.

Tomorrow morning we're going to have a meeting. I'll tell them then.

What if they won't let me leave? I don't really believe that's a possibility. But just what if they say I know too much now and I have to stay? What if they take a vote and decide that I actually am a spy or a rat and I should be shot and buried in the woods? We've talked about it enough, hypothetically, in our meetings, how 'rats' should be "offed" because how else can a guerrilla cell function without jeopardizing everyone's safety?

These thoughts are all jumping around inside me while we're all sitting at the table together, but I don't really believe them. I don't believe them enough to stop me from continuing to write the letter in my head, right there at the table while I'm passing Vinny the salt and pepper and reaching for the wine.

"I'm pregnant," RoAnne says when we're standing side by side at the sink washing dishes and the others are talking in the other room, and she looks at me with soft glowing eyes. Of course Roland is the father, I don't even ask. She tells me without the slightest intention of harm, as if the sharing of this news will bring me into her circle in an ever more intimate way. "Look," she says smoothing the loose sweatshirt she's wearing over the firm mound of her lower belly. "I'm just beginning to feel kicking inside."

Now I know why she's seems so calm and content. I know why she called me "sister" and linked my arm. It wasn't really about me at all, but just that she finally has what she's wanted and because I'm a woman too I should know. But I don't know. I don't feel what she feels. I am as empty and lost as she is full and secure. I have no home.

I slept on the couch in the small living room, preferring that to sharing floor space on an old rug with Vinny and Eddy in the spare bedroom upstairs. I kept the fire going all night, the flames lapping at the logs and the wood hissing as it burned. The flickering light inside the stove was just bright enough to write by— that, and the light of a waning moon brightening the snow-lit meadow. What I want to say to them comes pouring out and as I write I realize it has been gathering for some time—like a slow weather system with no particular moment of beginning, no particular cause, but a sum of events, of moments and choices that have built toward the crest of craziness of the ride north in the car today with Vinny and Eddy. I still don't know exactly whose idea it was to bring Eddy into the group, but it has fractured some belief I have in Roland's judgment, and without that I know I don't have the faith, can not proceed with all my doubts now amplified and with the real possibility at hand, even closer now than it had been with the bank robbery, the possibility of killing any other being "for the revolution".

I wrote for some time but my final draft was a short page, my longer explanations burned in the wood stove—each one too complicated in its diversions, intimate in ways I might have shared with one or another in a different time, but not with the group as a whole, this group with a lethal mission, and executors like Vinny and Eddy and maybe others I didn't even know. A short declaration of my intent would have to do, something I could read aloud to them at our meeting in the morning—that was my plan. But if I lost my nerve I would at least have something to send to them after we left to return to Portland the following afternoon.

I slept then for a few hours but woke at dawn next to a cold stove. The clear night had given way to snow while I slept, and when I went out to fetch more wood I could see that it was coming down steadily, had already laid a light feathery inch or more, and a new layer of silence as well. The woods beyond the meadow beckoned and I would have liked to walk there, but I couldn't just disappear, and probably, for security reasons, wouldn't be allowed to take a walk anyway. I watched the silent movement of the snowfall hoping for some inner silence as well, but I had loud voices in my head. After dinner last night, after we'd cleaned up and Roland and RoAnne had gone to their room, the remaining four of us played a few hands of poker, and it was okay until Vinny and Eddy couldn't help but start up with their ideas for how and where to use the dynamite—government offices, police barracks, homes of corporate executives and "pigs" they knew from the streets. A few sticks here, a few sticks there . . . there was a lot to "play with", as Eddy had said with his slippery high-pitched laugh. It was all more fantasy than real talk, nothing I hadn't heard before from them and from others in the movement, from Harlan's Big Black Book, from some of the newspapers and books and letters and talk that circulated the radical left, rhetoric that it seemed should slide off the tongue of the truly committed, that had always challenged my own "commitment", and hearing it from the crass mouths of these two just made all my misgivings and fears louder. I didn't think anyone else in the group would tolerate this careless talk, but then Devon didn't stop them, and Roland and RoAnne had, for reasons I wasn't privy to, invited Eddy into the group. There was no calm to be had, and the truth I had to swallow was that I wanted to be away from here, from this mission and these people, so badly that it was hard not to run.

We gather at ten o'clock, bringing the metal folding kitchen chairs into a circle in the upstairs room where Vinny and Eddy had slept, that room offering the most uncluttered floor space. The room is small, barely big enough to put the six chairs in a circle, and barely offering enough air for me to catch a full breath, and I want to be over with it, be out with it, and living in my truth again, even if my truth is made of a million contradictions. RoAnne has put her chair next to mine and I'm glad. She seems relaxed, her legs outstretched and crossed at the ankles and her fingers laced over her rounded belly, and she gives me a sisterly smile as she sits down. Vinny puts his chair on the other side of me, and Roland and Devon and Eddy make up the other half of the circle. I have the letter folded in my sweaty palms and I think it draws attention as no one else is carrying anything but a coffee mug except Roland who has a pad and pencil. I see him check out the paper in my hand and I'm sure he knows that something's up.

RoAnne rubs her belly and maybe the baby is kicking or rolling about, and I have a memory. I remember I'd felt that kicking once, from the outside—my hand on the taut stretched surface of the pregnant abdomen of a friendly high-school teacher of mine—and even though I was young and a little embarrassed to be waiting for long expectant moments to feel movements inside of another's body, an intimacy too close not to feel guilty of some transgression, even so, when the baby finally tapped twice against my palm and then heaved across it as it rolled over, I knew I had felt something completely fantastic, far beyond anything I could ever fully comprehend. And in a way it repelled me because of its strangeness, the small being growing in there too mysteriously, and for the humility that mystery demanded.

I wondered once again if it was love that guided this group toward this mythical future—the peaceful world born through violence, to be delivered to that very life in RoAnne's belly, though it might mean the sacrifice of that very life to accomplish our "mission". Would RoAnne be able to sign on to that? Would Roland? If that was so then it had to be a love beyond what I could imagine, or else, it seemed to me, it could be the greatest lie of all.

"So we're here to talk about how we're going to proceed now that we have the package delivered yesterday." Roland looked at me and to Vinny and Eddy with a small approving nod. "Good work, you all," and Vinny gave a raised fist salute and Eddy followed with his twisted smile. At least the two of them appeared clear-eyed and sober this morning. But of course Roland didn't know what had actually gone down on that ride, and I should speak up about that, I definitely should, but without one sure ally in this distant place and my return ride dependent on the other two, I know I won't. "The floor is open to suggest targets and I'll make a list so we can discuss each one at length," Roland says, a serious chairperson already making notes on his pad.

Now that I'm certain of the agenda, I know I can't be part of this discussion. It's information I don't need or want and I raise my hand before anyone else. "I have something to say . . . ." The voice I hear is suddenly sharper than I'd intended, claiming more space than I'd intended as all eyes look at me. "I have something I want to share with you all."

And so I do . . . I begin to read the letter . . . *When this underground cell formed over a year ago I became an above-ground liaison for this group. In that capacity I agreed to support the work of building a guerilla cell but stated that I was not willing to make the move into the underground at that time. Over the last year until now I have honored that commitment—I have bought weapons, housed and transported fugitives, provided financial support and, assisted in other actions which some of you, but not all of you may know about. This was done in support of our shared mission to help bring radical change to this country, a mission that I continue to believe in.*

"A mission I believe in . . . " With those last words out of my mouth, I suddenly doubted my own sincerity . . . was it a lie, this whole position that I'd concocted? A sham to pave the way for my separation? But I *do* want them to be strong freedom fighters. I do want this mission, some mission of resistance and change to succeed. I want to support them and I want to trust them and I don't—not all of them, not as a group.

I pause for a breath, and a quick glance around the circle to glean the energy there. It's a blur of motionless bodies and faces and I don't let my eyes settle on any one. I don't know who the person is who has the voice to say these things but it's my voice, a voice that's shaking, a mind that last night was convinced of the strength of my position and has now suddenly considered that Vinny, or more likely Eddy, or any one of them actually could be packing a weapon into this meeting as a matter of course, and that it could be produced after they've heard what I have to say, and then suddenly—the way a mind can travel infinite distances in a split second while still going forward into speech—suddenly I'm in the woods with Muck and RoAnne and Muck is making his bull's eyes with the loud report of his pistol, only *I* am the bull's eye and Eddy holds the gun and there is no one, no one in a hundred miles of this dense forest outside who will hear the shot or find my frozen body under the ever deepening snow.

But I've begun to read the letter and have taken the next breath to continue . . . there's no turning back and so I go on.

But my relationship to this group has to change now. I am not comfortable with participating in any actions that could potentially harm or end a life, any life. And therefore, I do not want to be linked to any actions of this group that could potentially cause harm to any person.

I don't use the word "kill", and why not? To protect them from my accusation, from my judgment? Who was I to judge if they were the right kind of warriors . . . and it was, I could still see, a kind of war that needed strong and dedicated soldiers of some kind to stop this ruthless monster of greed and death, resistance of *some* kind—but as long as I still had a choice I could not fight with these cadre—definitely not with Vinny and Eddy, no matter what their intentions.

I am willing to be an above-ground liaison, and as such, will maintain contact with you through a safe phone at regular agreed upon intervals, and if possible, will help you when I can and if I can.

By "help" I'm certain we all know that I mean money, and then all of the other necessities—false IDs, renting safe houses, giving transport or safe haven, and the other essentials required by those living underground in the heart of the beast. And I believe myself again as I read my offering to help, in my intention to be willing to take a stand—even if it's not true, not entirely true, not if Vinny calls me for a gun, or for money, or if Eddy calls me for any reason at all—but I want them to let me *out*, they have to let me out. I hear the conviction, the sincerity in my voice, and in a moment of confidence I look up again and around at each of them because, in this moment, this is truly what I believe I will do—but not only because of my support for the revolution, support that needs to be reconsidered now, but because it is my way, after all, as it has always been my way in my family group and then in every other group I have ever been a part of, to avoid that other death, the one of rejection, anger, contempt—to be "good" in the eyes of any beholder—even beholders that *I* hold in contempt, like Eddy, and maybe others now too—and in that way of my own weakness and skewed motives I cannot judge theirs. *"I'm not here to change you,"* I say. *"I'm not here to say whether you are wrong or right,"* I say. For me these certainties of right and wrong are way out of reach now—too perilous a course to lay claim to where one begins and the other ends. Every step along that continuum seemed relative to a moment, elusive and shifting. But I *won't* kill, or maim, or cause intentional suffering to any other being ever—that is my wish, my vow, and soon soon maybe the money will be gone—soon maybe I will give away the rest and then be living out from under that harm that is mine as well.

There is one more promise: *"In case I need to say it . . . I am not a rat,"* I tell them, *"and I have no intention of turning on you"*—a rat being the lowest moral form of life, an opportunist, and I'm certain I don't want to be responsible for sending anyone to prison.

After the few short minutes it took to deliver my speech there was silence, and I looked to Roland to give the first sign of acceptance but he wouldn't meet my gaze. I saw Devon raise his eyebrows and slowly shake his head, and I realized that in spite of my fantasies about Eddy and the gun in the woods that I had been sure they'd be okay with my plea, had convinced myself during my long night of writing drafts that all or most of them would understand, and that there'd be nods of assent for letting me move on.

"Let's take a vote," Devon said. "We need to know that everyone's okay with this. Anyone have anything to say?" But no one did—no one said a word—and for breathless moment I thought that it was actually possible that they wouldn't let me go.

It was RoAnne who spoke up. "It's okay with me. She's been a solid sister this far and I don't see that changing." And then there were nods of assent, because I had, certainly by all accounts, been a "solid sister" up till then, and they had been my comrades, my lovers even—men and women who would not intentionally kill or extort or "disappear" anyone they believed to be a comrade, or innocent in other ways, and some, and Roland, would not ever kill or harm anyone at all, ever, not in a rational moment, in a clear-headed moment, one such as this.

EPILOGUE

—————

There is a road, no simple highway, between the dawn and the dark of night. And if you leave, no one will follow. That path is for your steps alone . . . "

Jerry Garcia

Over the years that followed that weekend of my departure, I would try to push them all away, to scrub them out of my world, over and over, like blood on sheets, my blood, their blood, evidence that we'd lain together.

I'd agreed to stay in contact through the safe phone we'd established in the hospital lobby. I don't remember how long it was before I heard from them again. A few days? A few weeks? Now, these many years later, there are only fragments of moments that hold on—like the dutiful, ambivalent feeling I had as I sat in the cramped booth, the glass door shut tight to all the unsuspecting hospital lobby life passing by, and then picking up the phone on the first half of the first ring. It was Vinny, asking for money.

"We don't need much, maybe a few hundred."

And there it was again, all of the indecision and uncertainty. Blood money. Sins of your ancestors. I should say no. I should say yes.

"I'll think about it. I'll let you know next week, by the next call. Maybe I can—I don't know."

His request followed me like a stray cat trailing me everywhere, rubbing against my leg, begging for food . . . a cat that follows the scent of a full cupboard, the scent of possibility, and my heart torn between the desire to care and not to care.

But I missed the next call, pretending to myself that I'd forgotten, that it had slipped my mind, that I was caught in traffic, held up at my job. Who could challenge me? It was so easy that way, to lock the door, to lock the cat inside, to slip the key into the pocket I knew had a hole in it. To pretend I didn't hear it's faint thud on the dirt as it hit the ground. But the choice stayed with me, the lie of it, always there to remind me when my fingers found that hole.

I rubbed to get the stains out, and carried on with my life of numb and distanced performance at the hospital. One day, I woke up to headline news that there had been a bombing of a courthouse near Boston where several people had been injured, one very seriously, one who might die, who'd lost one leg, maybe two. I thought right away it was their doing, and in the same instant convinced myself that I couldn't know for certain, could I? Couldn't know for certain if it was the dynamite that I had transported that caused injury to those people. I turned away—I'd left the group after all, hadn't I? It wasn't blood on my hands, was it? I'd heard that a warning call to the courthouse had been delivered and ignored. Did that distribute any of the real blame? I turned away then—and again and again at every opportunity to find out more. I turned away to slip out from under the weight of that knowing, and pushed away the knowledge of those injuries, of my culpability, of the confusion it presented about their revolutionary tactics in this "war" to change the system, and I moved to a new city, into a new life.

But there is no such thing as "a new life", a new start, because you're always with yourself, sleeping in the same bed, the same sheets, with all of them and now with all those injured people as well. I didn't want to find out what happened next, where they went, what they'd decided to do. I avoided any of many possibilities of finding out. They were in the news—I stopped buying the paper. They were on TV—I didn't own one. But you hear things anyway. You read headlines over the shoulder of the man in the subway at rush hour, or the woman sitting next to you on the crosstown bus . . . Seventeen bombings and almost as many bank robberies all throughout the New York and New England area in those years after I left them—attacks on slave holders, murderers, earth killers . . . that was still "the good fight" wasn't it? And they remained, in some part of my desperately insistent mind, the true warriors—warriors whose contempt I feared as my own 'political' life felt sketchy, ambivalent, dabbling.

During those same years, I went to nursing school, moved from one apartment to another throughout Manhattan, did not find love or home but found a niche, eventually, working three to eleven in the emergency room of a major city trauma center where gunshots were routine, where everybody—patients and staff—was high on something, and where sometimes, for a few hours, I felt useful and alive again.

I shopped around, still looking for the tablet of commandments to live by, an exodus from contradictions. It wasn't enough to patch up, however kindly, the bloody drug-addicted lives of the people who'd been most blatantly victimized by the system. It wasn't enough.

For a brief period of time I became involved with a grassroots community-organizing group of Socialists and Communists, a substantial network of people who worked with a rabid energy to build a new political party in Manhattan. They were a family, an extended community that worked together, played together, often lived together. Early on in my apprenticeship their leaders, a group of four, invited me to a "closed" meeting to be interviewed for membership. It was made clear that not everybody was asked or offered this opportunity in front of me—to "turn my life over to the people", to make that lifelong sacrifice for "the struggle", a metaphoric blood seal. This time it wasn't difficult to decline—their power hierarchy was too questionable, their righteousness too insistent, and the community they offered too claustrophobic and cloying. In their attachment there was a chain of sorts that bound them together, that I was being asked to wear, not a liberation at all. It was my secret to know these things, to be suspect of their motives, to be suspect of everyone's motives including my own. Motive had become everything to me, and in my exploration of it the questions that haunted me became clearer: *When does the resistance to the exploitation of one become the exploitation of another? When does "knowing" become its own kind of blindness?*

Of course there was a massive manhunt for Roland and some of the others. Their pictures were in every post office, and sometimes I would pause in front of them, feign nonchalance while my heart beat wildly, as if to even look was tantamount to a confession—not to the FBI, but to Roland himself, as if in some prescient way I imagined I was suddenly before him, as close as I was to his picture, and that I was trying to justify again my choice to leave the group, to defend my fears that the group had taken an unconscionable turn, not a necessary one, and to explain why, since leaving them, my own politics and activism had become so ambivalent and undefined.

I remembered how Jo used to say, in reference to someone new who'd we'd met, or who she'd be describing, she'd say "Oh s/he's political" as if that said it all, as if that were the stamp on the hand that allowed you in and out of that inner circle without question. I'd had that stamp on my hand, however much I questioned my rights to it, but had I forfeited it entirely now? Did I want it back again?

Not surprisingly, the picture of Roland they'd chosen captured his most extreme darkness of expression, the wildest look in his eyes. His determined and dedicated heart was so far away in memory then that I wondered if maybe I'd been mistaken in my assessment of the goodness I'd known in him. He could be arrogant and cold, but wasn't that a cover for the good intent that truly motivated him? Or was he really motivated more by a vengeful anger fed by phantoms lurking in his own personal closet? But it was impossible to fully entertain these thoughts, to explore them in any honest way. To allow them was to invite the dismantling of so much else—not just that I'd been on the "right" side, but that there was a "right side" at all, and that "goodness" was capable of surviving in a political world.

The charges against Harlan were dismissed after a long trial. I never saw him or Jo ever again. About a year after I'd left for New York City, they found my address and sent me pictures—small snapshots of their kids doubled up on their Shetland pony, their little hands gripping the pony's thick brown winter coat. They had a farm in New England. They had the life I wanted—with kids, with animals, with land of their own on a farm and I was alone in my city life way out of reach of any of that. I remember feeling envious, and then lonely, and putting the pictures away where I wouldn't find them again for a long time.

Some of the memories gradually began to fade, to blend and blur, and I was grateful for that, impatient for that natural process to take its course, wishing for a tonic to a quicker forgetting, where I could honestly say to the judge, or a jury, or to the agent who would certainly someday legally corner me, "I don't remember. I don't remember." But some things, of course, you don't forget.

From time to time, the FBI would visit, our short conversations through my door chain. "Have you heard from any of them Miss Coleman?"

"I'm not talking to you. Go away." And that felt good, to be clear like that, to not have one breath of indecision about talking to them. But their visits just served to keep me close to a certain edge of knowing that someday, one day, they wouldn't leave when I told them to go.

They found my friends—friends I hadn't seen in years, and then they went to friends of friends. And certainly they must have found my parents, certainly my father, but I wasn't going to ask either of them if they'd had "visitors", not if they didn't bring it up. By then, they had troubles enough of their own. My father had been diagnosed with cancer and their world consumed in its own war zone of multiple surgeries and cancer treatments that ravaged them both and infected all of our family with an impending grief. It was enough for them to know that I was now a nurse, fully employed, living alone but not with "those people". They would not, did not inquire anymore . . . to inquire might invite more information than they might want or had the heart or life left to consider. It was enough that I showed up ready to care for my father at every crisis. Whatever that love I had for him was made of, it poured forth then without a moment's hesitation.

Vinny was caught first. He and Eddy had split off from the others (or had they been cut off?). They had had their own group of two, their own political bombing and robbing campaign. And soon after Vinny's arrest, Eddy was cornered after a 100 mph chase, his car packed with dynamite—a chase that ended with his car hugging a telephone pole, the dynamite intact, and Eddy quickly surrendering every bit of information he could muster as a government witness. Even though his testimony wasn't entirely reliable given his past record, it did implicate me in bank robbery, harboring fugitives, and transportation of explosives—all crimes with penalties that amounted to most of a lifetime behind bars. That was when the government convened the grand jury, when I got the knock on my door and was served with papers, and when I knew without a doubt that sooner or later I'd be called to testify.

Of course my father had been told of their arrests and of the grand jury call by someone in his law firm, and he and my mother called me together that same day. "You can choose your own lawyer, honey, but I have someone I think you would like . . . I wish you'd let me help you." I remember how his steady voice unleashed a deep tremor of anxiety I'd never felt before. I wanted to lean on him desperately, and I didn't want his help at all. He said if I'd just come to meet her I could always make up my mind later. And my mother had chimed in that it was the least I could do for my father, given all he'd been going through, to assure them both that I had good legal help. With the clipped accusation in her voice it was hard to admit to her that she was right, but I couldn't very well tell them that I had "other plans"—I had no idea what to do.

I wasn't supposed to like her, Laura, (an "enemy" lawyer of the ruling class), but immediately I did—a lovely sister of sorts who embraced me with an infectious and kind attention in spite of my judgments. And I wasn't supposed to let my father help me out either, adding to the debts of my privileged advantage. Could I justify? Could I explain? Could I tell about how he looked the morning that he introduced me to Laura—a morning four months before he died, a ghostly shell of his former self in a suit that hung on him like a sail without wind, barely strong enough to hold the hint of the reassuring smile that he managed, and to hold my arm as he guided me into her office. My jury who weighed my choices and transgressions at every turn might send me to some other form of hell, but I stayed with Laura.

Somewhere in that wandering I met my first husband. I married him, quickly, within a year of our meeting. If it had been up to him he might have waited a little longer, but I was driven, certain I didn't want to wait. He was the perfect man for me at the moment of our meeting—a moment I can see now was clearly overshadowed by my father's recent death, and the long cancerous decline that preceded it. I know now that it is not uncommon when you love someone who is ill and dies, when you are close enough to them to help care for their body—to dress their wounds, give them shots for pain as you watch them slip away—it's not uncommon to feel like you're dying too, that the wave that is carrying them under is sweeping you along with it, and so you grab at any proof of the vital opposite, at anything that teems with life. I think, in this way, I clung to my first husband.

He was a lawyer, like my father, sister, brother, but not from my class background and too independent to be headed for Wall Street. "How perfect," I thought, though thought had little to do with that mysterious intractable web spinning through those first moments of connection. He was grounded—I needed to be grounded. He was funny, so funny—I needed to laugh. And through his humor and eager generous attentions I believed that he saw the world as I did. I convinced myself that it was true and I'm certain that he did nothing to dissuade me of that impression for those first months of being together.

In 1984, in August, we were married. In November, almost ten years since I'd left the group, Roland and RoAnne were arrested, and their three young children taken into government custody. Shortly thereafter Devon and Sarah were caught as well, and their three children taken by the government. There was another couple that had been part of their group, arrested at the same time, but I didn't recognize their names.

I remember now one small piece of the day, the moment when my husband threw the newspaper onto the kitchen table, and slapped his finger onto the headlines, "Are these those friends of yours?"

It wasn't like I hadn't told him. It wasn't like a part of me didn't have to refrain from telling everyone, *I did that,* from wearing the story like some kind of badge of honor, some kind of evidence of rebellious courage that bought me license to exist with the story as my real substance, the outline finally all colored in. I don't remember how he'd responded when I'd told him initially, what his views were about my involvement with them before their capture. But I do remember the anger in his gesture that morning—it's surprising and sudden bite, how he spat out the word "friends" and how that moment seemed to be the birth of an intractable and often rage-full opposition to any and all of my inclinations to defend them. He was clear—so certain in his position, so articulate and forceful—and my own retorts, however passionate, sounded clumsy and naive. *So what if we hadn't done everything "right"—at least we'd tried!* At least they'd tried even more than I had to live their resistance to the violent hypocrisy of our government's genocidal policies. To the hidden brutalities in our prisons. To the racism that impoverished millions in our ghettos.

"That's a bunch of liberal apologist rhetoric and they're no better than street criminals," he'd say. He couldn't see their heroism, not one shining moment of it, and maybe that is why it was all that I could see at the time, all that I allowed myself to see, to saturate my entire being with their righteousness. Without it, I felt he could have simply and efficiently extinguished me.

But even so, I didn't follow the events subsequent to their capture, much in the same way I'd missed the second contact call in the hospital. Their trial hearings and arraignments were happening all around me in courts in Manhattan and I pretended not to know; did not make it my business to know. It was like avoiding eye contact with my neighbors in the apartment building where I lived, riding the elevator every day with no more than a perfunctory smile. It was impossible to know in advance what they might ask of me and what I might do, what I might agree to do if I invited them into my home.

But where was my home? Rarely, it seemed, in my husband's presence. Day after day of this first year of our marriage the distance between us grew as we pretended it did not. To be sure, there were moments when we'd speak in level tones about our differences, and then I could hear his concern, feel his love for me, and his own frantic confusion about how to navigate the storm we were in. We would come together for a time, but soon another squall would blow us apart. I turned away from the trial news, and instead focused on the work of keeping our marriage alive.

Even while I avoided news of their trial proceedings, I did learn how Roland and RoAnne had traveled from place to place with one, then two, then three children—always with alias identities, their children having to remember the details of every change, every different name and place and never, never slipping up—these children described by teachers and neighbors as "cooperative", "well adjusted" "very good students". Not that I doubted that they were well-loved—with respect, patience, kindness. But why had their parents made the choices to have children at all? To travel like that with children who had then to carry their own life-threatening secrets and undue burdens of responsibility? But I didn't, I couldn't allow myself to judge them—it threatened too much of the foundation I needed to defend them at all.

I know that in one analysis, however unpopular, however divorced from the pulse of the mainstream American culture of those years, that they were still fighting a war, the one that had begun in the civil rights and anti-war movements of the decades before. They were fighting what they believed was "the good fight"—to the end, to the other side, where the nirvana of justice and social equality we'd all envisioned would exist, and the "fair" world would shine forth. I could still feel the tug, the temptation of living in the belief of, and for, this idealism for the "right" way. In the wake of the absence of belief I stumbled into a great void, into the mind of not knowing, really, the answers to anything at all.

But if there is a "good fight", then there is "a right way". Everything falls precisely onto one or the other side of the war zone. Then it can neatly follow that the government is 'wrong' and the rebels are 'right', and to secure my place there, on that side of knowing, I should never have testified against them.

By the following summer—the summer after they were arrested—a grand jury was convened. Soon, I would be called to testify, and by then I was pregnant with my first child.

If you're called to testify in front of a grand jury you have three choices. You can cooperate, you can refuse to testify on the grounds that it will incriminate you because of your own involvement— at which point you are granted immunity from being prosecuted as long as you do testify, or, you can refuse to testify altogether, and instead go to jail for the life of the grand jury. In my case, that would mean up to two years and then the possibility of being indicted and tried for other crimes that Eddy had implicated me in. Still, I wore the possibility of going to jail like a life-vest in a storming ocean. Without it I would certainly drown.

I couldn't testify.

I would "do time" like the rest of them.

I would finally pay dues for my privilege, be absolved of my ancestral crimes, and suffer the consequences of my actions alongside my "comrades".

I would be re-deemed. Clean. No bad karma. No debt. Free.

I couldn't testify. It was against every moral fiber of my need to be on the "right" side. I wouldn't "rat" on these people I'd once called my friends, even if I now disagreed with their tactics. Hadn't I promised them as much in our last meeting at the farmhouse? I wouldn't be an "informer", a government witness. I would forever carry the weight of that blasphemy, the heaviest sort of drag on a soul; it's own kind of windowless walls. And if it meant going to jail for a few years, for two or four or five . . . . how many years would I accept as fair payment? After all, I'd left the group at the juncture when our positions on violence diverged. I'd left, but I'd carried with me my own uncertainties for doing so.

When I heard that they'd bombed the property of the Union Carbide Corporation for it's cooperation in the massacre of 1,000 people, mostly women and children, in the Soweto Uprising of 1976 in South Africa, I felt the justice in that. When I heard that they'd blown up the offices of US military contractors that had sent 750 pound fragmentation bombs to drop in El Salvador, bombs that were especially designed to explode before hitting the ground in order to kill more people, I silently cheered. As long as their own bombs didn't hurt anyone—that was my own line I'd decided not to cross. But what about the people who'd suffered injuries in that first bombing? How had the group continued on their campaign in the face of those victims? I'd heard that Devon was on trial for the death of a policeman who'd been killed in a shootout. Could the lives of those dead or injured be neatly excused as "war casualties'?

The "establishment" voices of some of my family and friends, certainly of my parents, cast them as dangerous criminals. Others, my sister and close friends more aligned with the left understood my struggle, and together we spent many long hours deliberating and weighing my options. There were voices inside me that had never fully answered how to overcome tyranny without violence, how to throw out the armed invader without armed resistance. So was it my strength or my cowardice that had turned me away from that path? And those voices still sought to convince me to sacrifice my own unborn child's well-being for the sake of a principle, the way that my former friends had done with their own children.

But how many years then would absolve me? Five, six, ten? I'd heard that Roland had been sentenced to forty-five years in one trial, and Devon a life sentence in another.

And honestly, I can say now, as I write this, that I was afraid of more than a life in jail. I'd convinced myself with the help of my own inner rhetoric, my lawyer's and parents' admonishments, and my husband's angry voice, that I might be in danger if I testified against them. It had been almost ten years. Ten years to balance and weigh the images and voices of memory—Roland the fierce warrior, Roland the lover, the principled student of revolutionary politics, the disciplined founder of an underground resistance cell. Could I trust my instincts that he would never support harming me no matter what the party line on informants? Yes! Of course, yes! That Devon, or Vinny or anyone else I'd known from that time would not harm me? I doubted it. I might have worried about Eddy but he'd been shuffled away in a witness protection program and he had no reason to be concerned with me now. And yet I'd let myself go there, into that paranoia that left me looking over my shoulder as I walked down the street, that kept the constant fine tremor in my hands and a nagging burning in my gut. I couldn't testify.

And finally, how could I offer evidence that would send them to jail, even for one day of the thousands that they would have to serve for their other crimes. Why should I get off, go free for the same criminal activities? And why hadn't I been indicted for these crimes in the first place? It reeked of class privilege again, of treatment that would never have been afforded me if I hadn't been my father's daughter, my grandmother's grand-daughter. I loathed the idea of that kind of help, and yet the contradiction was inescapable that I was now benefiting from the very privilege that I'd opposed.

My father and mother have now both passed on. I would like to take poetic license to create a scene where I ask each of them on their respective deathbeds if they had cut a deal for me, if they had used either their familial or legal status to protect me. My father would pat my hand reassuringly. He would say, "You'll see, when you have your own kids, dearie." My mother would frown, would wince as if the very reminder of that time brought on it's own physical pain. "You know," she'd say with a quivering lip. "I've always thought that what you did to us during those years is what brought on your father's illness."

I never did ask either of them. The truth is that I'm not sure what I would have wanted them to say in response.

I'd go to jail. For as long as it took. At least I would have a righteous foot to stand on when I got out, if I got out. Had I been alone, I'm certain that's exactly what I would have done. But I wasn't alone. I was newly married. And then I was pregnant, and that changed everything.

By September when I was finally called, I had felt my son's first quickening, the faint tapings of his certain life, and with it came a kind of love that insisted on every possible protection and guarding from harm's way. By then, there was no choice left at all.

United States Courthouse, Springfield, Massachusetts
January, 1989

. . . . "Listen, you're just one of two hundred witnesses called by the government in a trial that has been going on for months and will continue for many more . . . " Laura, my lawyer had said to me that morning, brushing one long hair from my blouse, patting me on the shoulder with her smiling reassurances. "Nobody's going to sink or swim based on what you say."

But those are empty words, filled with compromised values, platitudes to wash down this poison I am swallowing. 'Government witness' is branded on my back for all to see. Traitor. When they caught Eddy, he talked right away. But I'd promised never to talk. "I'm not a rat," I'd told them. I'd told the FBI too every time they came knocking at my door over the last twelve years. But here I am.

I can pretend I can't see them. I can preserve these last moments of our separate lives, the illusion of separate lives, but even in these blushing blurred moments I can't obliterate them entirely from my recognition. I lumber heavily by the long table on my left where Roland and RoAnne sit side by side with others I don't recognize. I don't have the time or the courage to study the crowd for faces I might know . . . certainly Devon and Sarah are there as defendants, and Harlan and Jo somewhere in the audience of spectators . . . .somewhere out in that judgmental sea of faces.

Roland is leaning towards RoAnne, not looking at me. He is whispering in her ear, and she is smiling. She smiles at me in that same half-shy, half-stubborn way that I recognize, that makes me certain that it is her, a smile that won't condemn me as Roland might, or Jo or any of the others, but I know she won't budge either from where she sits, where she has stayed for the last ten years. She has been charged only with harboring a fugitive, running with her fugitive, and carrying their one, then two, then three children with them for the ten years they ran underground. For the ten years when they allegedly stole over one million dollars in assorted bank robberies (money for "the revolution"), and bombed seventeen buildings—courthouses, corporate offices of war makers, slave holders, earth killers . . . "the most prolific left-wing terrorist group in the U.S." the F.B.I. had called them. "The most successful leftist propaganda campaign of the 1970's," some radical press called them.

My first son is at home with my husband, and along with my second child here inside me I will try to tell the whole truth and nothing but the truth.

The truth will set me free . . . .and help to put others in jail.

When I take my seat, all of the defendants and their lawyers are sitting directly across from me in a straight line of chairs behind tables, not twenty feet away. I can't bear to look at them, and I want to look each one directly in the eye. I want to stand upright for my children and my husband, for my life as it is, even with all of its contradictions, to stand upright and say to each of them I will not keep you as my judge and jury forever. I will not tell this judge or jury that it is okay to blow up buildings that might blow up people by mistake. Or to rob innocent people at gunpoint no matter how much money can be given to "the revolution". That is not my way. I have changed. That is not my way anymore.

And still I hesitate . . . .

Roland is his own lawyer in the tradition of other proud and poor revolutionaries without money to wage their own defense. And he will be cross-examining me.

Is that why I chose this particular blouse to wear, the African design that Laura had second thoughts about? Not your everyday bow-at-the-neck maternity garb. A small sign to him that I have not fallen entirely into the world of corporate enterprise. Do I care what he thinks of me? Yes. I care . . . I loved him once, and feared his judgment then, as I do now.

After I take my seat in the witness stand, I could be in a spotlight in this chair for all I can see, all I can allow myself to see in this crowd. I keep my eyes on my lawyer, Laura, who is as pregnant as I am and still manages three kids and a full time partnership at my father's law firm, who manages everything with her open smile, her re-assuring mother touch nursing me through this. My sister sits beside her, as she has sat beside me for weeks in preparation, and together the two of them will carry me through this day.

There is water in a glass in front of me. There is a box of tissues to the side.

Crying is out of the question.

Then it begins. The government man first, approaches me with his nondescript face, a well-suited government man. He wears horn-rim glasses and he doesn't really look at me, and I don't really look at him. He calls me "Ma'am" while he paces back and forth in front of the witness stand.

Ma'am would you state your name? . . . And would you tell us where you live? And what do you do, Ma'am? And do you know a person by the name of Roland Morand?

I do.

And do you see him in the courtroom today?

I do.

And could you point to him Ma'am?

I point to him, but my eyes are cast down, down and low like my voice. My voice is too low and the judge asks me to speak up.

And when was the first time you met Roland Morand?

I want to tell the whole story then, from the beginning, so that they'll all understand that there's no fault, no blame. We need to talk, to tell what happened. We need to all own up to our mistakes—those murderous mistakes in our country's foreign policy, and our own murderous responses to it—the boundaries of the law we'd each crossed.

But it's such a long story, and I'm not the best one to tell it, even if they'd listen. They can see that I'm still not clear about the choices I've made, am still mystified by how often clarity evades me—at least the kind of clarity where you decide for others what is right and wrong, whether someone should live or die—like the judge does, and like Roland and the others seemed ready to do as well. Perhaps I was clear in that way once, when I was surrounded by people with certainty, the one's who'd been so obviously and rudely used by the system; I felt clear for a moment about how to build a resistance to all the greed and evil-doing and could justify violence as a means to an end. I was filled with hope then and ready to birth a new world.

Maybe if I had "nothing left to lose" I would see more clearly, and it is this 'class cushion' that clouds my vision. But you see, Judge, how often you have to tell me to raise my voice? It's because I do see the "gray areas in something like this". I see that we are all culpable, and all innocent, and in a court of law there's no room for both.

I'm a stranger here and there is no room for that sort of explanation, or any explanation at all beyond the short concise answers I'm instructed to make. The prosecutor's questions come at me in a steady insistent monotone, are fractured by constant objections from the defense, and then the judge's tired "over-ruled". I would like to give the prosecution as little help as possible, in some subtle way to at least indicate that I am not entirely cooperative, that I would not be doing this if I hadn't felt cornered by circumstance, by my small circumstance in the scheme of it all.

"Could you repeat that question?" I say again and again, and my tongue is thick and slow in my mouth. There will never be enough water in the glass by my side.

Tell the truth. The truth will set you free . . . *and send others to jail.*

I am a clumsy walker along a path I have already cut for myself straight to their doorstep in my grand jury testimony four years ago. When I try to side step, to stray, the prosecutor reels me in.

After the bank robbery, do you remember any discussion concerning the gift-wrapped box that was brought into the car that you drove?

No . . . not specifically . . . no.

Ma'am, I'm going to show you your grand jury testimony. Please read lines three to ten on page thirty-five. Does that refresh your memory about the box?

Objection!

Over-ruled. The witness may answer. Does it jog your memory?

Well . . . not really. Not to as what was specifically said in reference to the box.

Ma'am, just say yes or no . . . .did you know what was in the box?

Objection.

Over-ruled.

Yes.

What was in the box Ma'am?

Money.

But I understood in some dim resistant way, the way that tried to keep all information about their circumstances sequestered into my lawyer's domain where she would "handle it", that the main purpose of this trial, the federal government's trial of sedition charges, was not to prove that the defendants had committed common felonies. Those would be, or already had been addressed in other trials. This trial, one of the longest and most expensive sedition trials in U.S. history, this nine month ten million dollar trial, was solely intended to prove that there had been a conspiracy—that the defendants had conspired to "overthrow the government", all six of them. It was a trial, in part no doubt, to warn other agitators, other political dissidents, organizers, revolutionaries, not to interfere with our government's foreign policy, clandestine attacks on civil liberties, imperialist greed in the name of democracy—conducting their all-too-often bloody business as usual. I hoped that at least I wouldn't have to feed right into the government's hands on that one. Even if I didn't want to align myself with the tactics of the group, I didn't have much allegiance to the way our country's great democratic principles were often demonstrated. I hoped that I could somehow hold back, twist the phrase, and convolute my responses so that the prosecution wouldn't have that satisfaction.

And Ma'am what was said at those meetings with you and the rest of the group that you've described?

I couldn't tell you specifically what was said.

Ma'am please state what was generally said at those meetings.

Objection.

Overruled.

Well, we discussed different things at different meetings. It was a long time ago . . . I don't really remember.

To the best of your recollection Ma'am.

Well, I guess generally it was a discussion of tactics around what an underground organization would do; what kinds of actions were consistent with the theories of the group.

What was said as to the theories of the group, Ma'am?

Well, there were different theories that we discussed.

Tell us, tell the court, what were those different theories.

I don't remember what was said exactly.

If he is exasperated with my evasions, he doesn't show it, rarely looks at me in fact, just persists doggedly with an almost tired certainty that he will arrive at his destination.

Tell us what you do remember.

Ah, well, we . . . I guess mainly we discussed different ways of going about changing the system.

And did you discuss the role of violence in changing the system?

Objection.

Overruled. Answer the question.

Well, sometimes I guess we talked about the role of violence in the theories we discussed.

In what context, Ma'am. In what context did you discuss the role of violence?

Ah . . . violence as a means, I guess, as a means to promote change in the system of government.

"As a means to promote change in the system of government." Is that correct?

Objection.

Over-ruled.

Yes.

No more questions, your honor.

And then Roland stands up. It's his turn and he comes towards me now with papers in his hand, looking down reading a last note, approaching me slowly, almost casually, as if he could pretend that I was just another one of the hundred witnesses he will have to cross-examine. He looks the same, is lithe and thin, thinner than I remember, dressed in black pants, a dark button-down shirt, his sleeves rolled up, his hair partly gray now and shoulder length, pulled back in a pony-tail. He delays looking directly at me, delays the moment until he is very close, very close, until I can feel the wave of the heat of him, until I can see beads of perspiration on his brow and the familiar weathered lines of his face, and as he comes towards me I feel an odd unsteady mix of some kind of desire to reconnect as we had once long ago, but confused now with fear, and then aversion as well. I'm surprised by the aversion, did not expect to feel the wave of it so clearly, but it's there in the mix of it. Could he obliterate me with his judgment now? Possibly. And I'm afraid of that as well. And when he does look up there's an entire journey that I take in an instant to find what is being communicated between us. It's a raw look we exchange, a naked moment, one that only has room for what is honest and true.

He rests his arm on the witness stand. His familiar hand is close enough to touch and all of the intervening years vanish for a moment, a terribly confusing moment.

"Hello, Linda. It's been a long time." His voice is low, is for me, is not for the audience. I think there is nothing at all accusing in it.

"Yes, a very long time," and we exchange a small smile.

Speak up. The witness must speak up.

"How long has it been?" he says. "Twelve years? Isn't that correct? I haven't seen you or talked to you in twelve years?" There are wet arcs of perspiration already under his arms and the very slightest tremor in his hand that holds the papers.

He lingers there, in front of me. I believe he lingers and I believe we rest together for a breath of a moment in a space where none of this is between us, and there are no roles to play, no class to belong to, no testimonies or betrayal, there is only the truth and mystery of the way our lives have intersected—a truth that I will try not to dis-honor.

There is only the moment that expands, expands, and sucks me in to all of that memory until it spits me back out into this place and he is gone, pacing back and forth in front of me, and I am a witness in his trial and he is cross-examining me.

To me, it seems that the government lawyer objects to every one of his questions. No matter what he asks, no matter which way he turns to try to find a way in to showing the goodness of our intent, the reasons—the humane reasons for trying to organize and resist the forces of darkness and greed wherever they'd presented themselves, forces that would allow the war in Vietnam to be all that it was, that would allow prison to be all that it was and is still, that would allow a police death squad to plan assassinations, and police attacks, and possibly a rape . . . no matter which door he opens they calmly, impassively close that door, and the next, and the next.

Do you remember the welfare rights work that we did?
Yes. I do.
Objection.
Sustained. Strike the answer from the record.
Do you remember the bail fund that we set up to help prisoners and their families?
Objection. Sustained.
Do you remember that our motto was "Serve the People"?
Objection.
Sustained.
Do you remember participating in the self-defense classes I taught for women and children?
Objection. Sustained.

I am on the edge of my seat. I want to fill in between the lines wherever I can, to show that *Yes!* We had organized all of that, and we did all of that, and it was good work, that work for poor people, imprisoned people, people who never got a break, got only broken. I want to tell them all of this because I know that this may be one of the last public forums for the world to find out, to hear anything about the courage and determination we all had, that *he* had, about the other Roland, before the bombings and the bank robberies. Not the one the government is so intent on portraying, but the man with all of that insistence on revealing the other side of the truth, even when it meant years of solitary confinement in prison, even when it meant police harassment at every turn, about the police death squad in his home town intent on assassinating him and others, for being a radical teller of that other truth.

I look at the prosecutor in his tailored suit, his laptop open on the table in front of him, and I wonder if he could possibly know what it's like to work in a factory or a mill, or to be a marine in Vietnam, or sentenced for five years for the sale of seven dollars of marijuana? Could the irony be lost on anyone here that with all the contradictions Roland's lived as a "free" American citizen that the system has made him the very revolutionary that it is now silencing?

I can hear the slight tenor of his voice increasing, the tension amplified. He pauses after each objection, nods his head, sometimes mutters beneath his breath.

Did you ever know me to take any money from anybody for anything I gave to them, any service I provided them?

The bookstore, the newspaper, the statewide prisoner's rights organization . . .

Objection. Sustained. Objection. Sustained. Objection. Sustained.

Do you recall one of our women workers being physically attacked and beaten and raped by men that we believed to be from the police department?

Yes, I remember.

Objection. Sustained. Strike the answer from the record.

Did you and I ever discuss that attack with her?

Objection. Sustained.

He is pacing, pacing. Every objection a whiplash. Why won't they let him ask a question . . . or let me answer?

Did she ever discuss this attack with you?

Objection. Sustained.

Is there any doubt in your mind at all about this attack having taken place?

Objection. Sustained.

He throws his hands in the air .
I'm beginning to feel like I've got handcuffs on up here, Judge!
Objection. Sustained. Mr. Morand, control yourself.

But there was an attack! Jo was raped . . . they should know about that. The jury should know, and how the bookstore was attacked and how it seemed like it had to be the police.

Mr. Morand, the judge says, *I'm going to direct you to focus your questions on those communications that were made to you, or data about which you were aware of which this witness knows.*

Again, I can see that I am a pawn that must be played correctly, expertly. But it seems that Roland is not an expert, and they are practiced, they are the "hired guns" that will stop at nothing to win this contest. They are making a fool of him, closing off his advances with every one of their objections. And he is working hard, so hard, to be the best revolutionary he can be . . . a kin to his deceased ancestors—George Jackson, Jonathan Jackson, Sam Melville, Che Guevara, Fred Hampton, Mark Clark, and so many others—men who had died "for the revolution". He is trying hard and I don't want to judge him but I do. I have this distrust in the mix of what I feel as I watch him pacing and working, and that is telling, that is truth as well, and I know that while I'm respectful of his effort, and I do want the whole truth of our circumstances to be heard, I don't trust him to be clear about his motives. I don't trust that familiar arrogance I can still see parading that invites too many romantic ideas about revolution, about being a revolutionary hero, living a story about a revolution that didn't exist, not really, not after the war had ended and all the opposition to it dispersed, and about "masses" that weren't ready and would not be made ready by bombs or bank robberies, and conviction that insisted on something as loud and deadly as a bomb that might take a life, like so many other bombs that had been dropped and millions who had been killed in the name of knowing.

He quits his traversing and approaches me in the witness stand. There is the half smile again, the eyes that stop their darting around the room and rest in an unsettling directness on me.

"You and I were very close friends back then, weren't we?"

Objection. Leading the witness.

Sustained.

"Were you and I close friends back then?"

Were we? Close friends? I wanted to know you, Roland, as much as anyone I'd ever met, but I was afraid. Afraid of everything I said—that any one of my words would find me guilty of some gross privilege, some ignorant moneyed perspective. Perhaps it wasn't your intention to judge me. Perhaps it was only the rhetoric you espoused that I used to judge myself. But with that tape I played over and over, I was as guarded as you were.

And then we are back in my alcove apartment the morning after our first night together, sitting on my bed with the quilt over our laps and the early sun on our skin and all of some kind of hopeful future there with us too. Maybe there were only those few hours that we were possibly "close", all the rest clouded by circumstance and guarding, and looking back on it as I watch him now, navigating this life and death struggle, I can see how young I was then, how naively hopeful and determined to embrace a path that had already claimed him irrevocably.

"Yes, we were close friends."

Earlier the prosecutor had asked me, *"Ms. Coleman. Do you think Mr. Morand is a violent man?"*

"No. Not a violent man . . . A man who espoused violence as a means to an end. There's a difference."

Oh . . . he might have asked. *And what is that difference? Could you describe it to the court?* Because he might have heard how my voice had faltered ever so slightly over those last qualifying words—there's a difference—my response crashing into the person I had grown to be in those ten years, one who truly deeply questioned violence as a means to any peaceful end, and yet still a person without the clarity of a solid alternative to offer.

But then it was over.

Suddenly over. Arriving at a dead end on a road I'd thought would go on forever.

That will be all, the judge said. The witness is excused.

Excused.

The witness may leave the room.

The witness may walk out of that door, that door on the left . . . yes . . . past the table where the defendants sit following your every move, past the sea of faces you imagine accuse you of treason of one sort or another, off of this stage, out of this episode of your life.

The witness may never think of these people ever again. Never wonder what has become of them.

The witness may choose not to remember every day that the defendants are in prison and to wonder what that is like for them, right now . . . . . and right now . . .

She may choose not to hold the entirety of her life up next to theirs . . . to dissect, to glean fault or merit, to look again and again, and then again . . . to understand the nature of these circumstances, to find the truth of the matter, and to ask herself, what is "right" and what is "wrong"?

But surely the witness must know the answer to that by now, after pondering these issues for so many years? She must have figured out by now what is just and what is unjust? And what exactly do we mean when we speak of violence? She may choose of course, not to ask herself these questions about violence—all the violence that consumes the world, and where does it begin? And who is responsible?

Postscript: 2014

All charges in the nine-month, ten million dollar federal sedition trial were dismissed on technicalities and prison sentences for the defendants were determined based on individual criminal activities. I have had no personal contact with any of the people mentioned, and thus the information below is what I have gleamed from internet searches.

Roland served 20 years of a 45- year sentence. He was released in 2004 on extended parole. He returned to New England and speaks out locally on prison and human rights issues. He and **Ro-Anne** are no longer married. After serving three years of her sentence of five for harboring a fugitive, she took up a career as a paralegal in New York.

Sarah was sentenced to fifteen years on bank robbery and bombing charges and was released after seven.

Devon is serving a life sentence for the killing of a state trooper, and for bombing and bank robbery charges.

With much difficulty, the six children born of these two couples were re-united with their families.

Vinny was arrested in 1977 and went to prison for seven years. After his release, he continued to be active and vocal in leftist politics in the New England area.

Eddy was put in a witness protection program. He was soon arrested on another criminal charge, was jailed again, and then charged with the murder of a fellow inmate. He remains in prison.

All charges against **Harlan** were dismissed after the lengthy trial in Denver. He and **Jo** moved to New England where they took up sheep farming. They raised their two children, Mark and Lou, and have kept their political focus on community and school issues.

To my knowledge, none of the eight children born to these three couples have spoken out about their experiences. I hope that someday their voices will be heard.

During those years after my trial appearance, after my marriage had ended and my mother had also died of cancer, I continued to be employed as a nurse, and then as a nurse practitioner. As I grew deeper into adulthood and parenting two sons, I began to accept the inevitability of living a life with contradictions, with "gray areas" and inconsistencies. Scrub as I might, I could never remove the taint of class privilege in my life; nor could I deny my deep feelings of appreciation, love, and gratitude for my parents and their efforts on my behalf. I awakened to their contributions as citizens as well; my mother in particular had been an activist in her own right who had, in spite of multiple serious health crises, made nationally recognized contributions to human rights causes and health services.

In my own way, much smaller in scope, I followed her lead in living a life of service, intent on alleviating the suffering of others. In that quest, I've been both supported and informed by a deep inquiry into the study and practice of Zen Buddhism, the teachings of which are all about both the source and relief of the deep dis-ease that imprisons so many humans. As part of this practice, for some time every day I sit and follow my breath. I follow my breath and watch the barrage of thoughts, the urgencies of body and mind that arise and then fade and then arise again. Thoughts, with their insistence and desires, their judgments and discriminations, muddy and obscure a deeper stillness. Sometimes, when all this activity of mind settles, and I can be with the totality of life as it is in this moment, I know the peace and freedom that belongs to us all.

From 2003 to 2012, I co-facilitated weekly memoir writing workshops for women incarcerated in the Suffolk County Correctional System. We worked with over 1500 students and published three anthologies of their writings, now used in several college criminology curriculums and as educational material for legislative change.* Since 2012, I've been working with youthful male offenders (16-19 years old) in the same jail in a weekly program we call "Transitions to Freedom" where, collectively, we investigate what keeps us "locked up" in mind, regardless of external circumstances. Through these many years of bearing witness to the deepest truths and often darkly shattered lives of others, I'm certain I've learned more from my "students" than they have from me . . . about forgiveness, resilience, and what it means to be free.

In entering jail, I recognize its insanity—a failed system for most, based on shame and punishment for largely non-violent deeds born out of circumstances that left little room for other choices or outcomes. In the United States today incarceration is big business—unprecedented numbers of people are locked in our jails and prisons†, the vast majority being poor and of color. Clearly, we are a punitive and racially divided nation that grows richer on the business of incarceration despite the tsunami of troubled impact that rips through generations of families, communities, and our entire nation.

Several years ago, when I first began work on this memoir, I spoke with my older son, then eighteen, about some of the violent activities I'd been involved in. "I understand that things needed to change," he said, "but how could you have thought that violence

---

* For more information and/or to order these books contact www.herstorywriters.org)
† As of February 2008, about 2.3 million adults were incarcerated in the U.S., or 1 in 100 Americans. 85,000 "do their time" in extended solitary confinement. Of this total population, 70 percent are non-white. The U.S. has the highest per capita rate of incarceration in the world. Source: *New York Times* and the Department of Justice Statistics.

would do any good?" I was caught off guard, suddenly speechless in the face of his unassuming clarity. Yes . . . how could I have? I offered some explanation of "the times"—how "revolution" was in the air and we were certain that the world had had enough of capitalism and imperialism, of the necessity of standing up to tyranny, along with a defensive reminder that most all revolutions have their armed warriors. But my words lacked conviction and sounded foreign to the woman I had become. "I don't know," I said finally. "Maybe in writing about it, I'll find out."

I do know that the events and choices I made during those years, and then during the subsequent years when I was called to testify, these have shaped my adult life. What constitutes "right action" in the face of tyranny? Who determines the parameters of "self-defense" or "justifiable" attack in the face of all forms of exploitation of person, property, or our shared environment? An even cursory look at military conflicts worldwide during and since the Vietnam War will show that one person's "terrorist" is another's "freedom fighter". Our own government seems no less vague in its definition or intent when one looks into the laundry list of brutal dictators and regimes we have covertly supported, or those we have overtly attacked in the name of "freedom".

As a pacifist, one who has been an ordained Buddhist monk since 2004, who has taken Buddhist vows "Not to Kill", I live this investigation. Does violence always beget violence? Sometimes, it seems, violence begets the cessation of violence. Violence can beget submission, or, release from submission. As a pacifist, when does one "turn the other cheek" to an attacker? The same son who wondered how I could think that violence would ever "do any good", later said he certainly hoped I'd defend him and his brother from attack, even if I had to kill someone. What would I do?

The Buddha said: "*Monks, even if bandits were to savagely sever you, limb by limb . . . . even then, whoever of you harbors ill will at heart would not be upholding my Teaching . . . we shall remain full of concern with a mind of love, and we shall not give in to hatred."*

Which sounds like the "revolutionaries" that Che Guevara spoke of—guided by love—but minus the gun.

One thing I have learned is that, while intentions may seem wholesome, the road to hell is certainly paved with them. We humans, so fraught with a deep angst, are so easily swept away by rhetoric and righteousness, drawn to those articulate and charismatic beings determined to show us The Way. Violence begins in the mind, as the Buddha taught, with "the thought that becomes the deed", and under the right circumstances, I imagine that each of us is arguably capable of any act of violence ever committed; only the moment determines what any of us will do.

In looking deeply through memoir into the mind and spirit of the young woman I was during those years, I sought, in part, to unravel how much of her path towards violent action had been propelled by anger at her parents and the family system she grew up in. Certainly that was some of the fuel for her fire then (though I've since, thankfully, moved well beyond any feelings of "blaming" my parents), but it hardly shows the full picture. It is said in Zen practice that the student is ready to become a teacher when her own understanding surpasses her teacher's (when she "stands on the shoulders" of her teacher). When I am hopeful about our human presence on this planet I think it is like that; not that we are superior to our elders, but that in standing on the shoulders of their wisdom as well as their mistakes, we manifest the change. And so with each new generation, as we evolve so very, very slowly towards "a more perfect union", as we seek other avenues of resolution beyond the insanity of war and hatred of others, as we wake up finally to our careless destruction of our planet, and as there is less separation altogether in this age of internet communion, I do see the possibility of our world finding a more co-operative, respectful, and pacific formation. In this pursuit, our country's founding documents have the potential to be of great service, even while our economic system may fuel the greed of the world and thereby invite our obliteration.

Still, "Injustice anywhere is a threat to justice everywhere", said another great teacher, Dr. Martin Luther King Jr., and clearly there is much to be done. My own efforts have been focused locally in community action—helping to found a local free alternative health clinic, working on diversity issues in schools and community, and in expanding the reach of the Herstory Writers Workshop where, as a participant I wrote the first drafts of this memoir, and later, as a trained facilitator, I was able to bring this writing method into our jail program.

I'm guided as well by the vows of a Zen Peacemaker before taking action, (a vow being a promise of intention and daily investigation) : to bear witness without judgment, in a space of "not knowing" the answer, and allowing action to emerge from that space. This vow in particular has been the backbone of our work in the jail as mentors. In this circumstance, most any judgment closes doors and blocks the intimacy and trust necessary to write deeply and to share openly. In being received without judgment, even the hardest of hearts readily softens. I do this work of mentoring in the never forgotten context of my own privilege—living in the relative peace, safety, and economic security that my life has afforded me, and that all beings deserve. I don't forget that.

One question that circulated the Left during that time of such radical choices: *How will you live your life so that it doesn't make a mockery of your values?* To the jury: Has the defendant let her life become a mockery of her values? My jury, both inner and outer, is still divided in moments, and non-existent in others. By some scorned, and by others accepted as I am in this moment . . . and then as I am changed in the next . . . always held in the totality and mystery of our collective Being—perfect as I am, as we all are, and forever after with endless room for improvement.

May all beings everywhere be free from suffering and the causes of suffering.
May all beings be free.

ACKNOWLEDGEMENTS

To my top shelf publisher, editor, and friend Bill Henderson. Luck was mine when I met you. Your epic and humble dedication to writers everywhere, and to this book, has given me the final push and courage to bring this story out of hiding.

A book written over many years can test the true grit of those kin on the sidelines, and without their tireless support, I would have floundered long ago. Endless thanks to my endlessly patient husband Geoff, dear sons Dan and Evan, sisters Susan and Penny, and encouraging friends and readers Virginia, Phillip, Gene, Ann, Wendy, Sam, Jeanie, Terry, Jane, Rachel, Laurel, Peter, Henry, and Mary.

Thanks to Pat Gorman for the title; Wendy Vitolo for her initial cover design; Sam DeWitt for endless computer help; and Alison Anthoine for generous legal advice.

Thanks to those women of the Herstory Writers Workshop who, under the inspired guidance of founder Erika Duncan, joined me week by week and then year by year in crafting book length projects and life-long friendship—Patra Apatovsky, Beth Heyn, Madeleine Cranston, Tina Curran, Christine Giordano, Pat Gorman, Hazel Saunders, Karen Wagner, Lonnie Mathis, and many others who came and went and encouraged me to persist.

Thanks to the many hundreds of incarcerated women of the Suffolk County Correctional facilities who joined me in small weekly circles and shared their deepest truths and hidden stories—your courage and honesty has fed my own.

Bows to my Zen teachers and Sangha of the Ocean Zendo—your revolutionary spirits and friendship have guided me home.

And to Peter Matthiessen—teacher, mentor, friend—it has been my great fortune to have been recognized by you.